Jennifer Love Hewitt's

MUSIC BOX

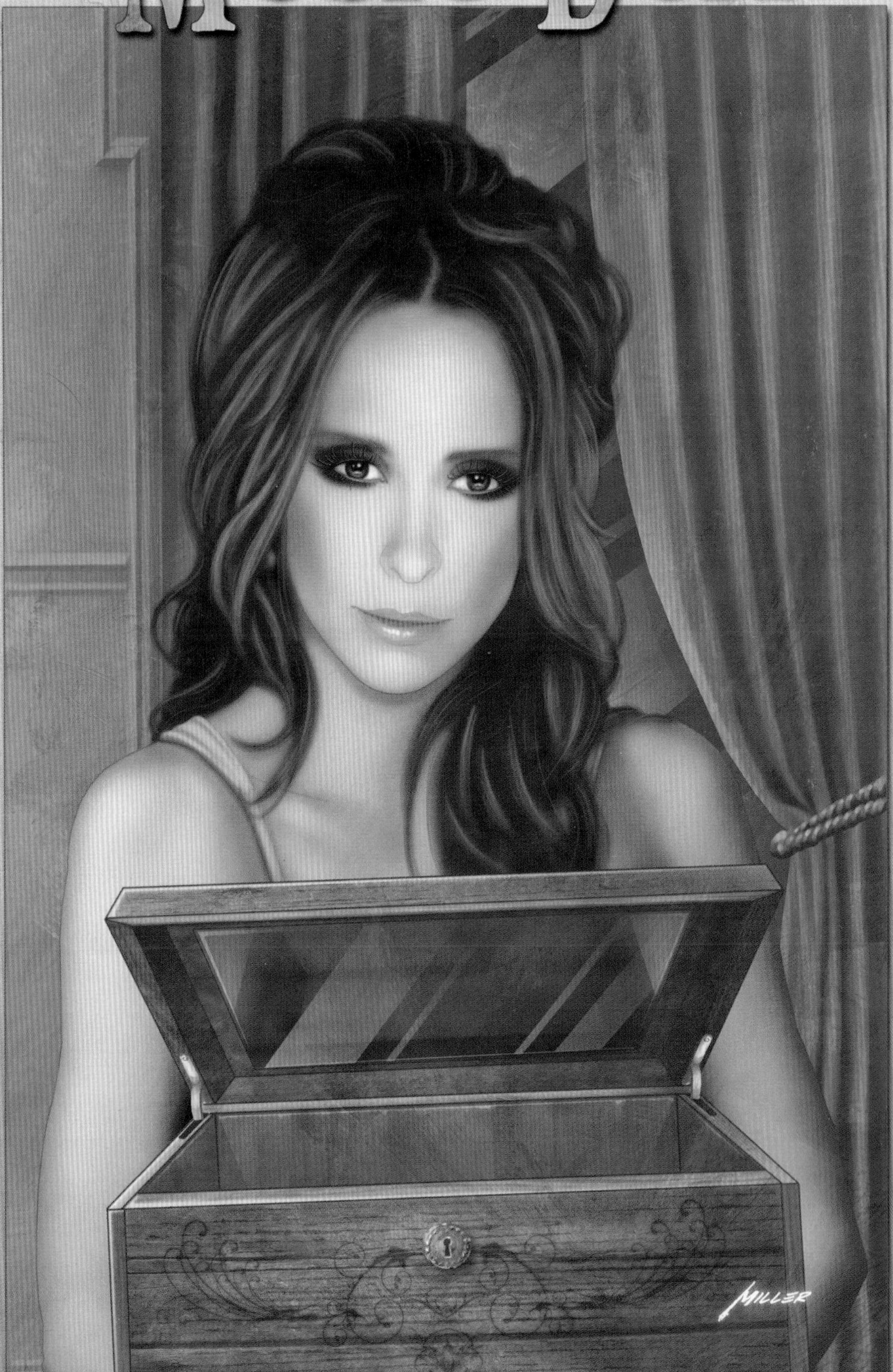
MILLER

Jennifer Love Hewitt's MUSIC BOX

Created by
Jennifer Love Hewitt

Stories by
Jennifer Love Hewitt and Scott Lobdell

Written by
Scott Lobdell

"Endnotes" art by Amber Shields
Lettering by Chris Mowry

Original series edits by Tom Waltz
Collection Design by Chris Mowry
Collection edits by Justin Eisinger and Mariah Huehner

Special thanks to A.J. Rinella for his invaluable assistance.
www.IDWPUBLISHING.com   ISBN: 978-1-60010-693-4   13 12 11 10   1 2 3 4

Operations: Ted Adams, Chief Executive Officer • Greg Goldstein, Chief Operating Officer • Matthew Ruzicka, CPA, Chief Financial Officer • Alan Payne, VP of Sales • Lorelei Bunjes, Dir. of Digital Services • AnnaMaria White, Marketing & PR Manager • Marci Hubbard, Executive Assistant • Alonzo Simon, Shipping Manager • Angela Loggins, Staff Accountant • Cherrie Go, Assistant Web Designer • Editorial: Chris Ryall, Publisher/Editor-in-Chief • Scott Dunbier, Editor, Special Projects • Andy Schmidt, Senior Editor • Bob Schreck, Senior Editor • Justin Eisinger, Editor • Kris Oprisko, Editor/Foreign Lic. • Denton J. Tipton, Editor • Tom Waltz, Editor • Mariah Huehner, Associate Editor • Carlos Guzman, Editorial Assistant • Design: Robbie Robbins, EVP/Sr. Graphic Artist • Neil Uyetake, Art Director • Chris Mowry, Graphic Artist • Amauri Osorio, Graphic Artist • Gilberto Lazcano, Production Assistant • Shawn Lee, Production Assistant

JENNIFER LOVE HEWITT'S MUSIC BOX, VOLUME 1. JULY 2010. FIRST PRINTING. © 2010 Lovespell Films, Inc. and Idea and Design Works, LLC. All Rights Reserved. IDW Publishing, a division of Idea and Design Works, LLC. Editorial offices: 5080 Santa Fe St., San Diego, CA 92109. All Rights Reserved. Any similarities to persons living or dead are purely coincidental. With the exception of artwork used for review purposes, none of the contents of this publication may be reprinted without the permission of Idea and Design Works, LLC. Printed in Korea. IDW Publishing does not read or accept unsolicited submissions of ideas, stories, or artwork.

OPENING NOTES

By Jennifer Love Hewitt

What happens when the song in the music box is playing for you?

That's the question repeatedly asked throughout the pages of the graphic novel you are about to experience. In the five stories that follow, you will learn what it means when the twisted notes of a bizarre music box entwine themselves around—and into—the lives of five unsuspecting victims. Five seemingly normal people—men and women—from all walks of life... from different times in history, even. What happens when the tune is theirs—when the music turns its dark attentions... and intentions... toward them? Well, you'll have to turn the page to find out. I only promise the answers you discover will always be sure to strike the creepiest of chords.

The title of this book is *Jennifer Love Hewitt's MUSIC BOX,* and though I am extremely proud to be the creator of the stories that you are about to read, nothing in the comic book industry happens in a vacuum... or without a little help from friends. First and foremost, I'd like to thank writer Scott Lobdell, who took my ideas and expertly fashioned them into the fantastic scripts that were the blueprints for the five stories contained within. To the many artists who took Scott's scripts and rendered them into the hauntingly beautiful graphic tales they were meant to be—Michael Gaydos, Casey Maloney, Adam Archer, Renae De Liz, Dan Duncan, Brian Miller, Josh Perez, and Ray Dillon—please know your efforts are truly, truly appreciated. To series editor Tom Waltz, thank you for keeping the music flowing so smoothly with such a diverse cast of creators. To trade editors Justin Eisinger and Mariah Huehner, a huge thank you for taking five separate comic books and transforming them into one gorgeous graphic novel. To letterer and production designer Chris Mowry, your ability to make words, captions, and balloons blend so seamlessly into the artwork never failed to impress. And, to IDW Publishing, it's been great working with you again, and I hope we have many more collaborations awaiting us in the future.

And, last but surely not least, to you, our wonderful readers, a heartfelt thank you for taking a chance on our graphic novel. It is to you that we dedicate the *Music Box.*

So, lift the lid and turn the page...

If you dare.

Jennifer Love Hewitt
May 2010

Chapter One: "Details"

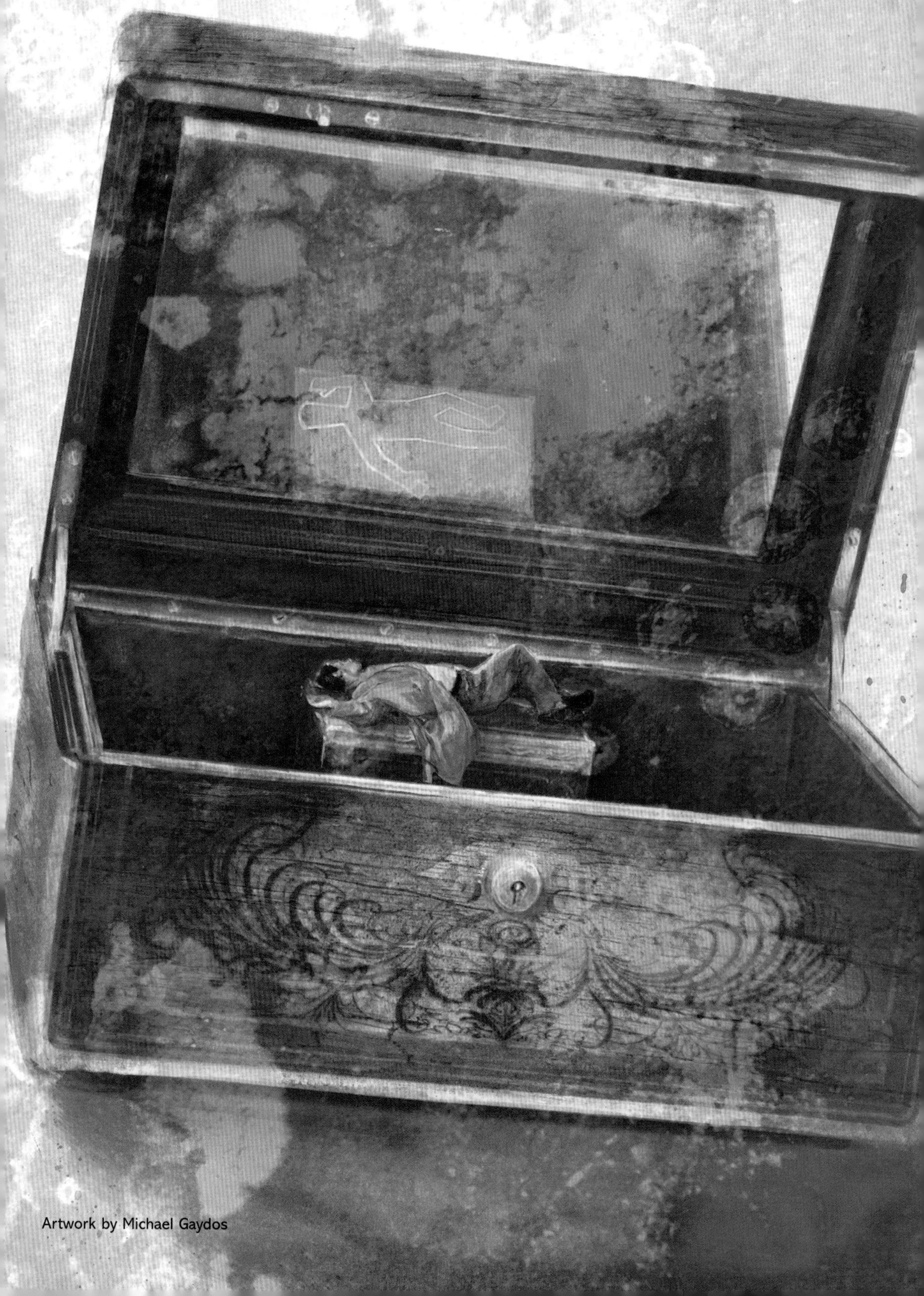

Artwork by Michael Gaydos

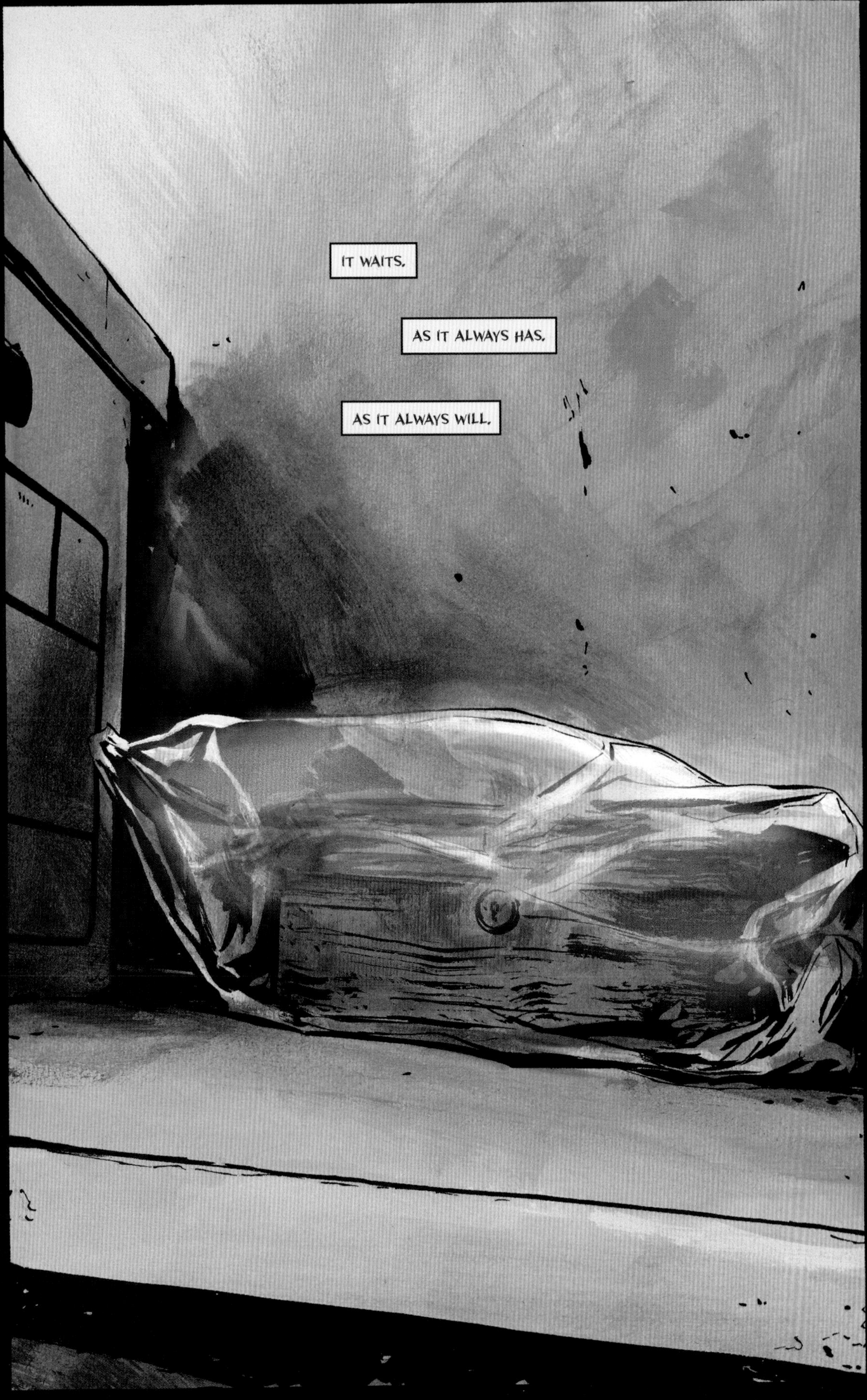
IT WAITS.
AS IT ALWAYS HAS.
AS IT ALWAYS WILL.

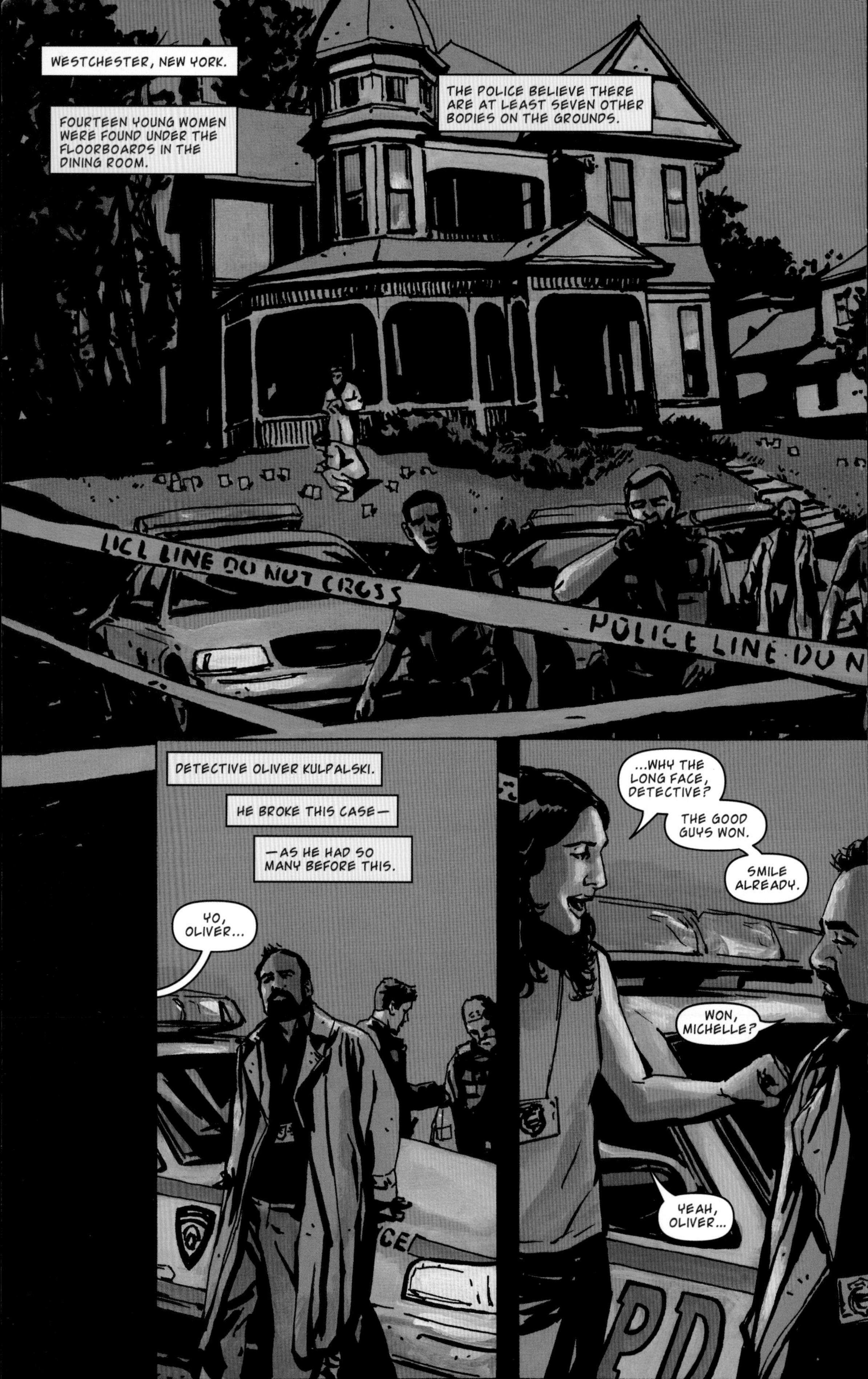
WESTCHESTER, NEW YORK.
FOURTEEN YOUNG WOMEN WERE FOUND UNDER THE FLOORBOARDS IN THE DINING ROOM.
THE POLICE BELIEVE THERE ARE AT LEAST SEVEN OTHER BODIES ON THE GROUNDS.
DETECTIVE OLIVER KULPALSKI.
HE BROKE THIS CASE—
—AS HE HAD SO MANY BEFORE THIS.
YO, OLIVER...
...WHY THE LONG FACE, DETECTIVE?
THE GOOD GUYS WON.
SMILE ALREADY.
WON, MICHELLE?
YEAH, OLIVER...

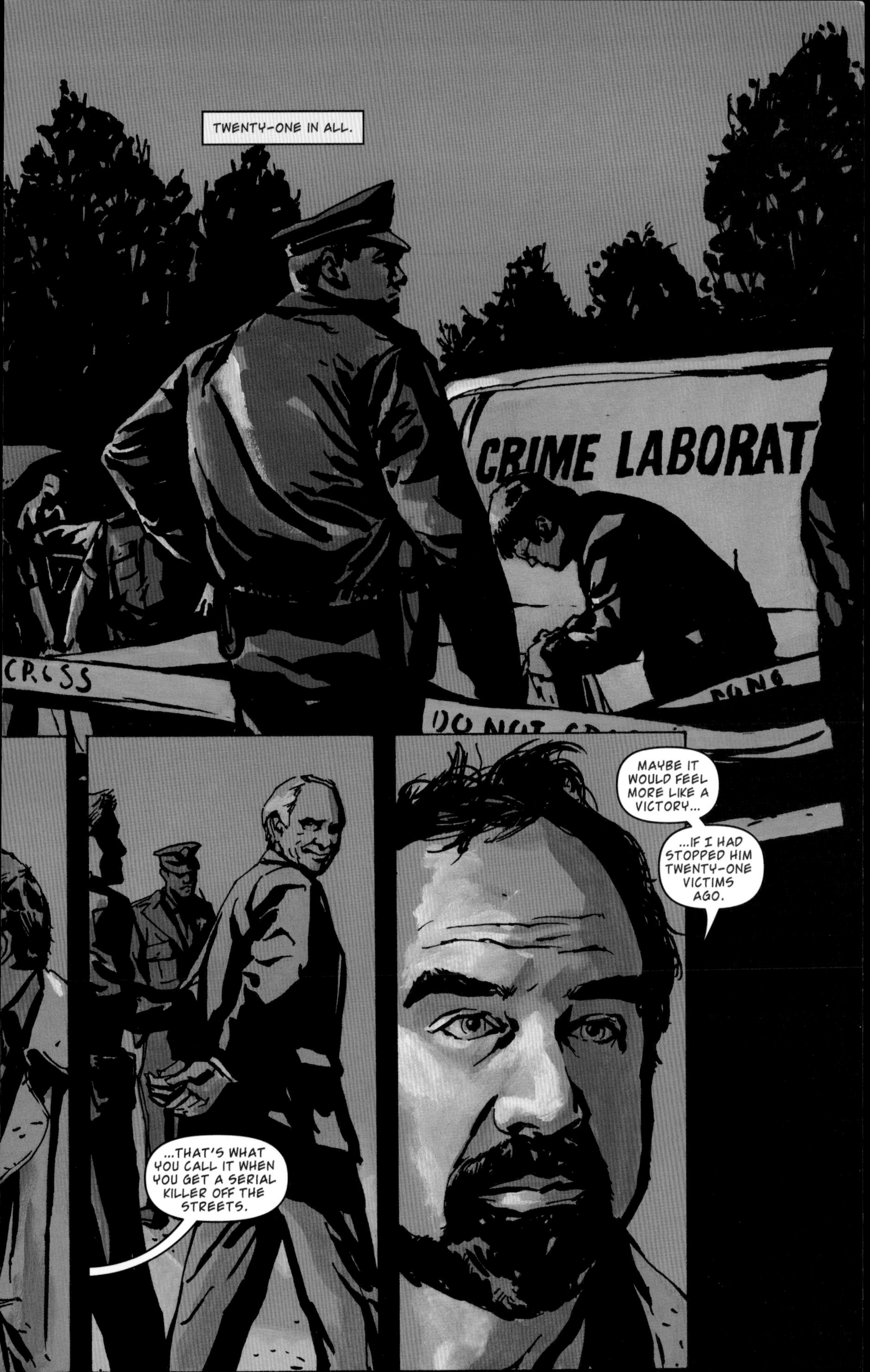
TWENTY-ONE IN ALL.
CRIME LABORAT
...THAT'S WHAT YOU CALL IT WHEN YOU GET A SERIAL KILLER OFF THE STREETS.
MAYBE IT WOULD FEEL MORE LIKE A VICTORY...
...IF I HAD STOPPED HIM TWENTY-ONE VICTIMS AGO.

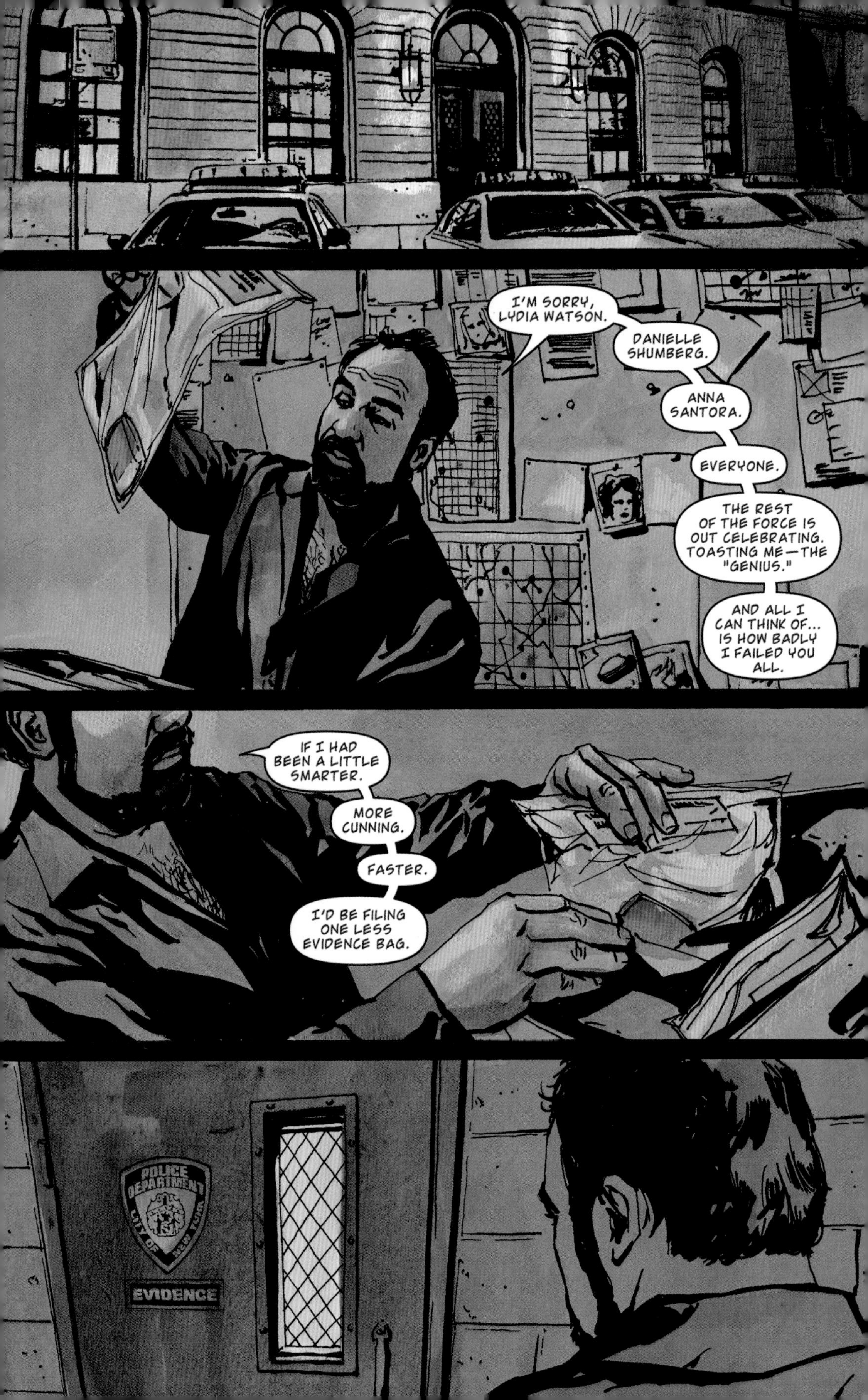
I'M SORRY, LYDIA WATSON.
DANIELLE SHUMBERG.
ANNA SANTORA.
EVERYONE.
THE REST OF THE FORCE IS OUT CELEBRATING. TOASTING ME—THE "GENIUS."
AND ALL I CAN THINK OF... IS HOW BADLY I FAILED YOU ALL.
IF I HAD BEEN A LITTLE SMARTER.
MORE CUNNING.
FASTER.
I'D BE FILING ONE LESS EVIDENCE BAG.
POLICE DEPARTMENT
CITY OF NEW YORK
EVIDENCE

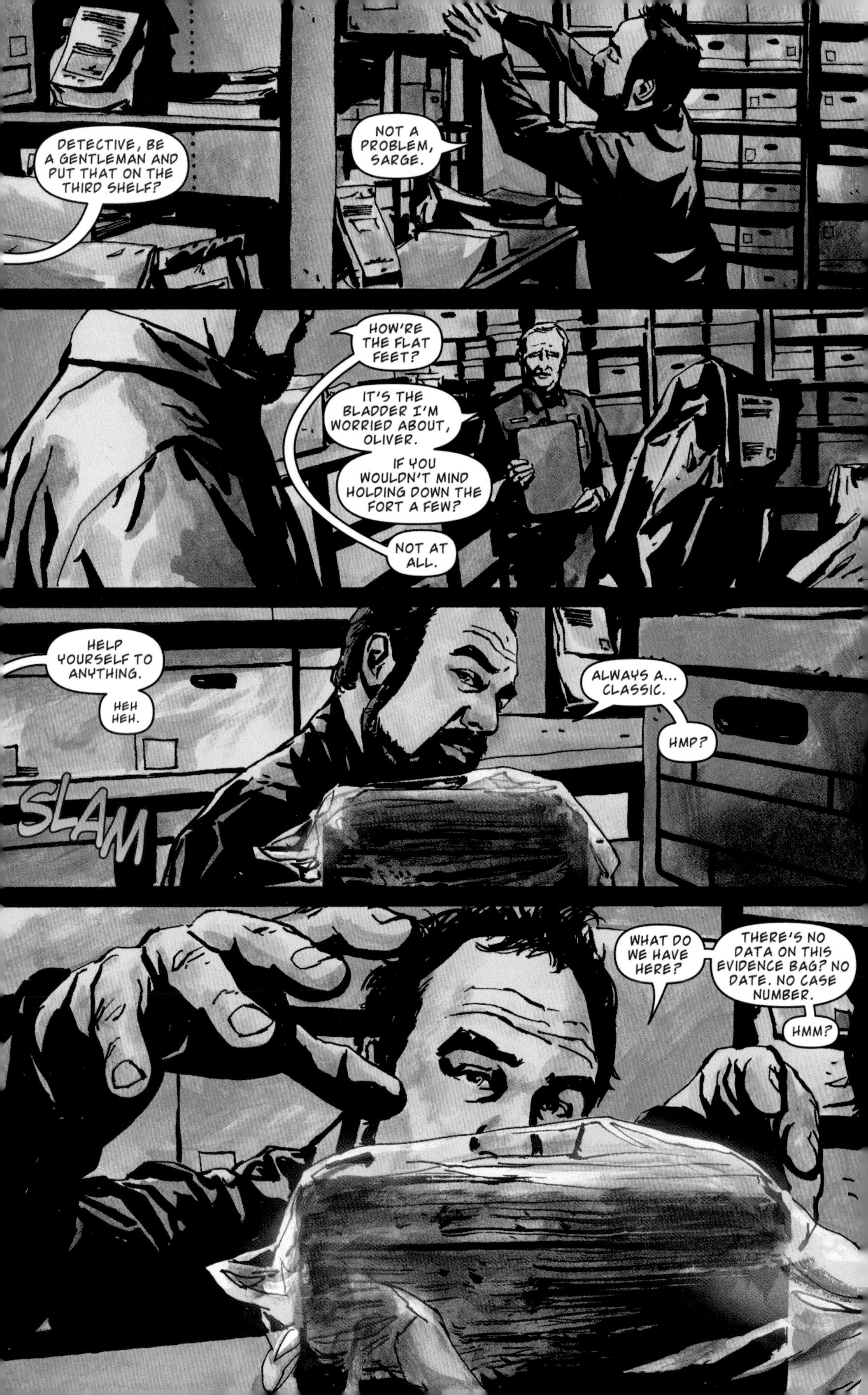
DETECTIVE, BE A GENTLEMAN AND PUT THAT ON THE THIRD SHELF?
NOT A PROBLEM, SARGE.
HOW'RE THE FLAT FEET?
IT'S THE BLADDER I'M WORRIED ABOUT, OLIVER.
IF YOU WOULDN'T MIND HOLDING DOWN THE FORT A FEW?
NOT AT ALL.
HELP YOURSELF TO ANYTHING.
HEH HEH.
ALWAYS A... CLASSIC.
HMP?
SLAM
WHAT DO WE HAVE HERE?
THERE'S NO DATA ON THIS EVIDENCE BAG? NO DATE. NO CASE NUMBER.
HMM?

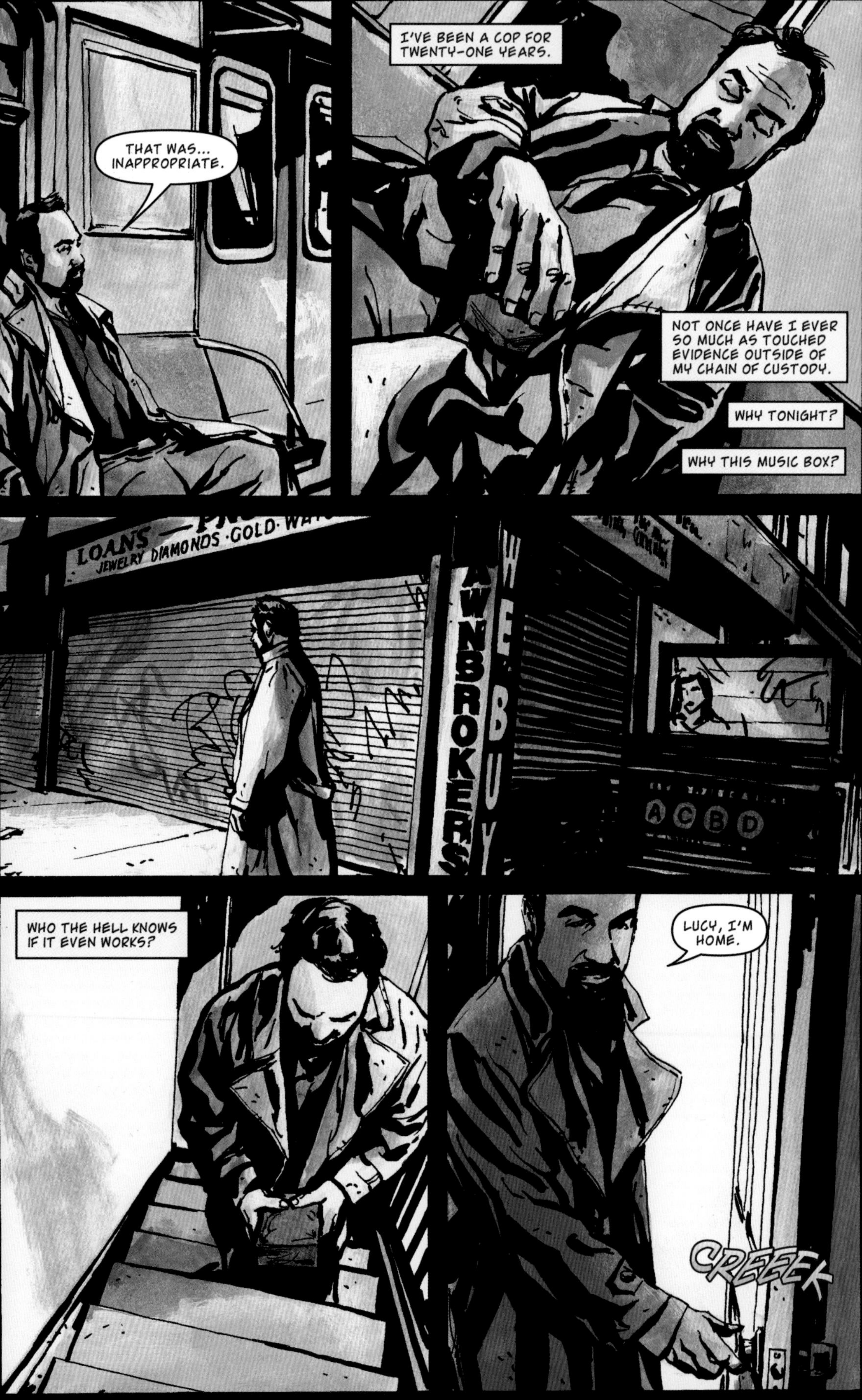
THAT WAS... INAPPROPRIATE.
I'VE BEEN A COP FOR TWENTY-ONE YEARS.
NOT ONCE HAVE I EVER SO MUCH AS TOUCHED EVIDENCE OUTSIDE OF MY CHAIN OF CUSTODY.
WHY TONIGHT?
WHY THIS MUSIC BOX?
LOANS
JEWELRY DIAMONDS ·GOLD·
AWNBROKERS
A C B D
WHO THE HELL KNOWS IF IT EVEN WORKS?
LUCY, I'M HOME.
CREEEK

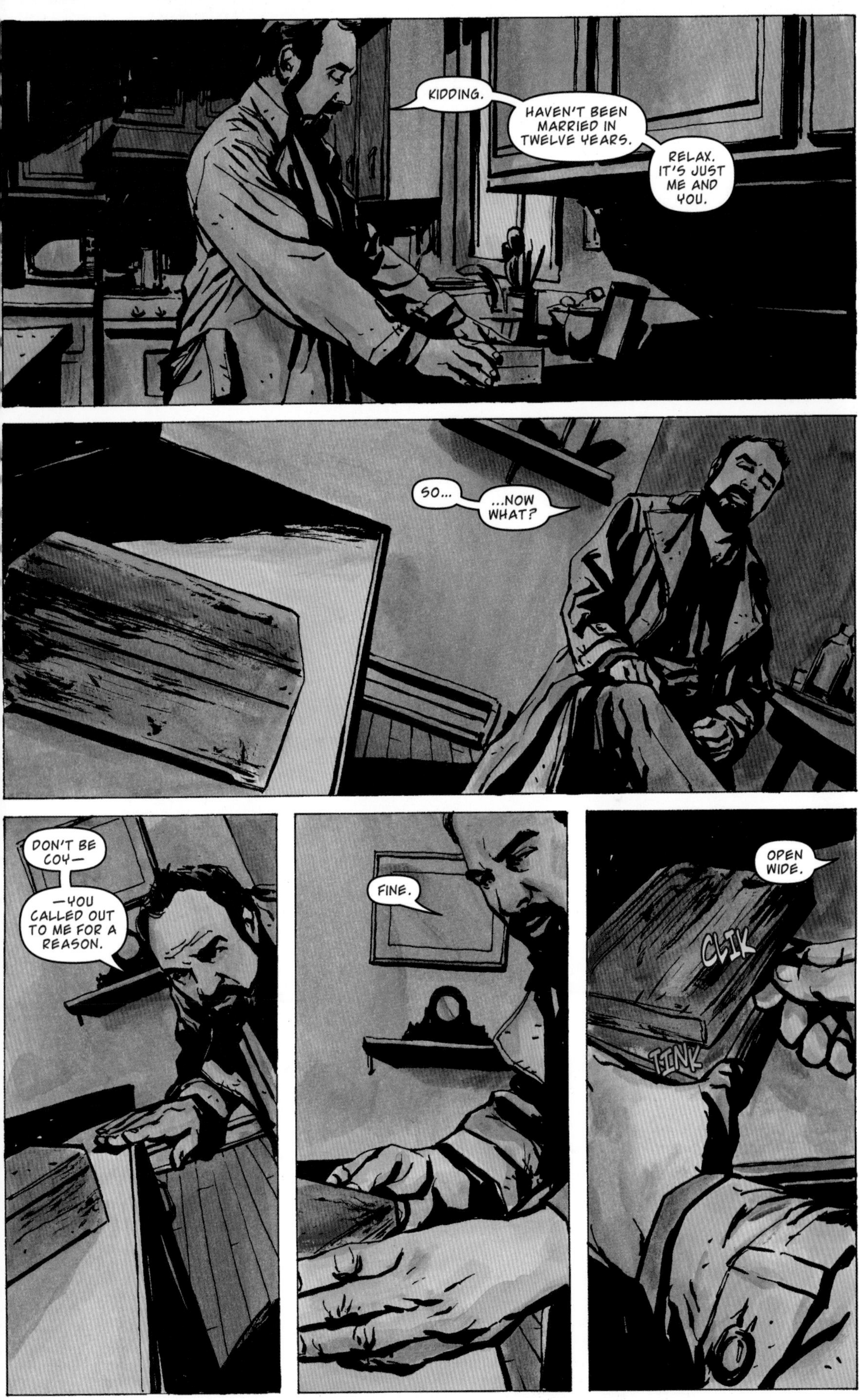
KIDDING.
HAVEN'T BEEN MARRIED IN TWELVE YEARS.
RELAX. IT'S JUST ME AND YOU.
SO...
...NOW WHAT?
DON'T BE COY—
—YOU CALLED OUT TO ME FOR A REASON.
FINE.
OPEN WIDE.
CLIK
TINK

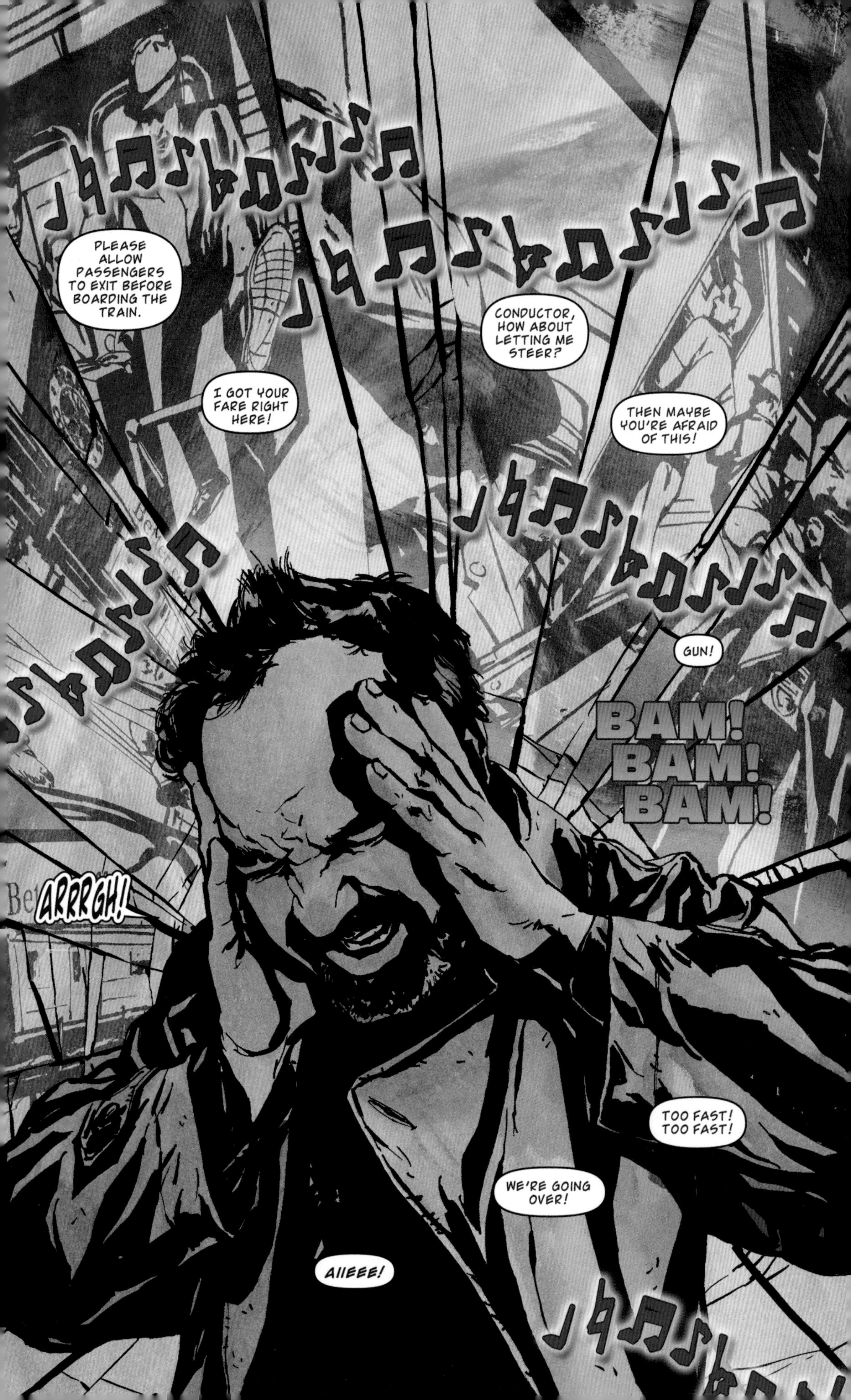
PLEASE ALLOW PASSENGERS TO EXIT BEFORE BOARDING THE TRAIN.
CONDUCTOR, HOW ABOUT LETTING ME STEER?
I GOT YOUR FARE RIGHT HERE!
THEN MAYBE YOU'RE AFRAID OF THIS!
GUN!
BAM! BAM! BAM!
ARRRGH!
TOO FAST! TOO FAST!
WE'RE GOING OVER!
AIIEEE!

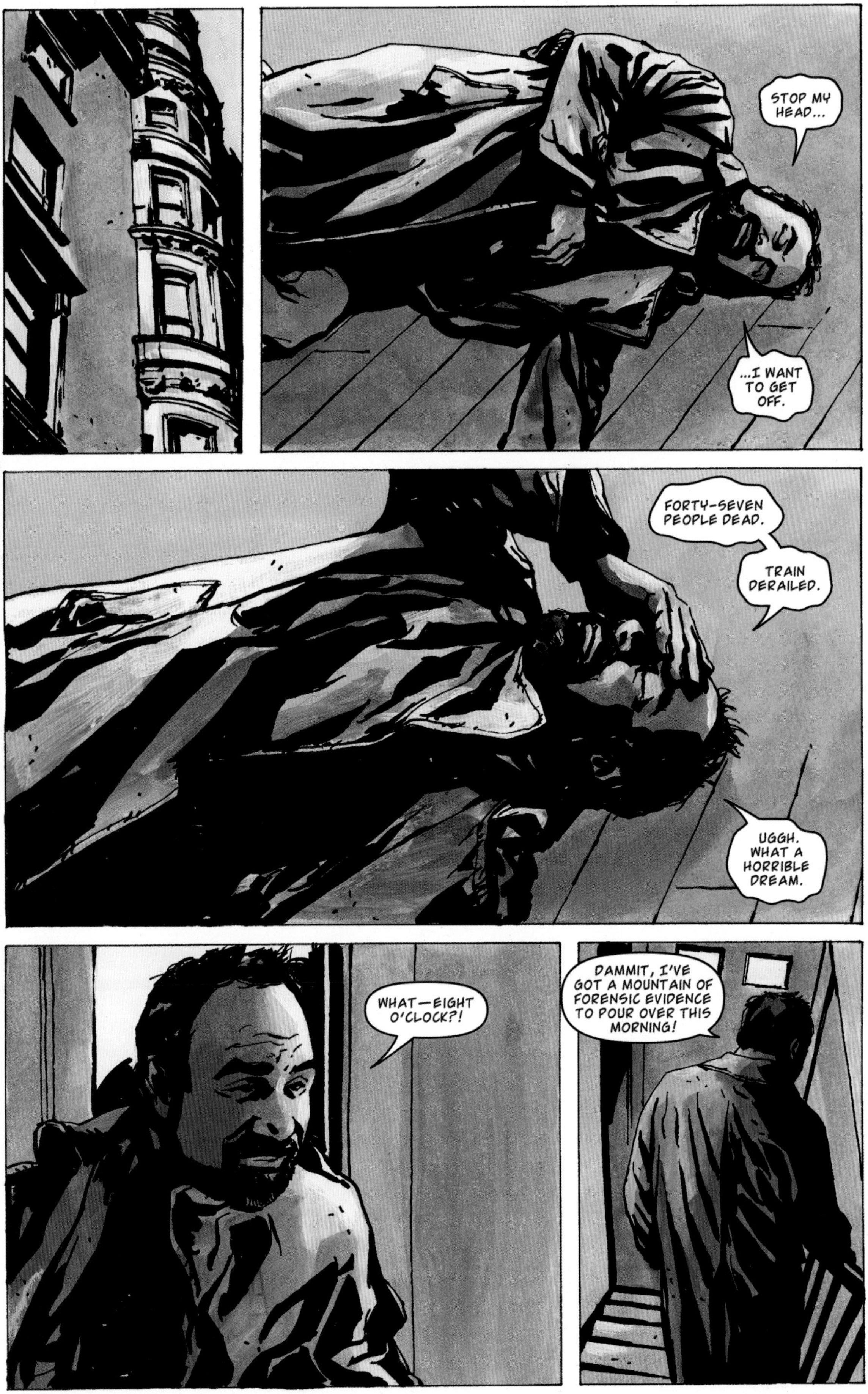
STOP MY HEAD...
...I WANT TO GET OFF.
FORTY-SEVEN PEOPLE DEAD.
TRAIN DERAILED.
UGGH. WHAT A HORRIBLE DREAM.
WHAT—EIGHT O'CLOCK?!
DAMMIT, I'VE GOT A MOUNTAIN OF FORENSIC EVIDENCE TO POUR OVER THIS MORNING!

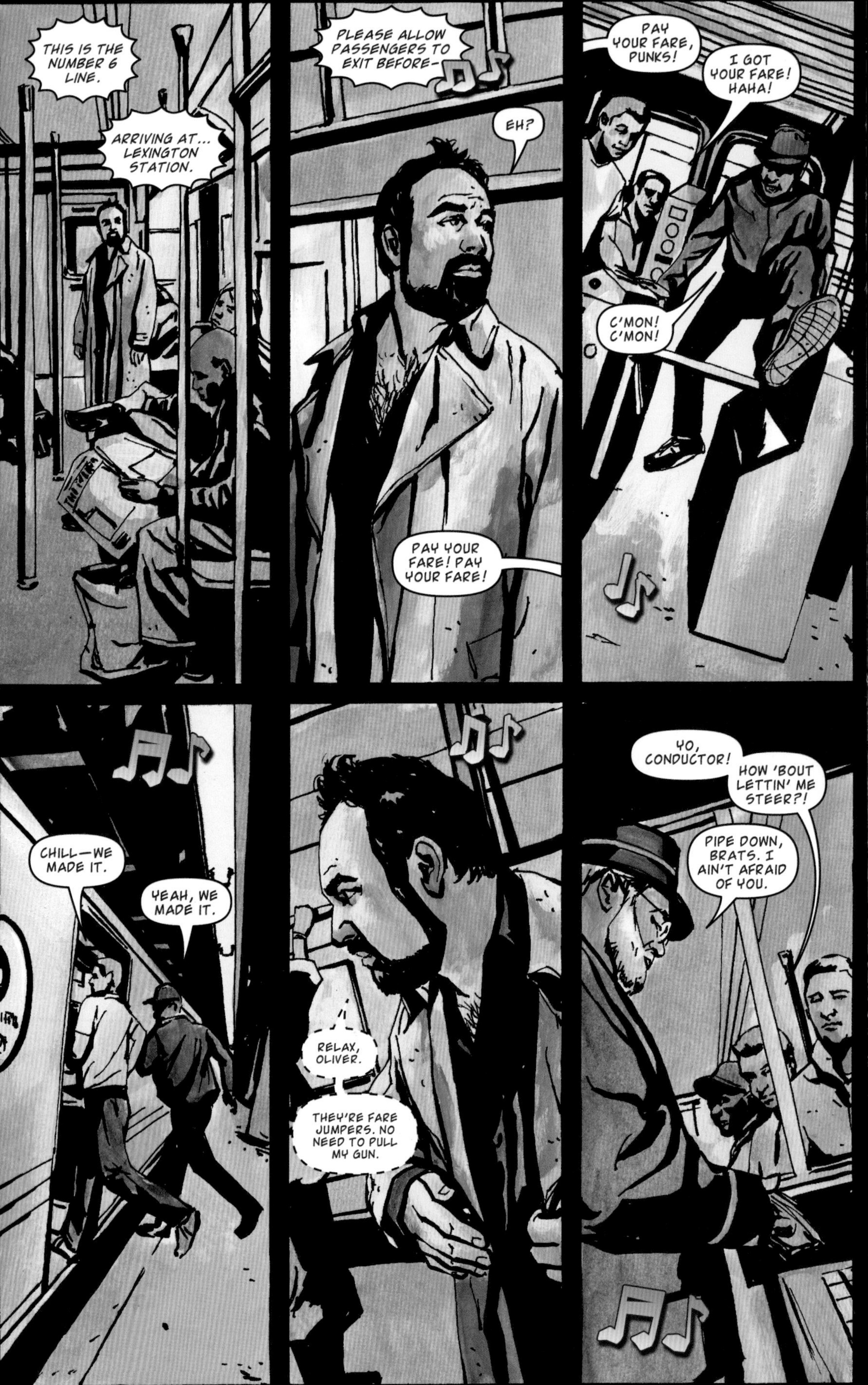
THIS IS THE NUMBER 6 LINE.
ARRIVING AT... LEXINGTON STATION.
PLEASE ALLOW PASSENGERS TO EXIT BEFORE–
EH?
PAY YOUR FARE! PAY YOUR FARE!
PAY YOUR FARE, PUNKS!
I GOT YOUR FARE! HAHA!
C'MON! C'MON!
CHILL—WE MADE IT.
YEAH, WE MADE IT.
RELAX, OLIVER.
THEY'RE FARE JUMPERS. NO NEED TO PULL MY GUN.
YO, CONDUCTOR!
HOW 'BOUT LETTIN' ME STEER?!
PIPE DOWN, BRATS. I AIN'T AFRAID OF YOU.

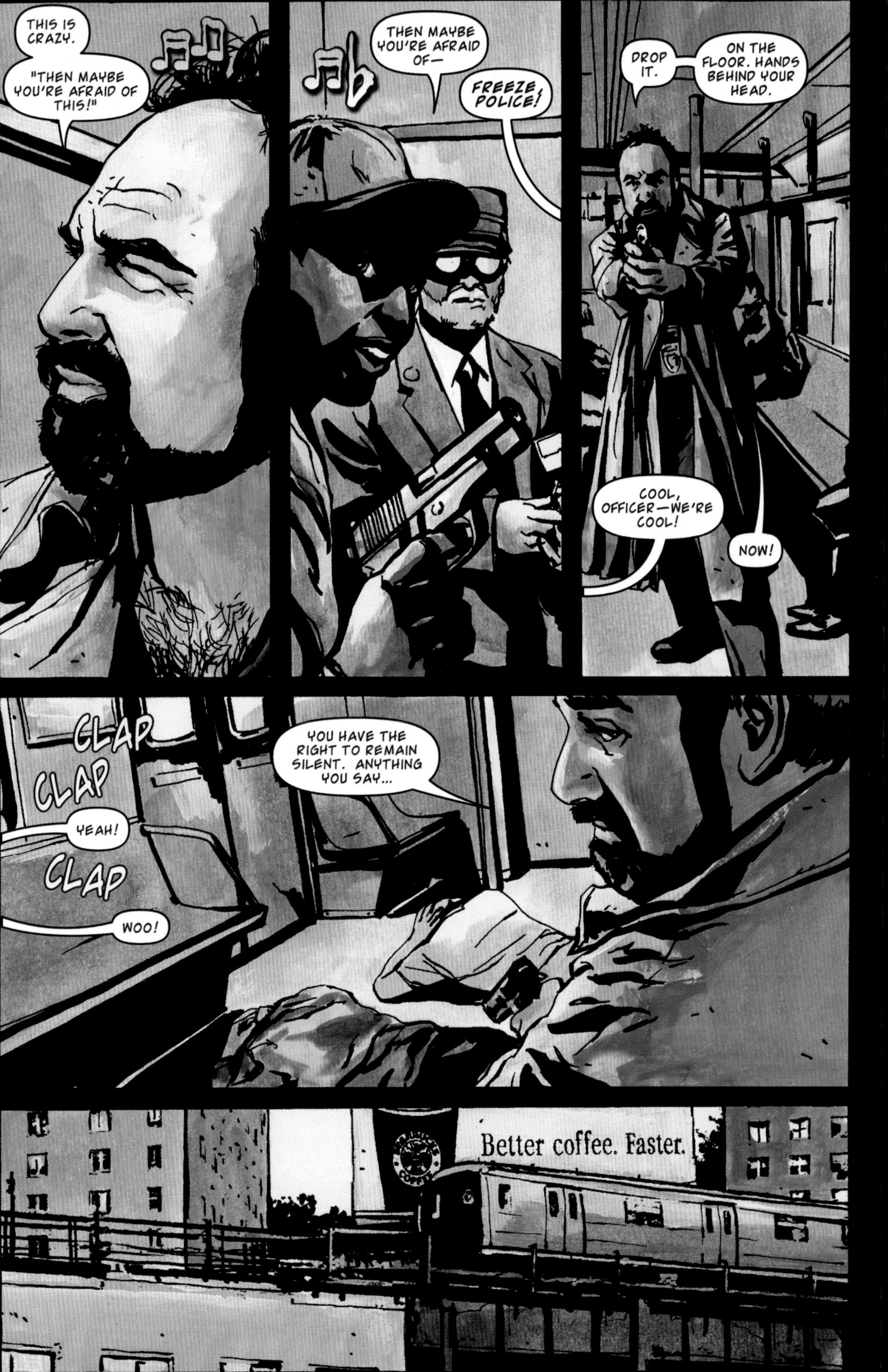
THIS IS CRAZY.
"THEN MAYBE YOU'RE AFRAID OF THIS!"
THEN MAYBE YOU'RE AFRAID OF—
FREEZE, POLICE!
DROP IT.
ON THE FLOOR. HANDS BEHIND YOUR HEAD.
COOL, OFFICER—WE'RE COOL!
NOW!
CLAP
CLAP
YEAH!
CLAP
WOO!
YOU HAVE THE RIGHT TO REMAIN SILENT. ANYTHING YOU SAY...
Better coffee. Faster.

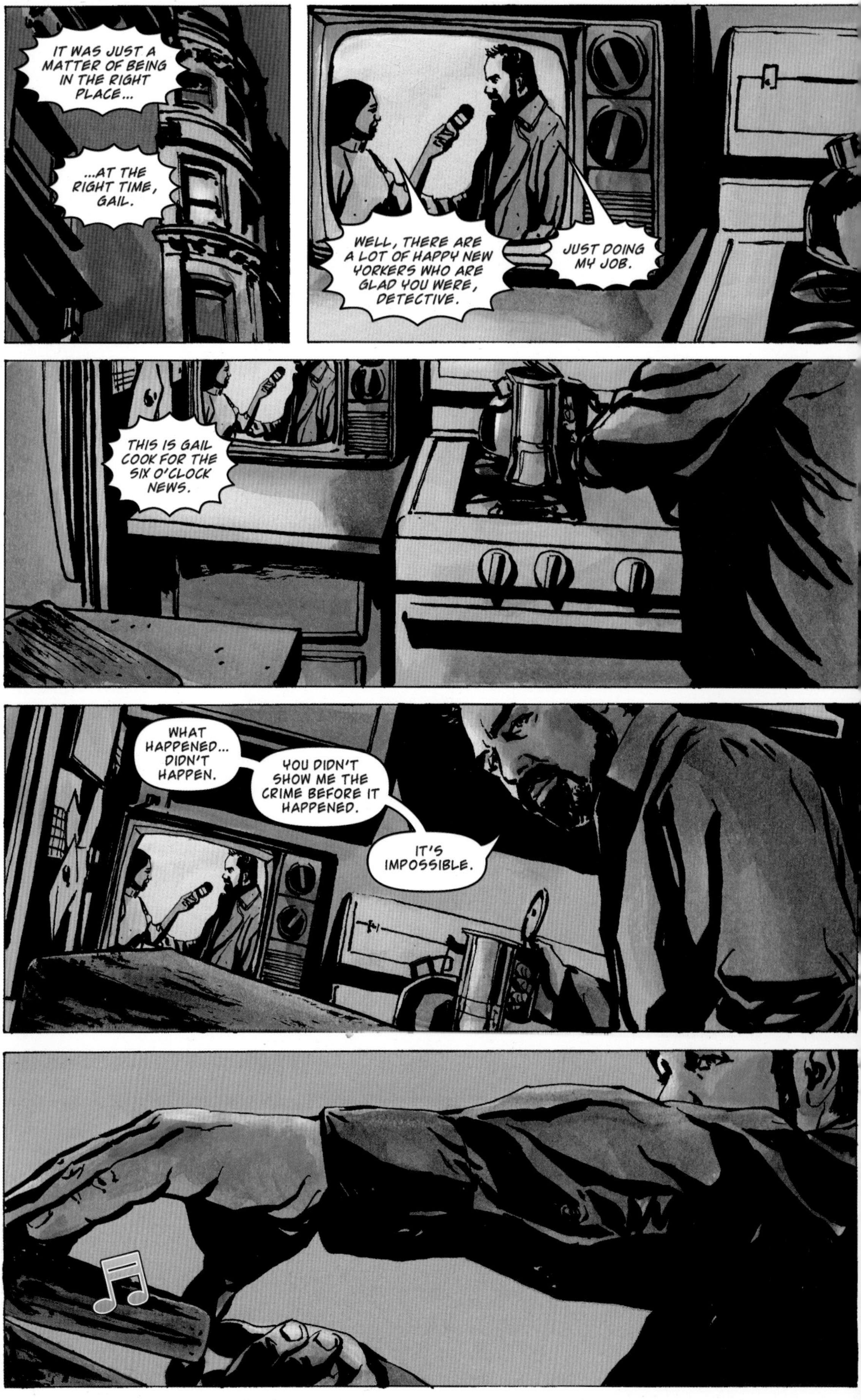
IT WAS JUST A MATTER OF BEING IN THE RIGHT PLACE...
...AT THE RIGHT TIME, GAIL.
WELL, THERE ARE A LOT OF HAPPY NEW YORKERS WHO ARE GLAD YOU WERE, DETECTIVE.
JUST DOING MY JOB.
THIS IS GAIL COOK FOR THE SIX O'CLOCK NEWS.
WHAT HAPPENED... DIDN'T HAPPEN.
YOU DIDN'T SHOW ME THE CRIME BEFORE IT HAPPENED.
IT'S IMPOSSIBLE.

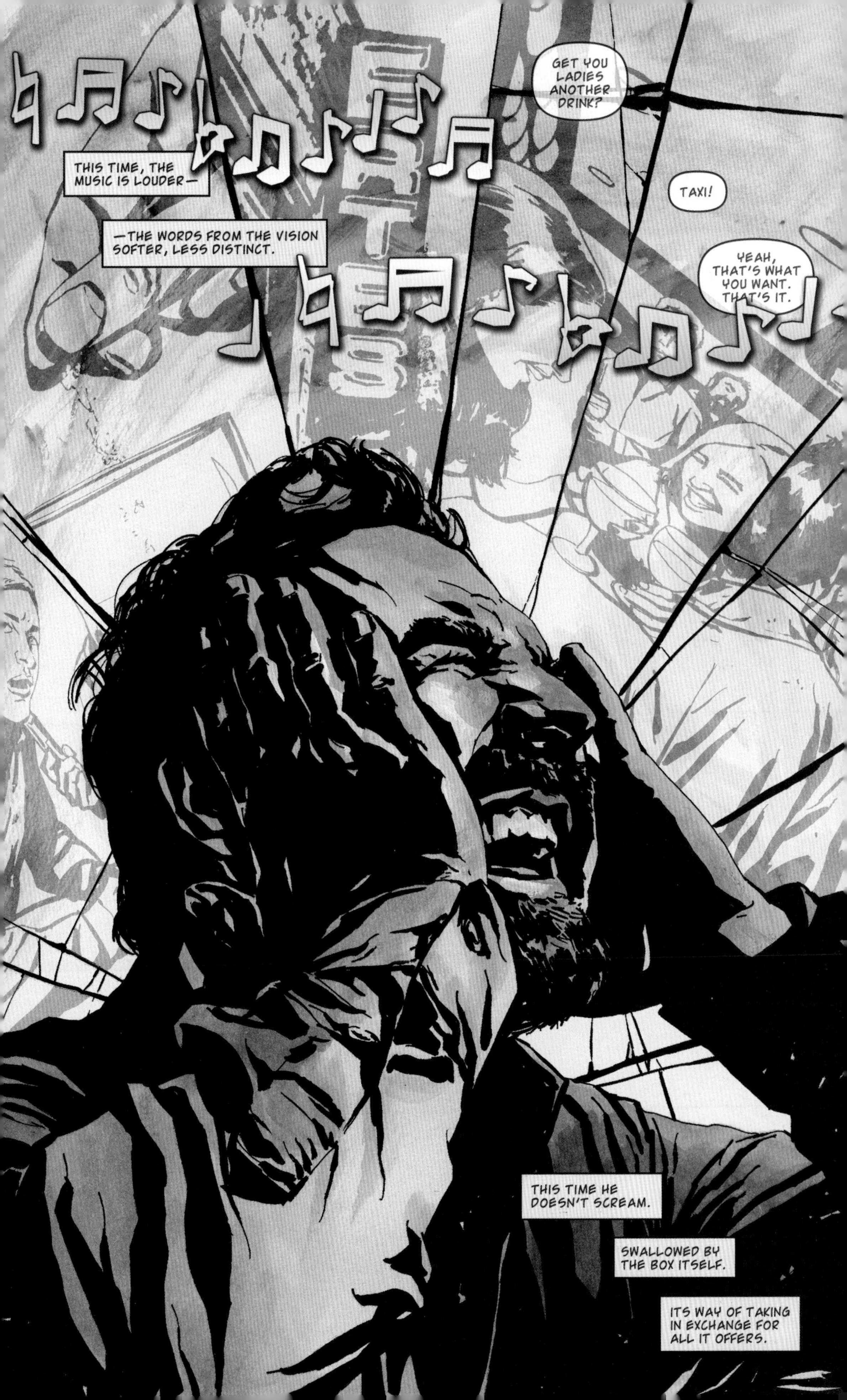
GET YOU LADIES ANOTHER DRINK?
THIS TIME, THE MUSIC IS LOUDER—
—THE WORDS FROM THE VISION SOFTER, LESS DISTINCT.
TAXI!
YEAH, THAT'S WHAT YOU WANT. THAT'S IT.
THIS TIME HE DOESN'T SCREAM.
SWALLOWED BY THE BOX ITSELF.
ITS WAY OF TAKING IN EXCHANGE FOR ALL IT OFFERS.

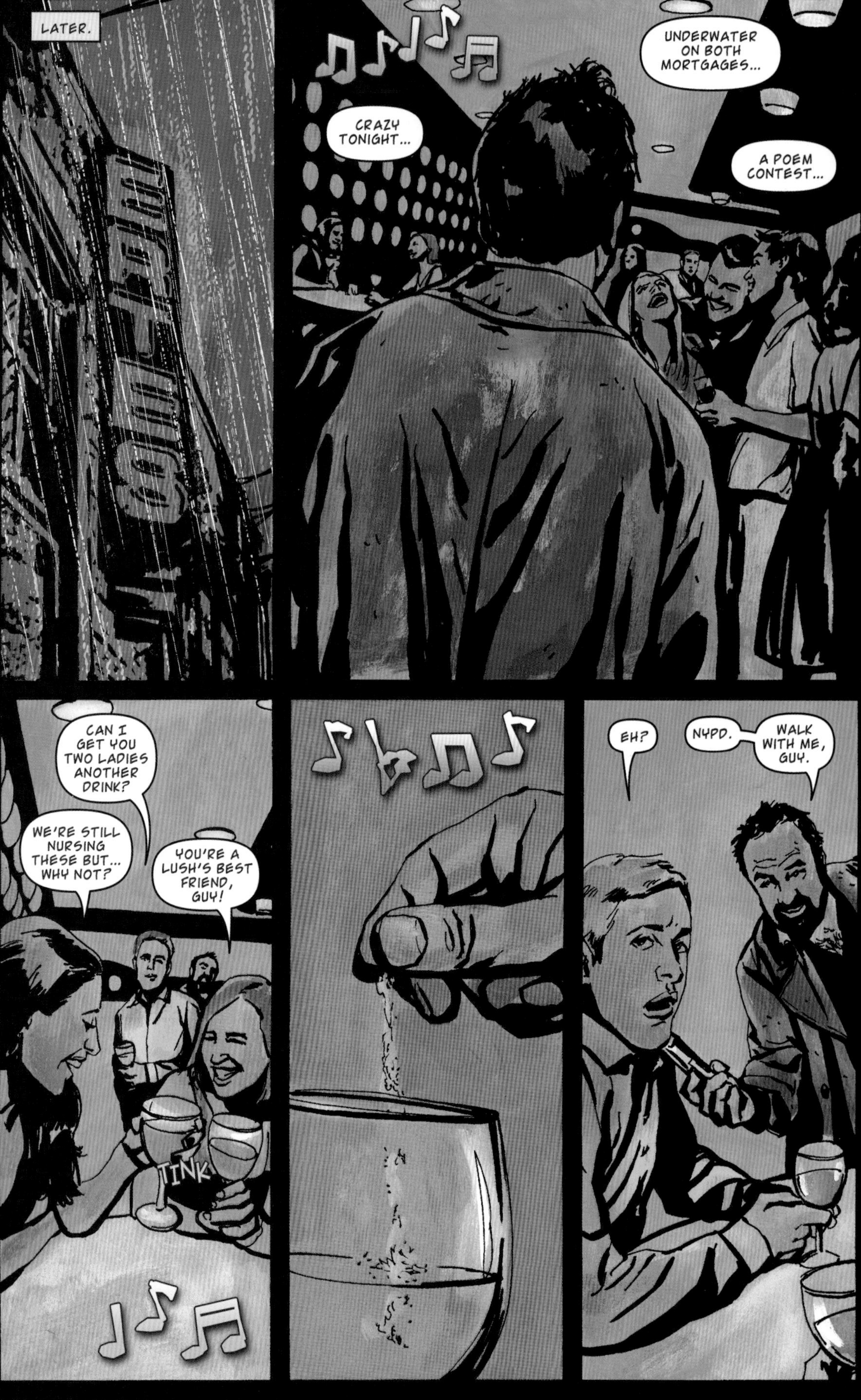
LATER.
UNDERWATER ON BOTH MORTGAGES...
CRAZY TONIGHT...
A POEM CONTEST...
CAN I GET YOU TWO LADIES ANOTHER DRINK?
WE'RE STILL NURSING THESE BUT... WHY NOT?
YOU'RE A LUSH'S BEST FRIEND, GUY!
TINK
EH?
NYPD.
WALK WITH ME, GUY.

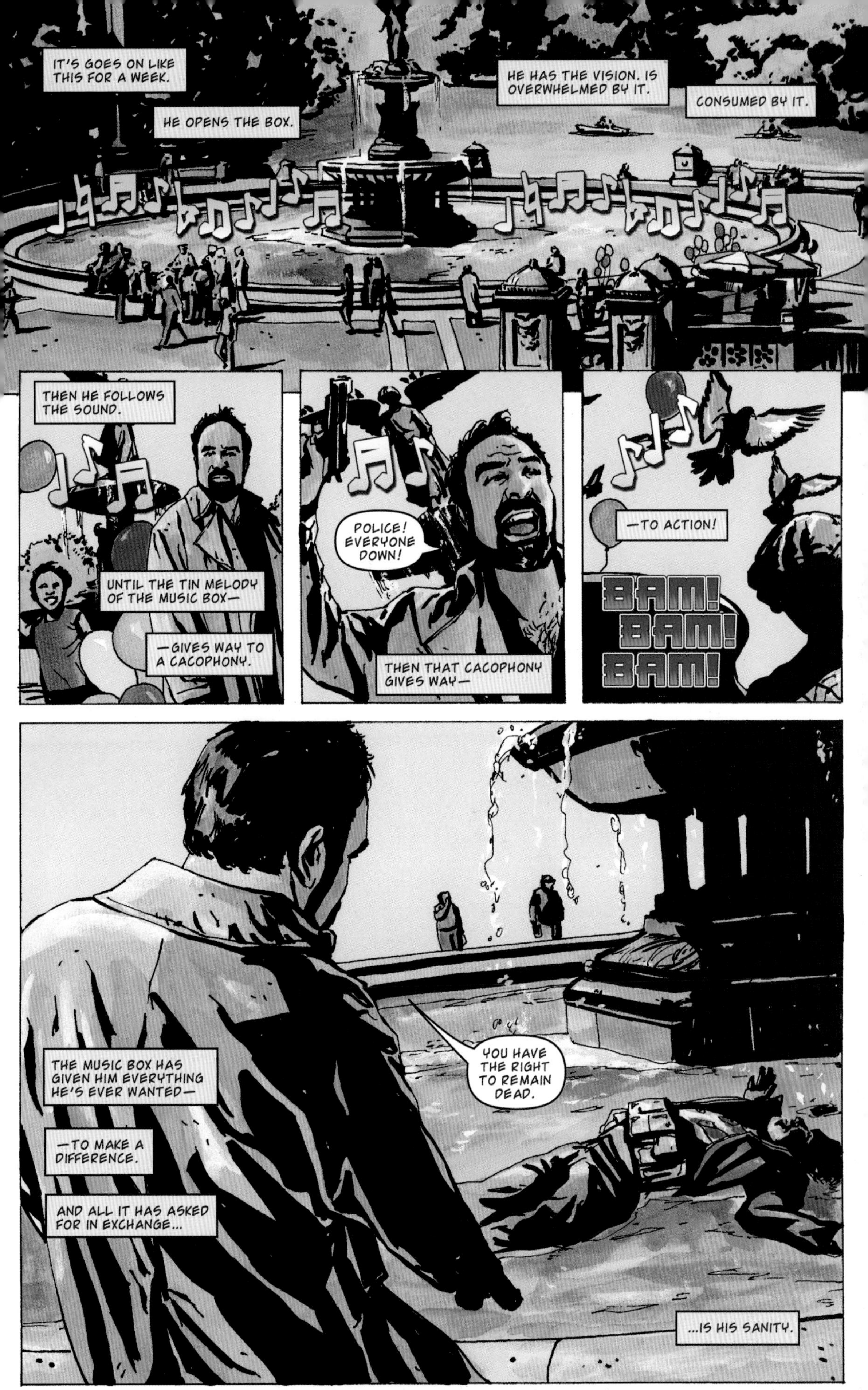
IT'S GOES ON LIKE THIS FOR A WEEK.
HE OPENS THE BOX.
HE HAS THE VISION. IS OVERWHELMED BY IT.
CONSUMED BY IT.
THEN HE FOLLOWS THE SOUND.
UNTIL THE TIN MELODY OF THE MUSIC BOX—
—GIVES WAY TO A CACOPHONY.
POLICE! EVERYONE DOWN!
THEN THAT CACOPHONY GIVES WAY—
—TO ACTION!
BAM! BAM! BAM!
THE MUSIC BOX HAS GIVEN HIM EVERYTHING HE'S EVER WANTED—
YOU HAVE THE RIGHT TO REMAIN DEAD.
—TO MAKE A DIFFERENCE.
AND ALL IT HAS ASKED FOR IN EXCHANGE...
...IS HIS SANITY.

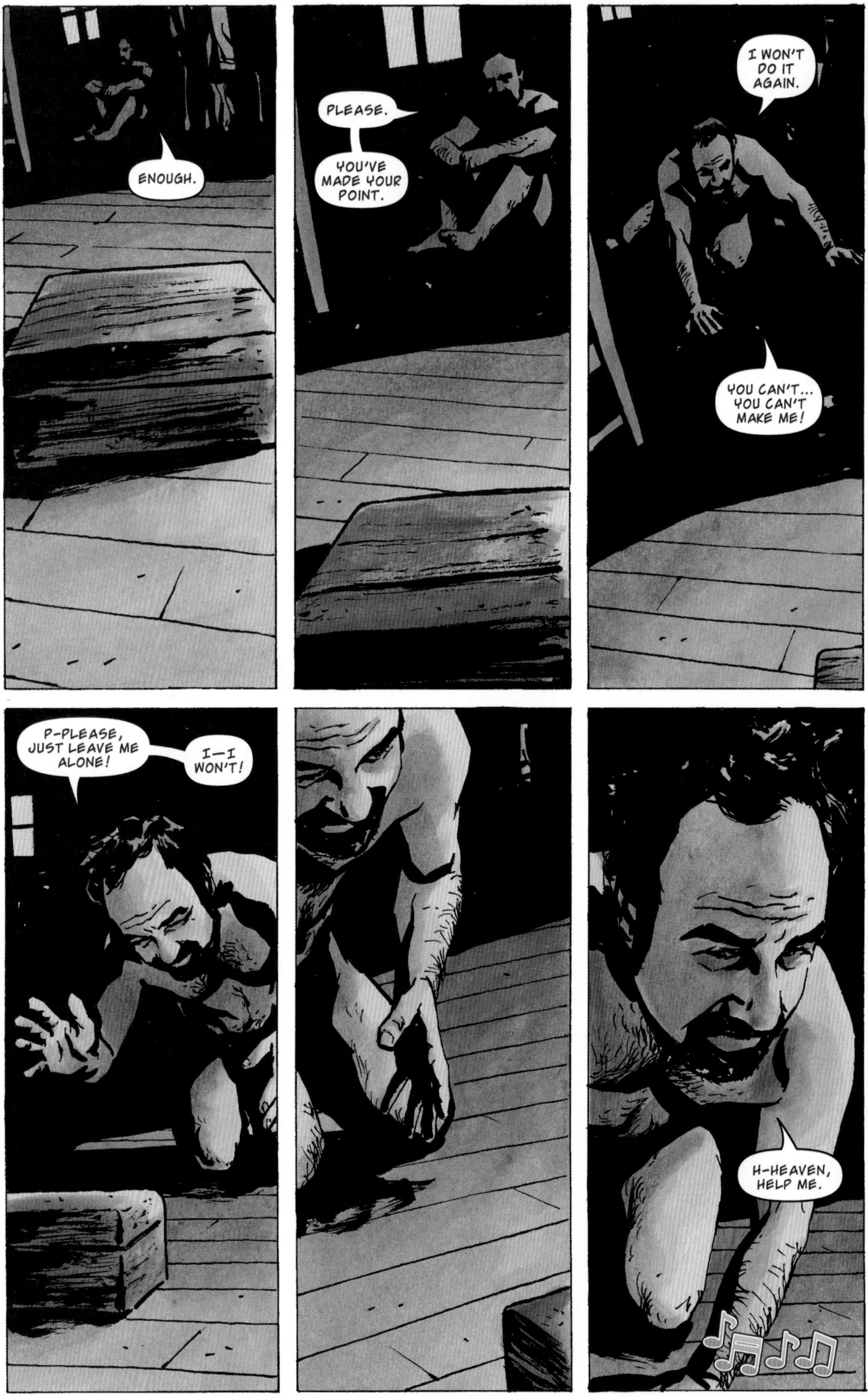
ENOUGH.
PLEASE.
YOU'VE MADE YOUR POINT.
I WON'T DO IT AGAIN.
YOU CAN'T... YOU CAN'T MAKE ME!
P-PLEASE, JUST LEAVE ME ALONE!
I--I WON'T!
H-HEAVEN, HELP ME.

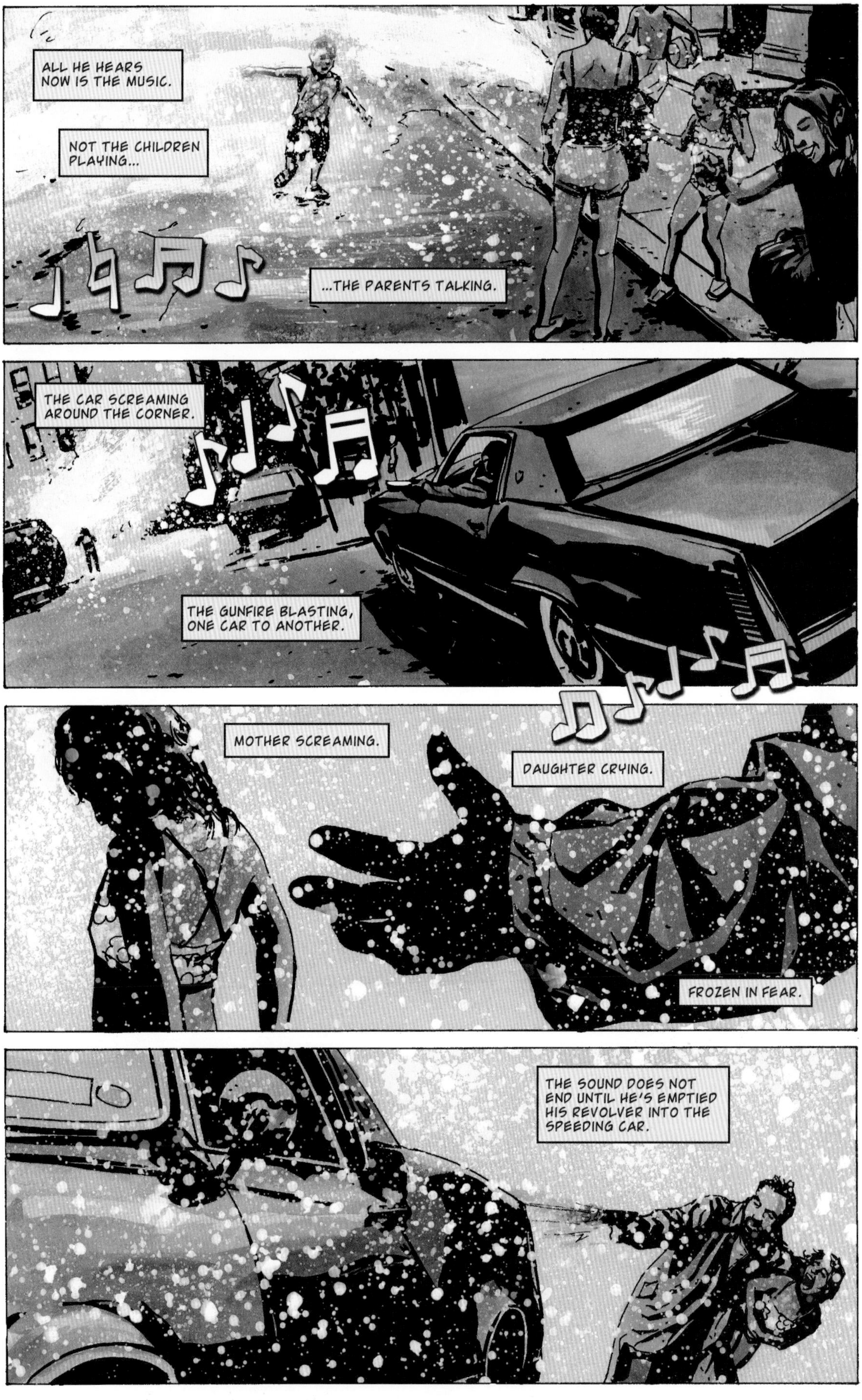
ALL HE HEARS NOW IS THE MUSIC.
NOT THE CHILDREN PLAYING...
...THE PARENTS TALKING.
THE CAR SCREAMING AROUND THE CORNER.
THE GUNFIRE BLASTING, ONE CAR TO ANOTHER.
MOTHER SCREAMING.
DAUGHTER CRYING.
FROZEN IN FEAR.
THE SOUND DOES NOT END UNTIL HE'S EMPTIED HIS REVOLVER INTO THE SPEEDING CAR.

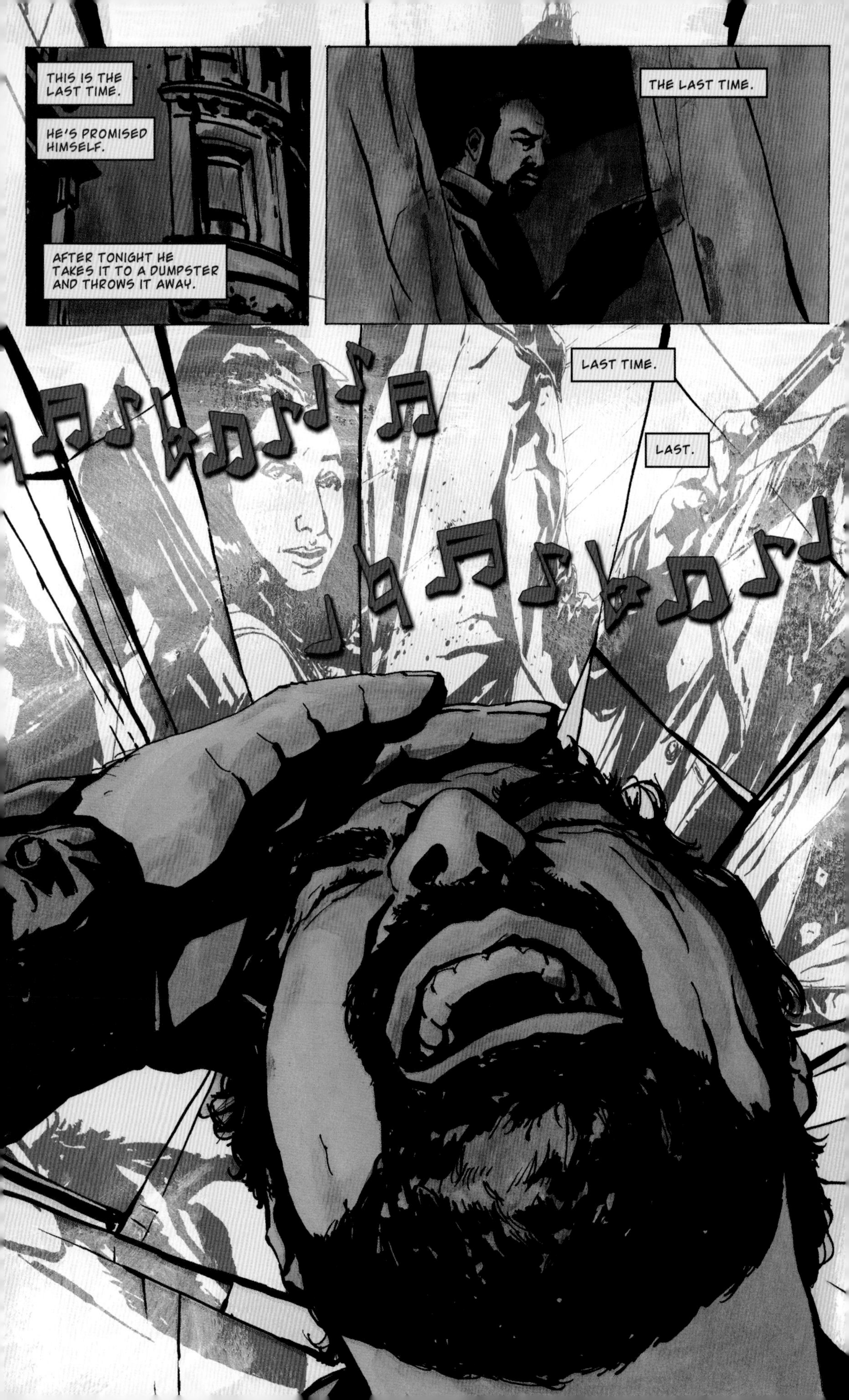
THIS IS THE LAST TIME.
HE'S PROMISED HIMSELF.
AFTER TONIGHT HE TAKES IT TO A DUMPSTER AND THROWS IT AWAY.
THE LAST TIME.
LAST TIME.
LAST.

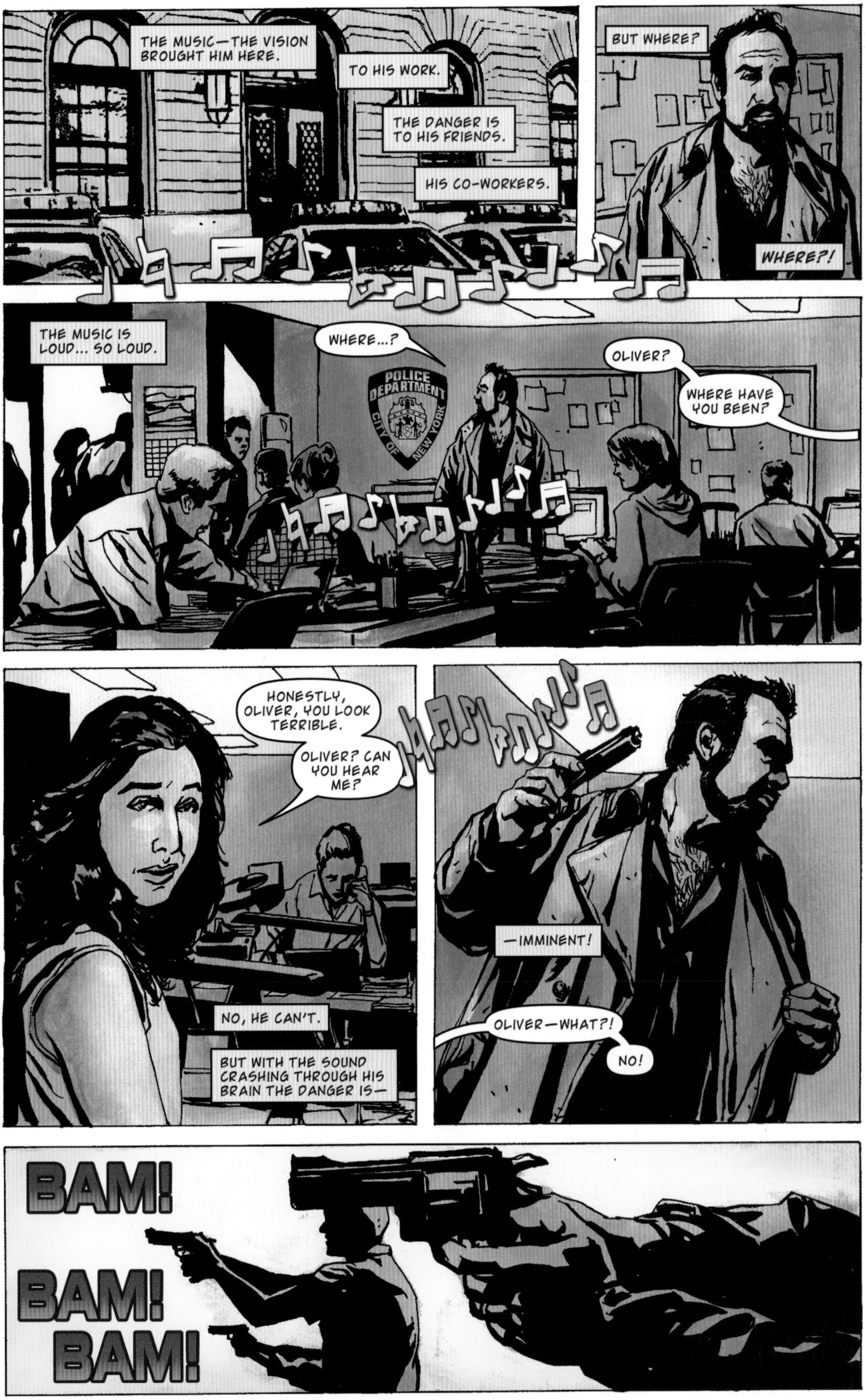
THE MUSIC—THE VISION BROUGHT HIM HERE.
TO HIS WORK.
THE DANGER IS TO HIS FRIENDS.
HIS CO-WORKERS.
BUT WHERE?
WHERE?!
THE MUSIC IS LOUD... SO LOUD.
WHERE...?
POLICE DEPARTMENT CITY OF NEW YORK
OLIVER?
WHERE HAVE YOU BEEN?
HONESTLY, OLIVER, YOU LOOK TERRIBLE.
OLIVER? CAN YOU HEAR ME?
NO, HE CAN'T.
BUT WITH THE SOUND CRASHING THROUGH HIS BRAIN THE DANGER IS—
—IMMINENT!
OLIVER—WHAT?!
NO!
BAM!
BAM!
BAM!

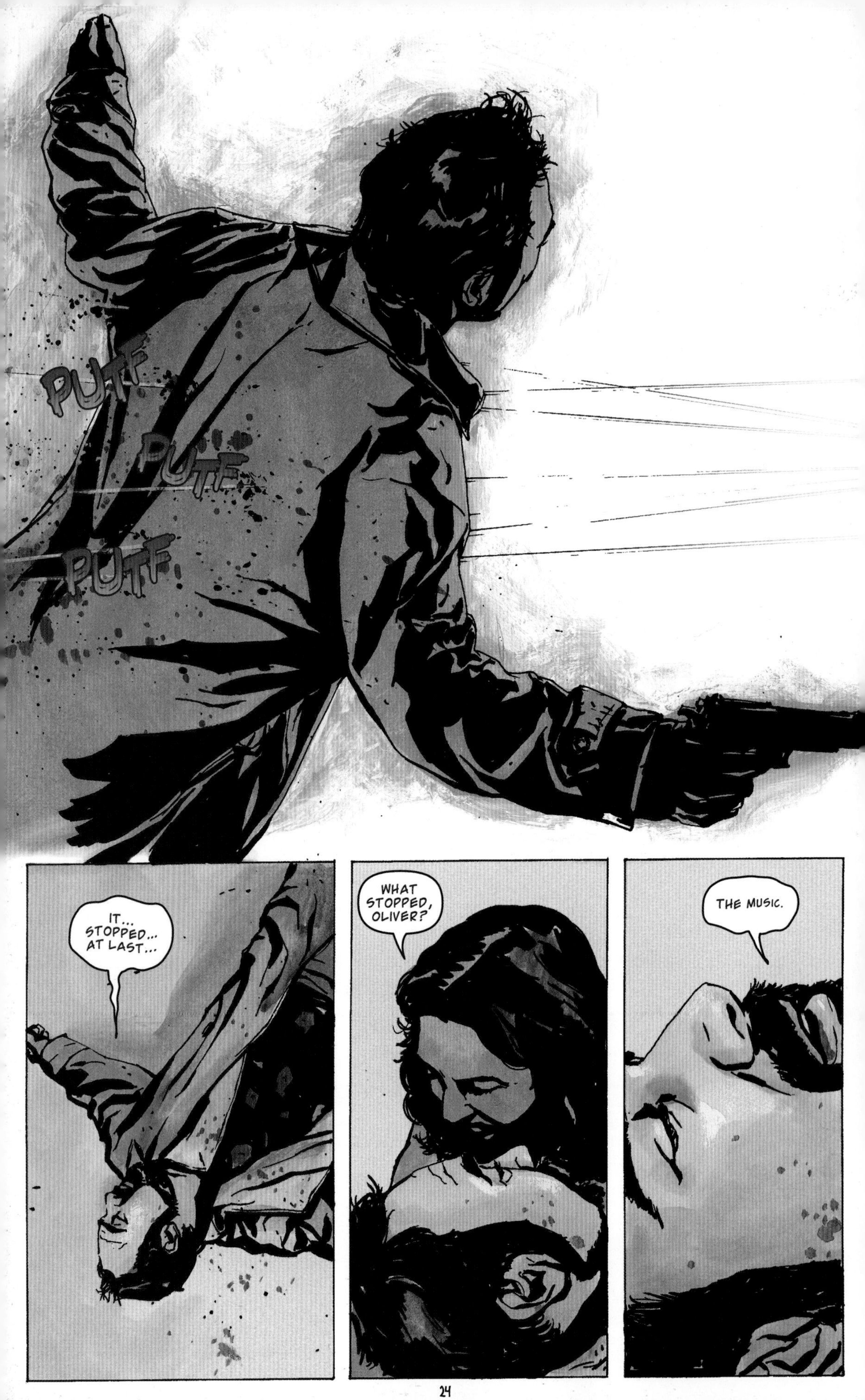
PUTF
PUTF
PUTF
IT... STOPPED... AT LAST...
WHAT STOPPED, OLIVER?
THE MUSIC.

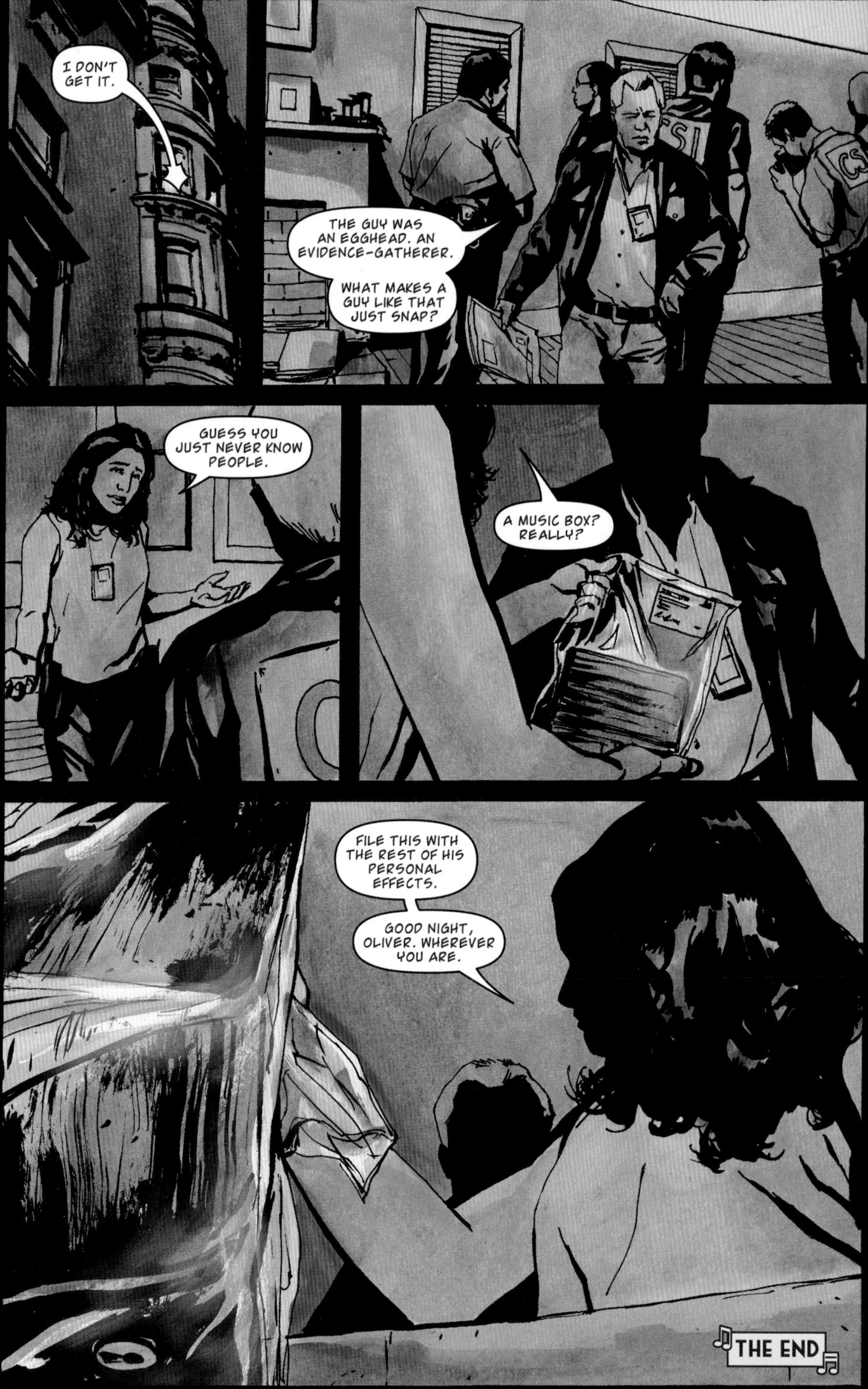
I DON'T GET IT.
THE GUY WAS AN EGGHEAD. AN EVIDENCE-GATHERER.
WHAT MAKES A GUY LIKE THAT JUST SNAP?
GUESS YOU JUST NEVER KNOW PEOPLE.
A MUSIC BOX? REALLY?
FILE THIS WITH THE REST OF HIS PERSONAL EFFECTS.
GOOD NIGHT, OLIVER. WHEREVER YOU ARE.
THE END

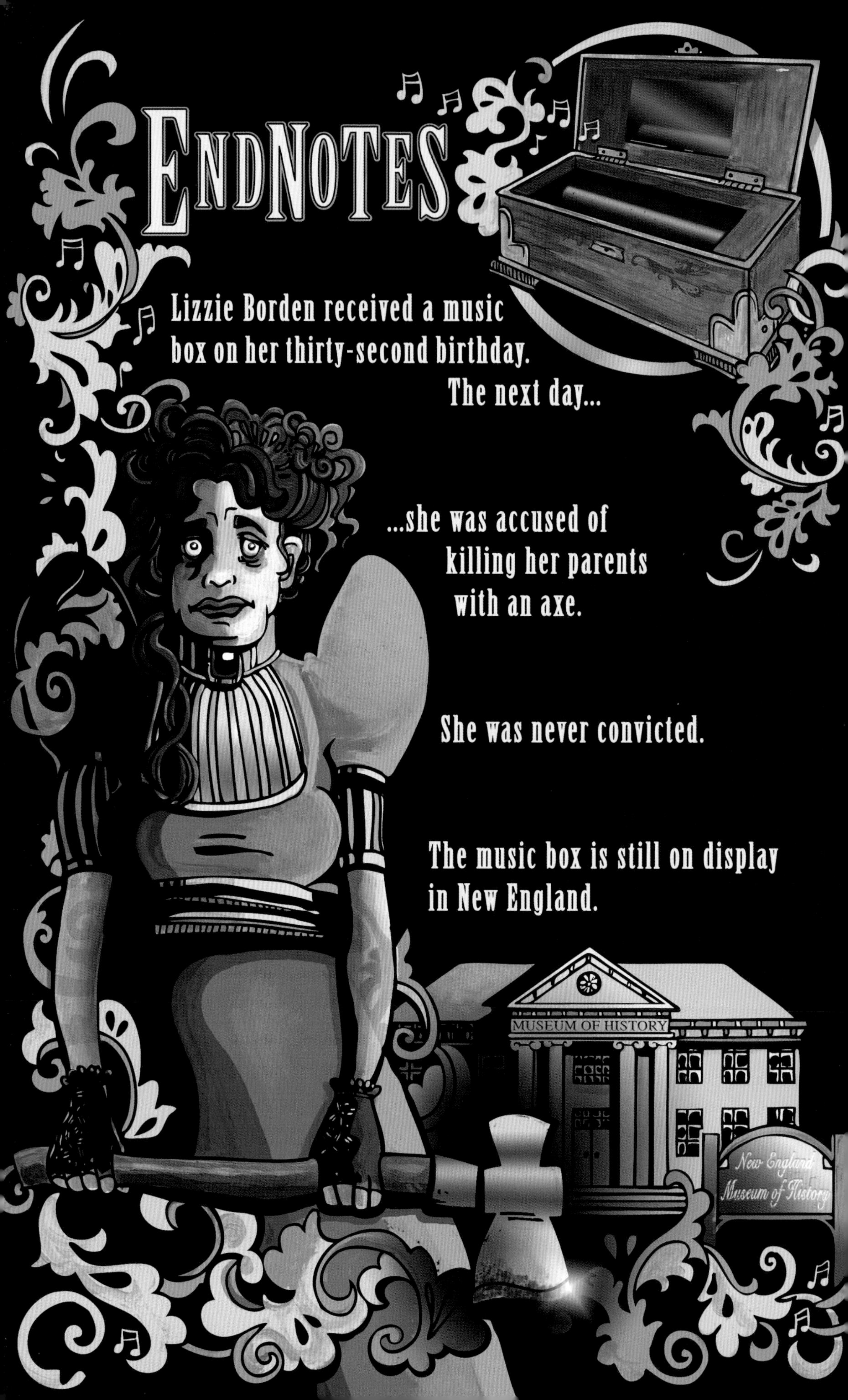
EndNotes
Lizzie Borden received a music box on her thirty-second birthday.
The next day...
...she was accused of killing her parents with an axe.
She was never convicted.
The music box is still on display in New England.
MUSEUM OF HISTORY
New England Museum of History

Chapter Two: "Wishes"

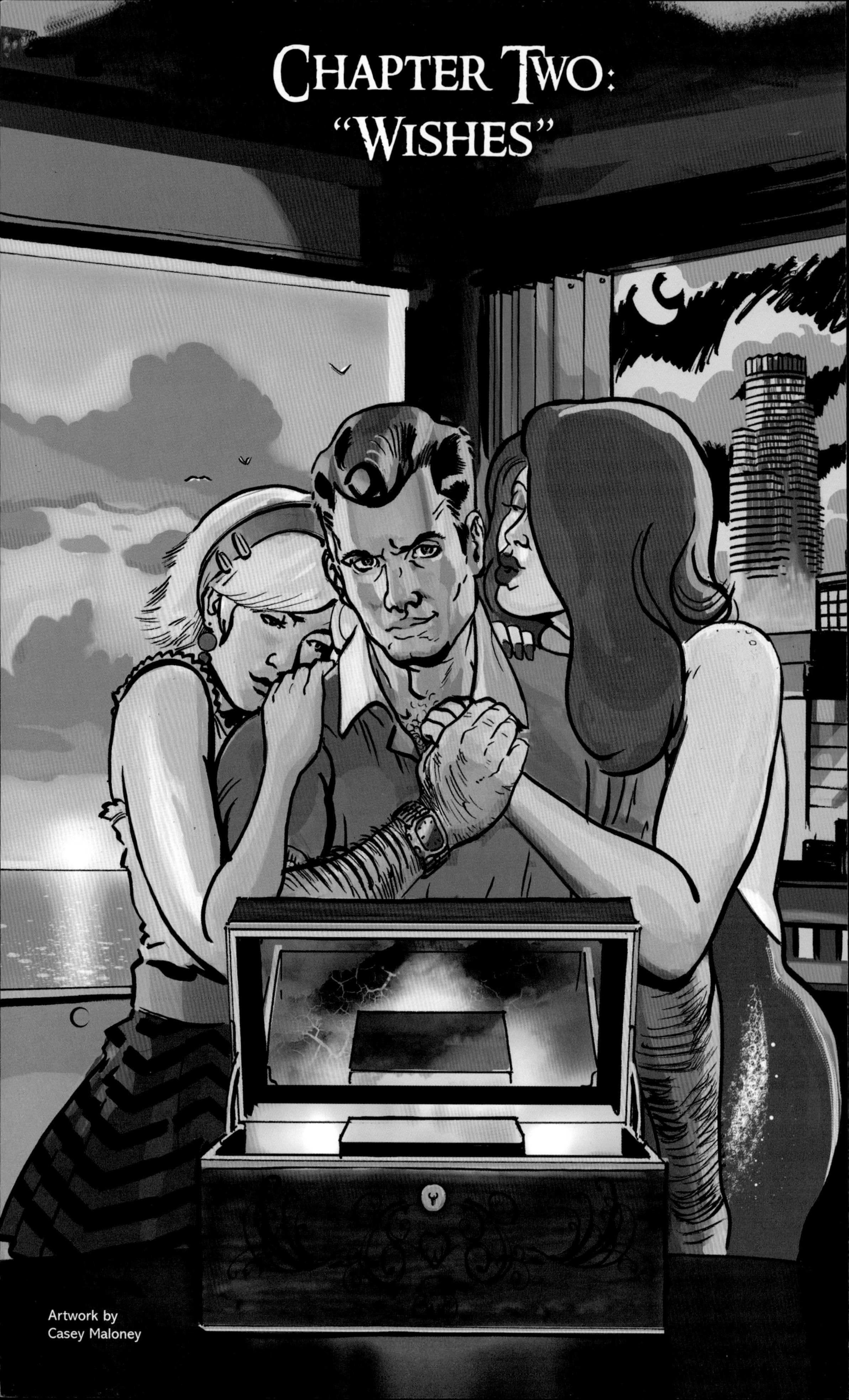

Artwork by
Casey Maloney

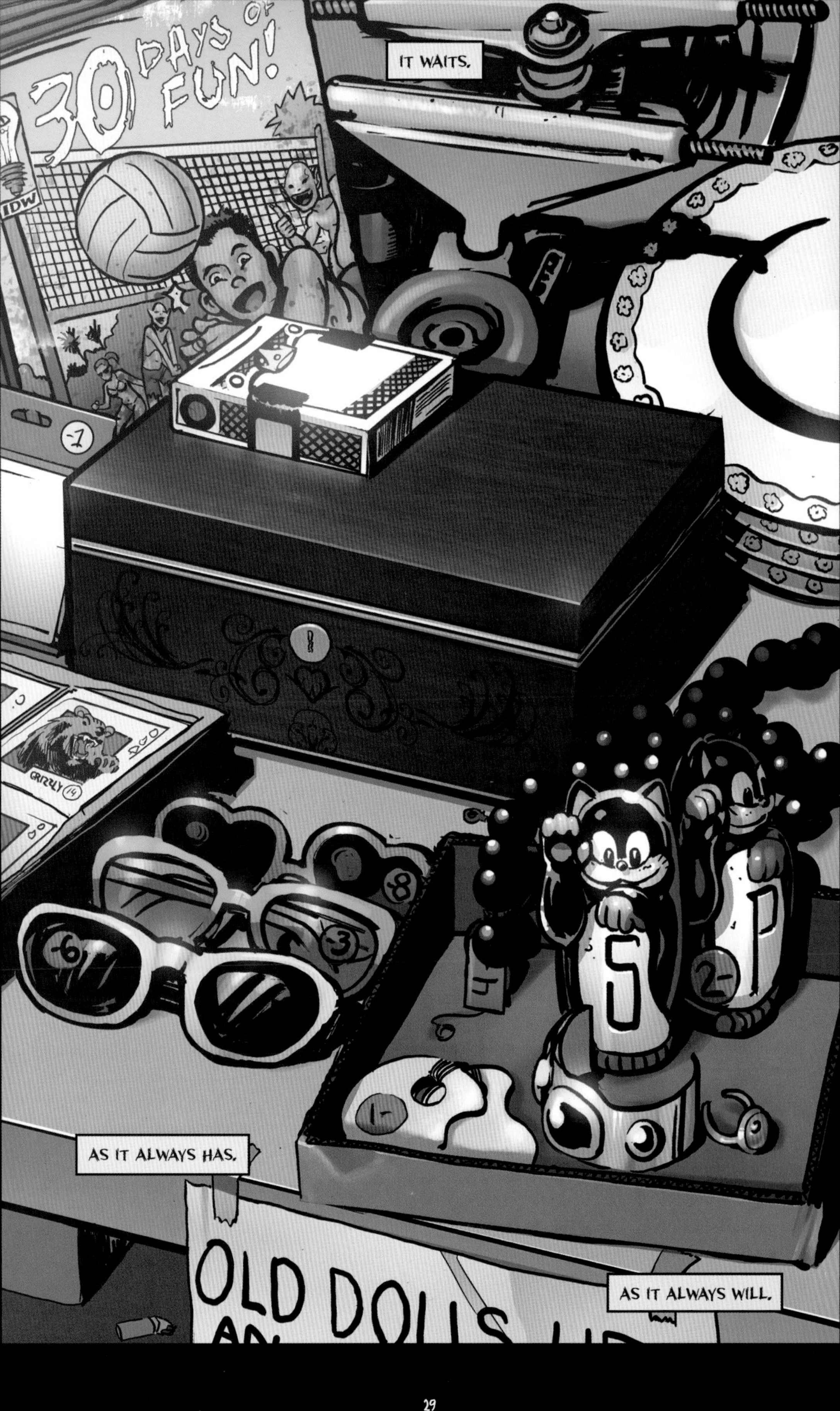
30 DAYS OF FUN!
IDW
IT WAITS.
GRIZZLY 14
AS IT ALWAYS HAS.
OLD
AS IT ALWAYS WILL.

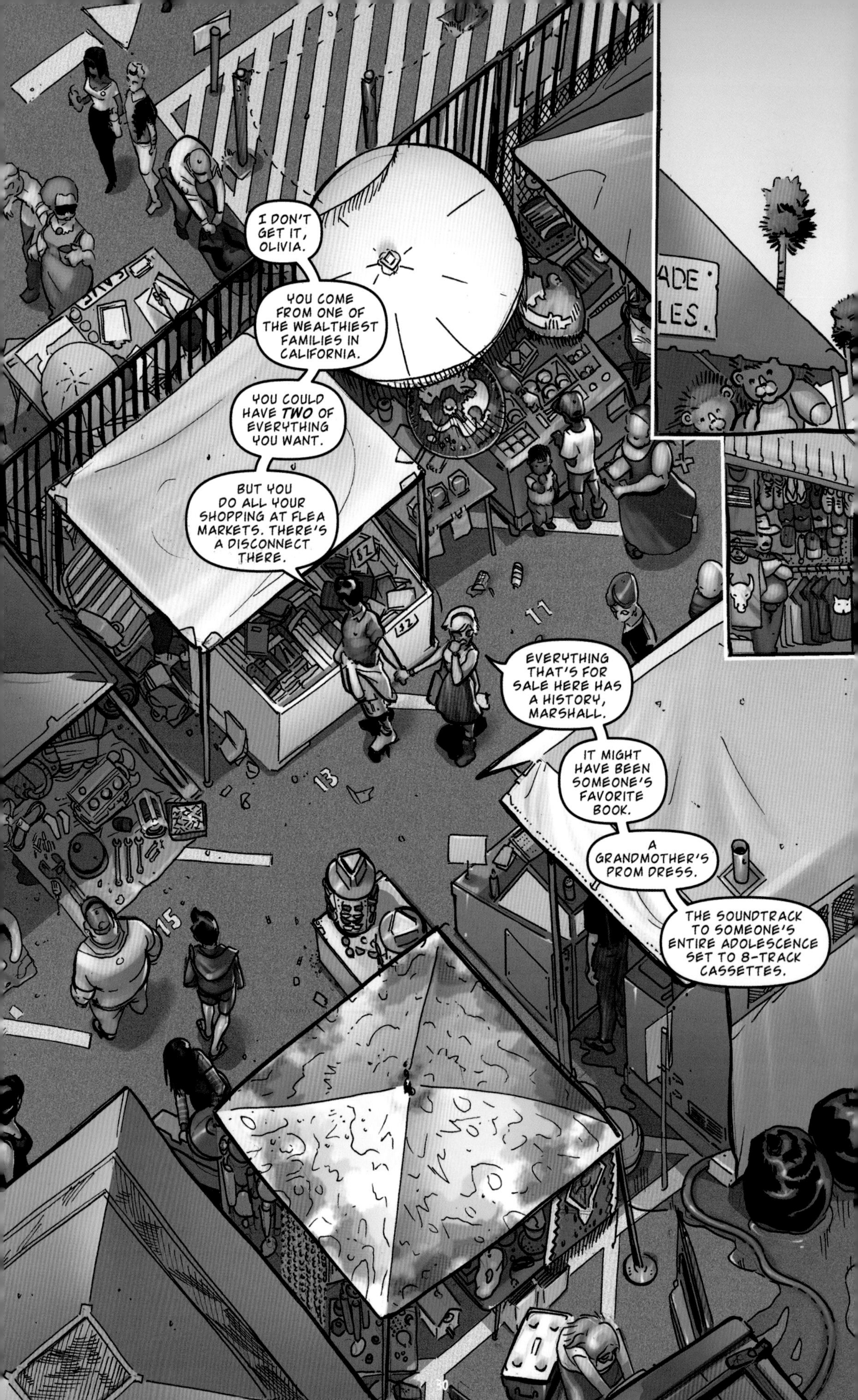
I DON'T GET IT, OLIVIA.
YOU COME FROM ONE OF THE WEALTHIEST FAMILIES IN CALIFORNIA.
YOU COULD HAVE **TWO** OF EVERYTHING YOU WANT.
BUT YOU DO ALL YOUR SHOPPING AT FLEA MARKETS. THERE'S A DISCONNECT THERE.
ADE
LES.
EVERYTHING THAT'S FOR SALE HERE HAS A HISTORY, MARSHALL.
IT MIGHT HAVE BEEN SOMEONE'S FAVORITE BOOK.
A GRANDMOTHER'S PROM DRESS.
THE SOUNDTRACK TO SOMEONE'S ENTIRE ADOLESCENCE SET TO 8-TRACK CASSETTES.

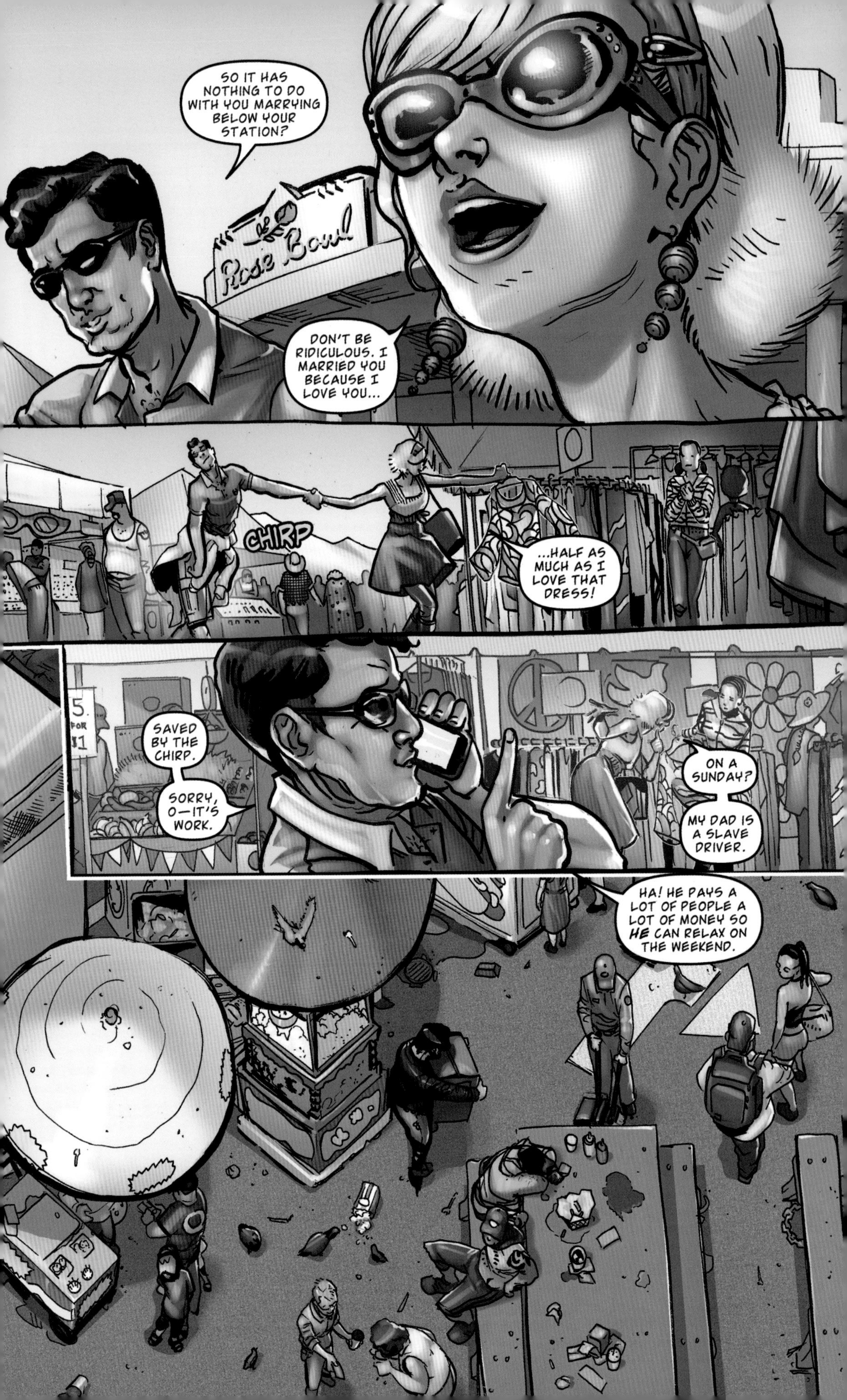
SO IT HAS NOTHING TO DO WITH YOU MARRYING BELOW YOUR STATION?
Rose Bowl
DON'T BE RIDICULOUS. I MARRIED YOU BECAUSE I LOVE YOU...
CHIRP
...HALF AS MUCH AS I LOVE THAT DRESS!
5 FOR $1
SAVED BY THE CHIRP.
SORRY, O—IT'S WORK.
ON A SUNDAY?
MY DAD IS A SLAVE DRIVER.
HA! HE PAYS A LOT OF PEOPLE A LOT OF MONEY SO *HE* CAN RELAX ON THE WEEKEND.

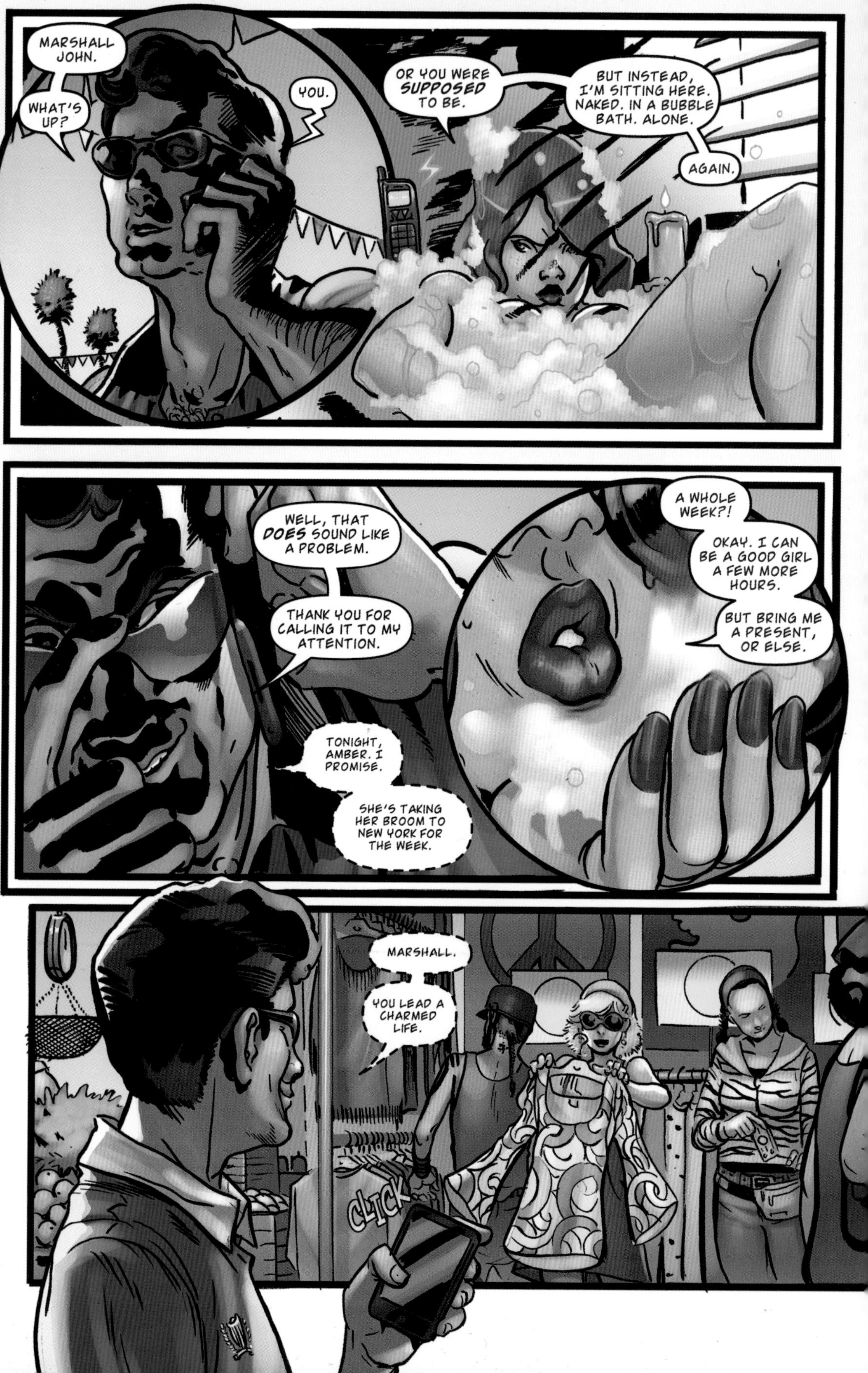
MARSHALL JOHN.
WHAT'S UP?
YOU.
OR YOU WERE SUPPOSED TO BE.
BUT INSTEAD, I'M SITTING HERE. NAKED. IN A BUBBLE BATH. ALONE.
AGAIN.
WELL, THAT DOES SOUND LIKE A PROBLEM.
THANK YOU FOR CALLING IT TO MY ATTENTION.
A WHOLE WEEK?!
OKAY. I CAN BE A GOOD GIRL A FEW MORE HOURS.
BUT BRING ME A PRESENT, OR ELSE.
TONIGHT, AMBER. I PROMISE.
SHE'S TAKING HER BROOM TO NEW YORK FOR THE WEEK.
MARSHALL.
YOU LEAD A CHARMED LIFE.
CLICK

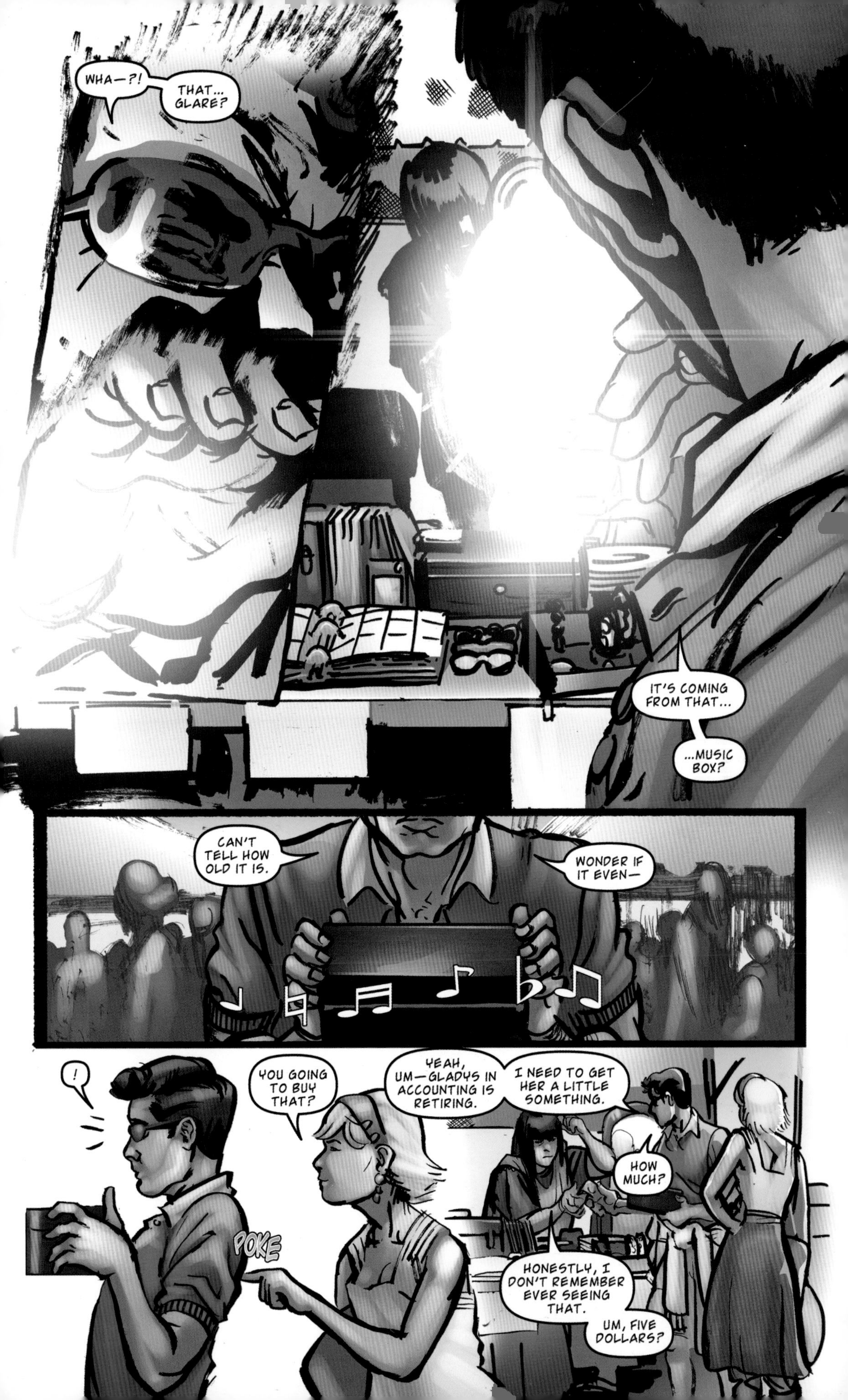
WHA—?!
THAT... GLARE?
IT'S COMING FROM THAT...
...MUSIC BOX?
CAN'T TELL HOW OLD IT IS.
WONDER IF IT EVEN—
!
YOU GOING TO BUY THAT?
POKE
YEAH, UM—GLADYS IN ACCOUNTING IS RETIRING.
I NEED TO GET HER A LITTLE SOMETHING.
HOW MUCH?
HONESTLY, I DON'T REMEMBER EVER SEEING THAT.
UM, FIVE DOLLARS?

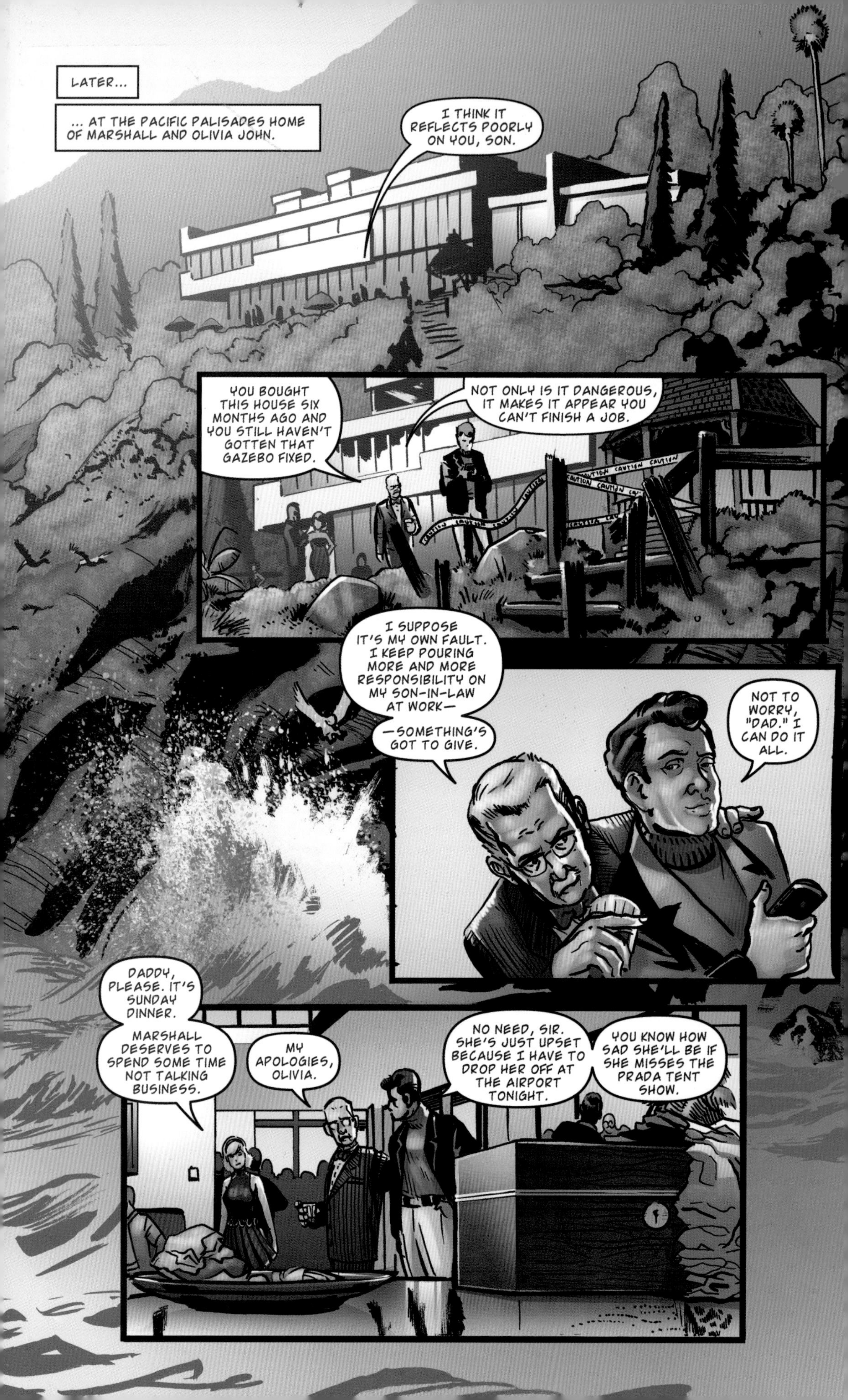
LATER...
... AT THE PACIFIC PALISADES HOME OF MARSHALL AND OLIVIA JOHN.
I THINK IT REFLECTS POORLY ON YOU, SON.
YOU BOUGHT THIS HOUSE SIX MONTHS AGO AND YOU STILL HAVEN'T GOTTEN THAT GAZEBO FIXED.
NOT ONLY IS IT DANGEROUS, IT MAKES IT APPEAR YOU CAN'T FINISH A JOB.
I SUPPOSE IT'S MY OWN FAULT. I KEEP POURING MORE AND MORE RESPONSIBILITY ON MY SON-IN-LAW AT WORK—
—SOMETHING'S GOT TO GIVE.
NOT TO WORRY, "DAD." I CAN DO IT ALL.
DADDY, PLEASE. IT'S SUNDAY DINNER.
MARSHALL DESERVES TO SPEND SOME TIME NOT TALKING BUSINESS.
MY APOLOGIES, OLIVIA.
NO NEED, SIR. SHE'S JUST UPSET BECAUSE I HAVE TO DROP HER OFF AT THE AIRPORT TONIGHT.
YOU KNOW HOW SAD SHE'LL BE IF SHE MISSES THE PRADA TENT SHOW.

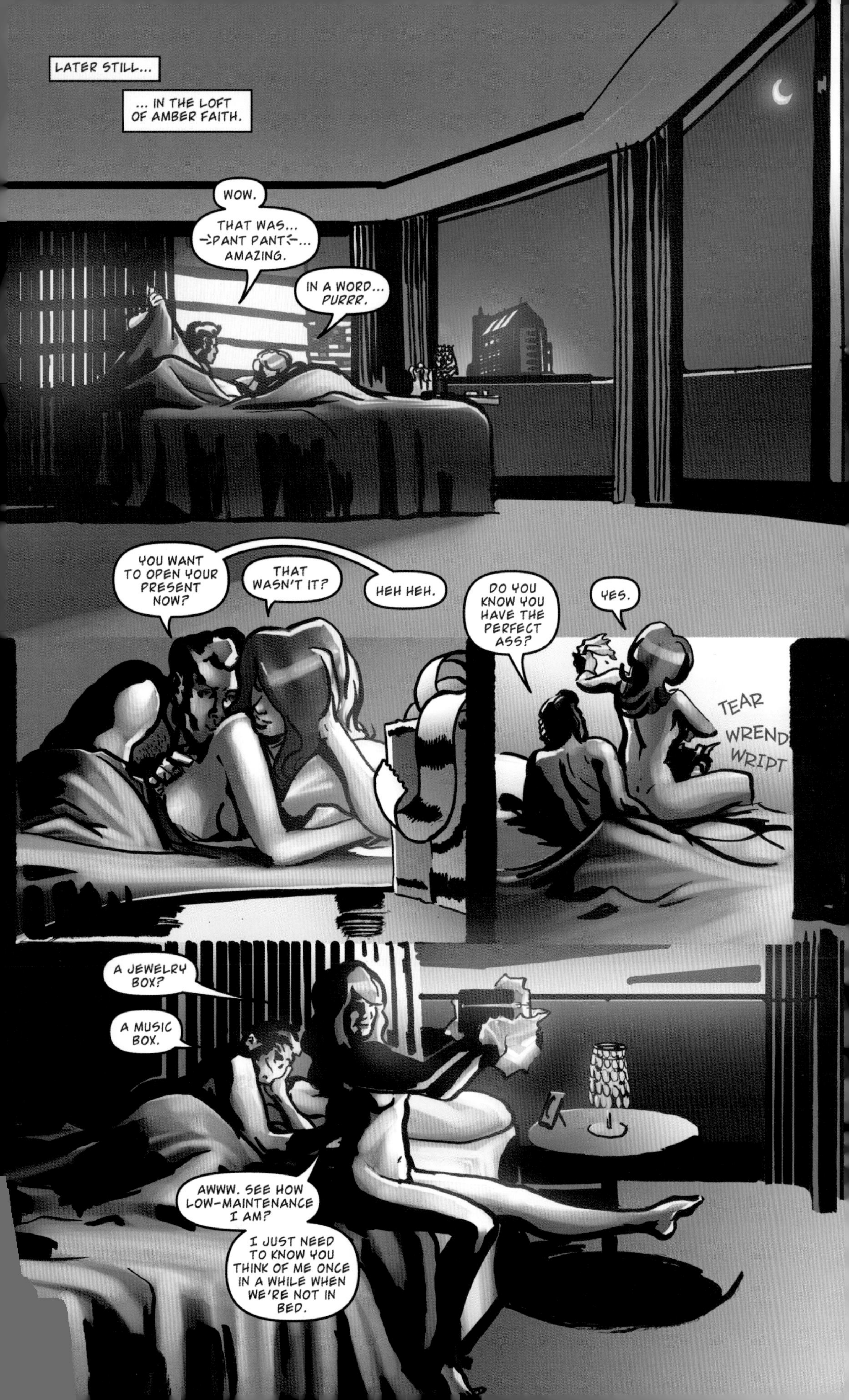
LATER STILL...
... IN THE LOFT OF AMBER FAITH.
WOW.
THAT WAS... -PANT PANT-... AMAZING.
IN A WORD... PURRR.
YOU WANT TO OPEN YOUR PRESENT NOW?
THAT WASN'T IT?
HEH HEH.
DO YOU KNOW YOU HAVE THE PERFECT ASS?
YES.
TEAR
WREND
WRIPT
A JEWELRY BOX?
A MUSIC BOX.
AWWW. SEE HOW LOW-MAINTENANCE I AM?
I JUST NEED TO KNOW YOU THINK OF ME ONCE IN A WHILE WHEN WE'RE NOT IN BED.

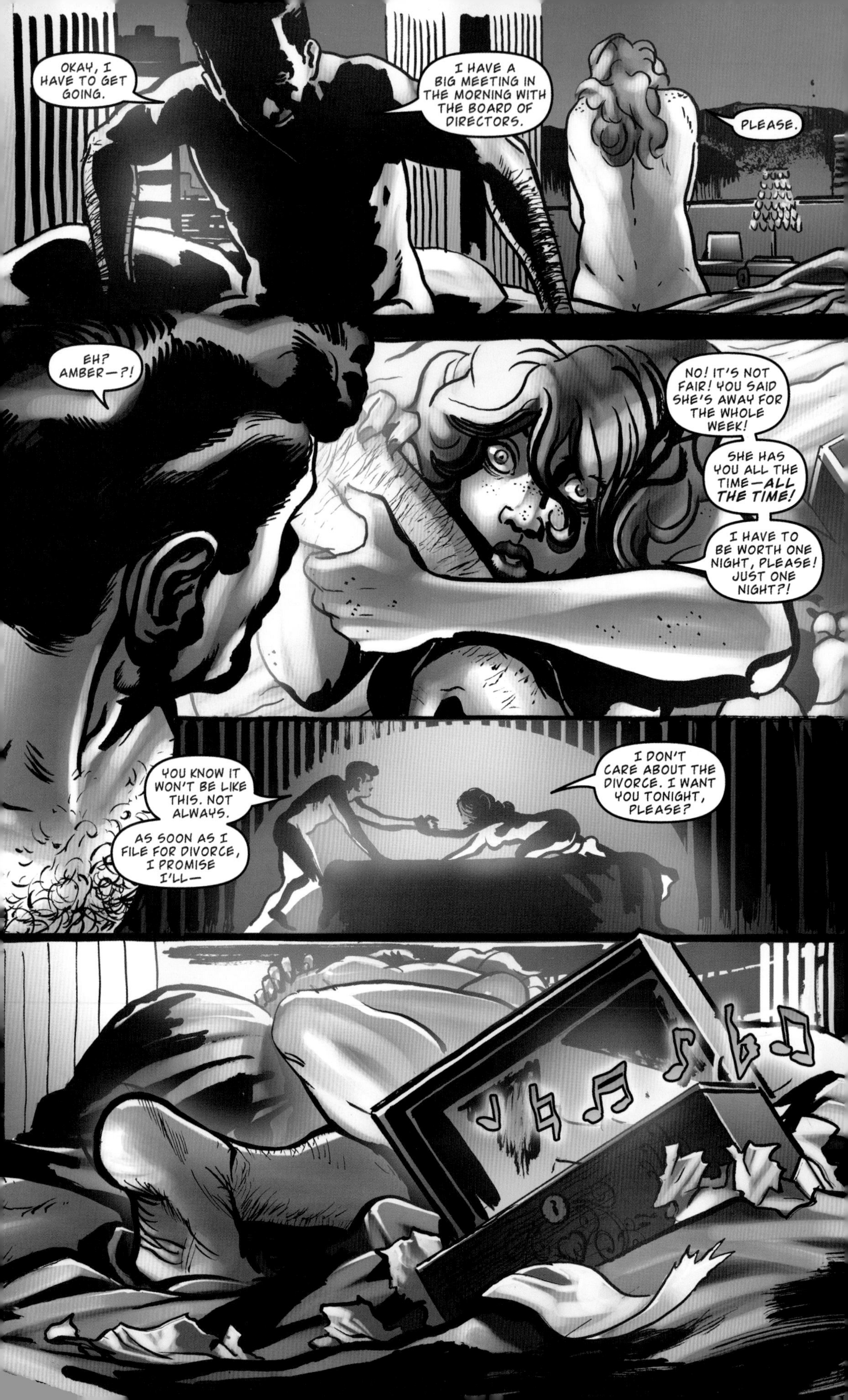
OKAY, I HAVE TO GET GOING.
I HAVE A BIG MEETING IN THE MORNING WITH THE BOARD OF DIRECTORS.
PLEASE.
EH? AMBER—?!
NO! IT'S NOT FAIR! YOU SAID SHE'S AWAY FOR THE WHOLE WEEK!
SHE HAS YOU ALL THE TIME—ALL THE TIME!
I HAVE TO BE WORTH ONE NIGHT, PLEASE! JUST ONE NIGHT?!
YOU KNOW IT WON'T BE LIKE THIS. NOT ALWAYS.
AS SOON AS I FILE FOR DIVORCE, I PROMISE I'LL—
I DON'T CARE ABOUT THE DIVORCE. I WANT YOU TONIGHT, PLEASE?

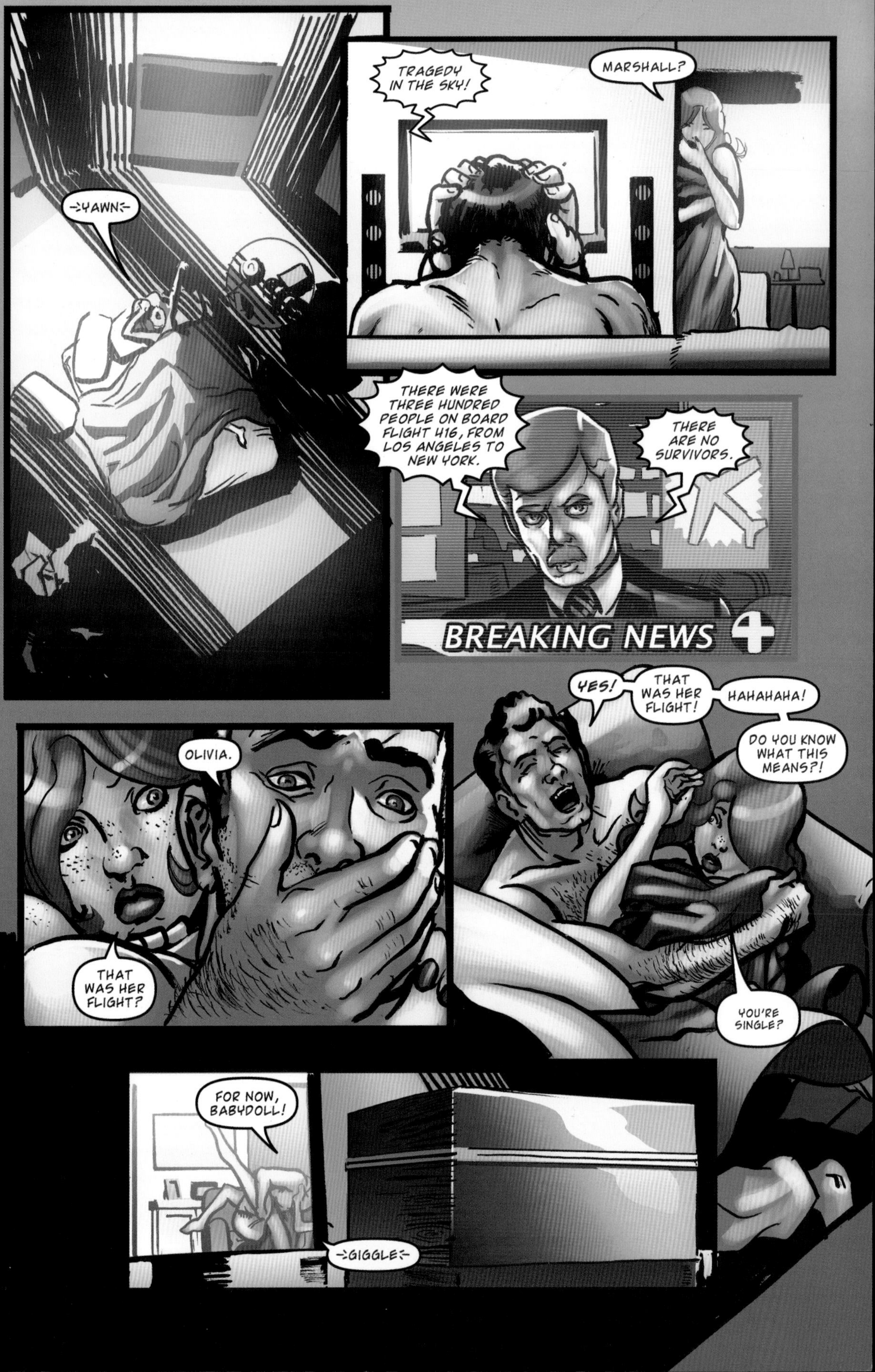

-YAWN-
TRAGEDY IN THE SKY!
MARSHALL?
THERE WERE THREE HUNDRED PEOPLE ON BOARD FLIGHT 416, FROM LOS ANGELES TO NEW YORK.
THERE ARE NO SURVIVORS.
BREAKING NEWS 4
OLIVIA.
THAT WAS HER FLIGHT?
YES!
THAT WAS HER FLIGHT!
HAHAHAHA!
DO YOU KNOW WHAT THIS MEANS?!
YOU'RE SINGLE?
FOR NOW, BABYDOLL!
-GIGGLE-

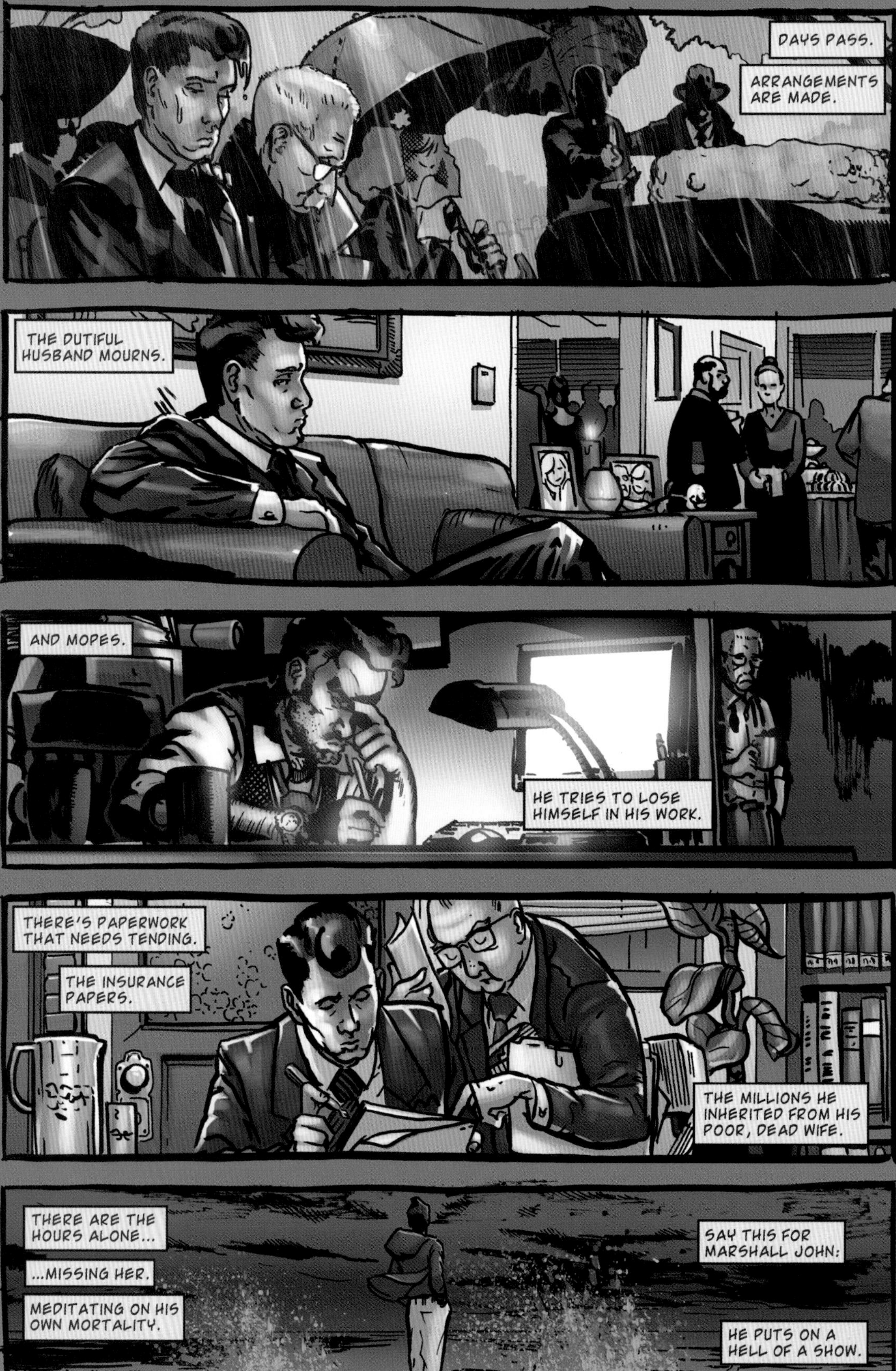
DAYS PASS.
ARRANGEMENTS ARE MADE.
THE DUTIFUL HUSBAND MOURNS.
AND MOPES.
HE TRIES TO LOSE HIMSELF IN HIS WORK.
THERE'S PAPERWORK THAT NEEDS TENDING.
THE INSURANCE PAPERS.
THE MILLIONS HE INHERITED FROM HIS POOR, DEAD WIFE.
THERE ARE THE HOURS ALONE...
...MISSING HER.
MEDITATING ON HIS OWN MORTALITY.
SAY THIS FOR MARSHALL JOHN:
HE PUTS ON A HELL OF A SHOW.

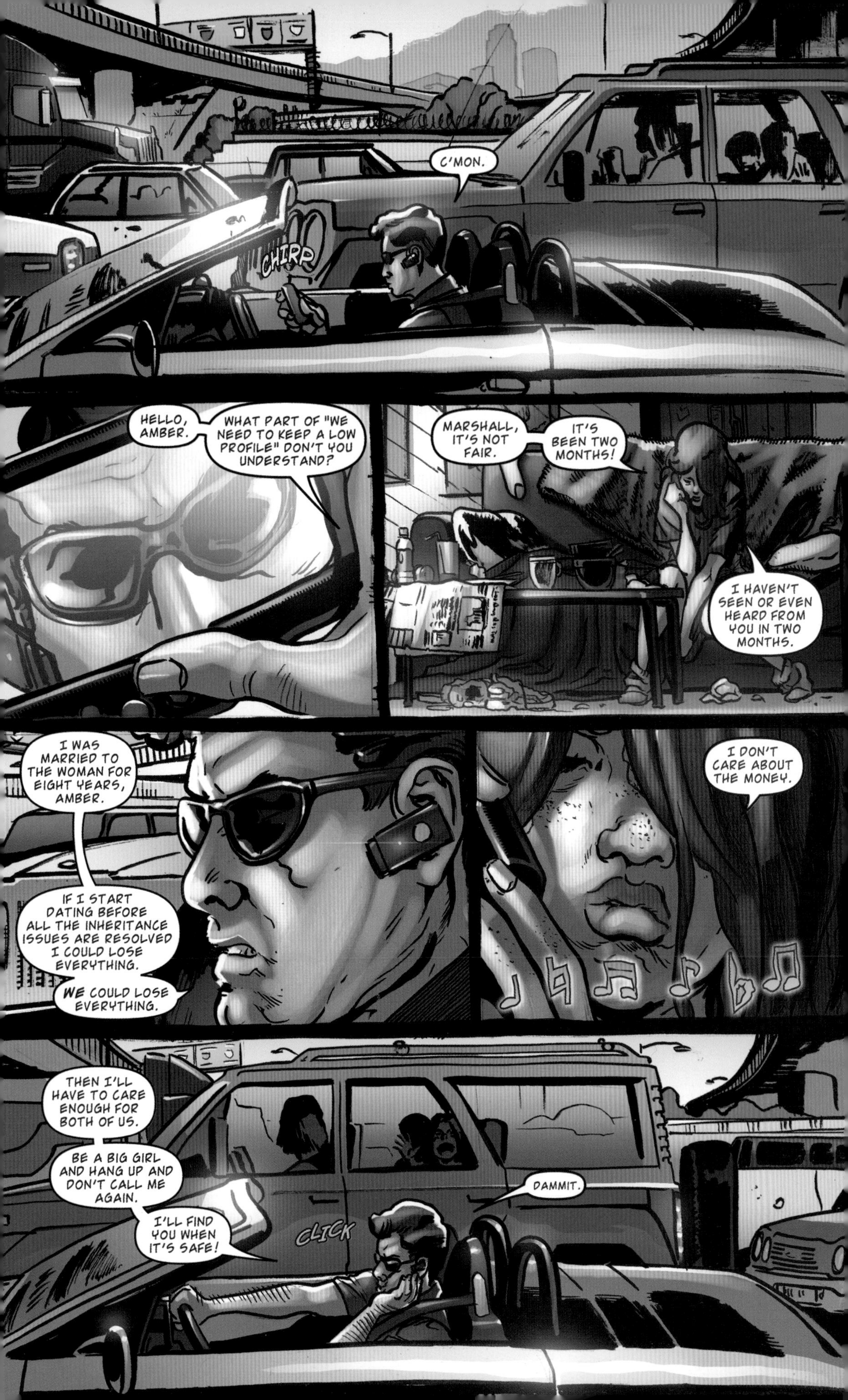

C'MON.
CHIRP
HELLO, AMBER.
WHAT PART OF "WE NEED TO KEEP A LOW PROFILE" DON'T YOU UNDERSTAND?
MARSHALL, IT'S NOT FAIR.
IT'S BEEN TWO MONTHS!
I HAVEN'T SEEN OR EVEN HEARD FROM YOU IN TWO MONTHS.
I WAS MARRIED TO THE WOMAN FOR EIGHT YEARS, AMBER.
IF I START DATING BEFORE ALL THE INHERITANCE ISSUES ARE RESOLVED I COULD LOSE EVERYTHING.
WE COULD LOSE EVERYTHING.
I DON'T CARE ABOUT THE MONEY.
THEN I'LL HAVE TO CARE ENOUGH FOR BOTH OF US.
BE A BIG GIRL AND HANG UP AND DON'T CALL ME AGAIN.
I'LL FIND YOU WHEN IT'S SAFE!
CLICK
DAMMIT.

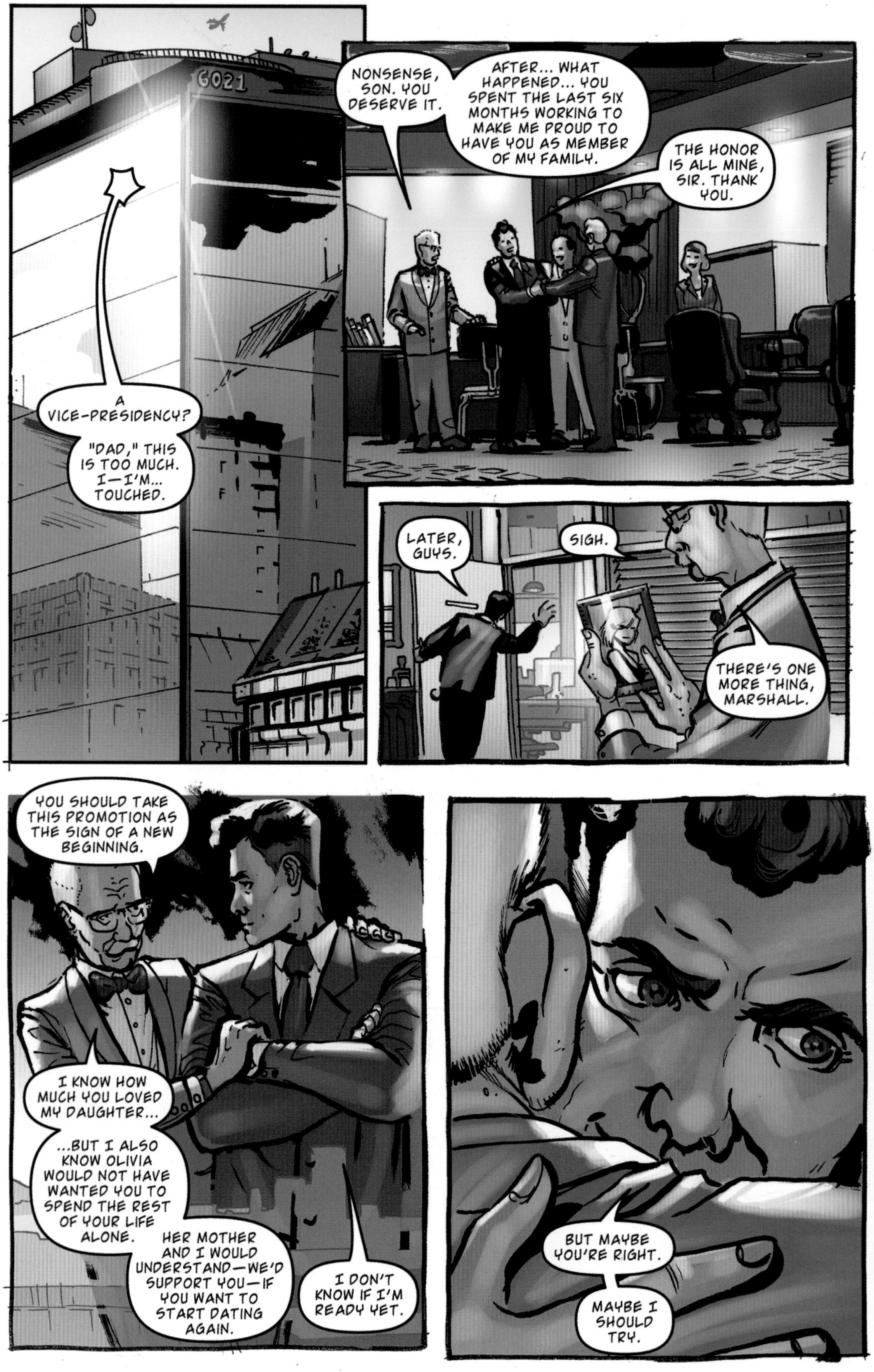
6021
A VICE-PRESIDENCY?
"DAD," THIS IS TOO MUCH. I—I'M... TOUCHED.
NONSENSE, SON. YOU DESERVE IT.
AFTER... WHAT HAPPENED... YOU SPENT THE LAST SIX MONTHS WORKING TO MAKE ME PROUD TO HAVE YOU AS MEMBER OF MY FAMILY.
THE HONOR IS ALL MINE, SIR. THANK YOU.
LATER, GUYS.
SIGH.
THERE'S ONE MORE THING, MARSHALL.
YOU SHOULD TAKE THIS PROMOTION AS THE SIGN OF A NEW BEGINNING.
I KNOW HOW MUCH YOU LOVED MY DAUGHTER...
...BUT I ALSO KNOW OLIVIA WOULD NOT HAVE WANTED YOU TO SPEND THE REST OF YOUR LIFE ALONE.
HER MOTHER AND I WOULD UNDERSTAND—WE'D SUPPORT YOU—IF YOU WANT TO START DATING AGAIN.
I DON'T KNOW IF I'M READY YET.
BUT MAYBE YOU'RE RIGHT.
MAYBE I SHOULD TRY.

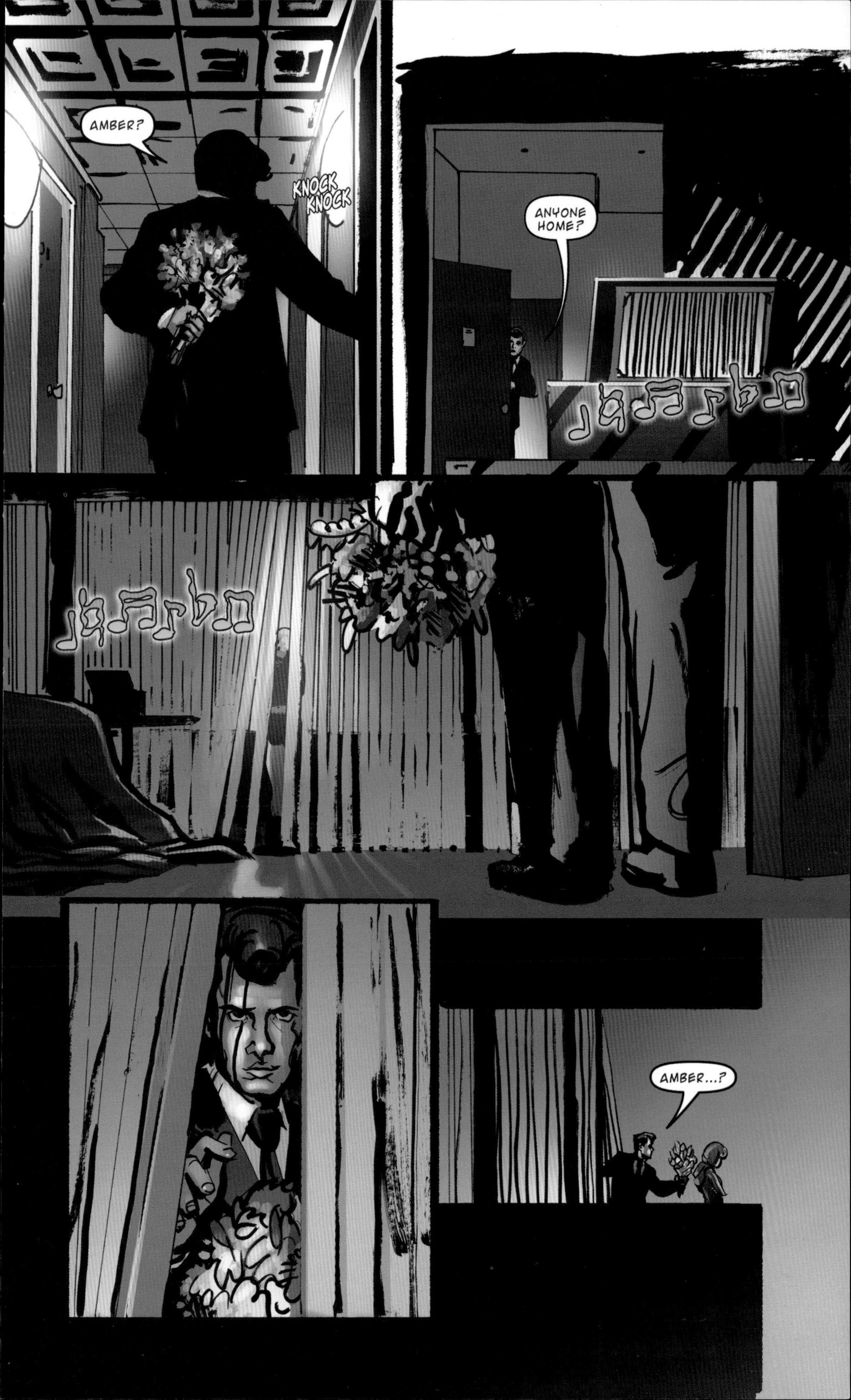
AMBER?
KNOCK KNOCK
ANYONE HOME?
AMBER...?

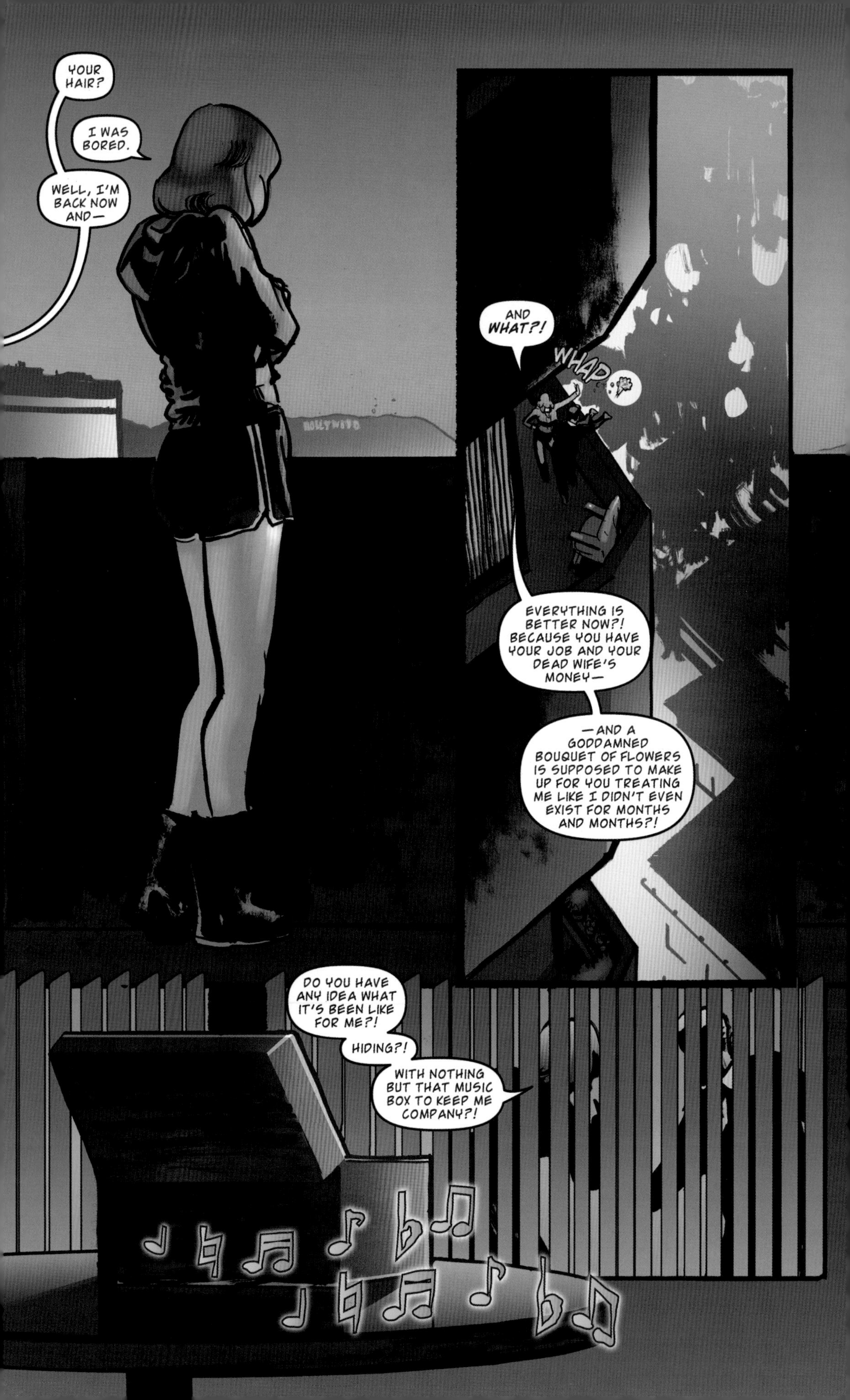
YOUR HAIR?
I WAS BORED.
WELL, I'M BACK NOW AND—
AND WHAT?!
WHAP
EVERYTHING IS BETTER NOW?! BECAUSE YOU HAVE YOUR JOB AND YOUR DEAD WIFE'S MONEY—
—AND A GODDAMNED BOUQUET OF FLOWERS IS SUPPOSED TO MAKE UP FOR YOU TREATING ME LIKE I DIDN'T EVEN EXIST FOR MONTHS AND MONTHS?!
DO YOU HAVE ANY IDEA WHAT IT'S BEEN LIKE FOR ME?!
HIDING?!
WITH NOTHING BUT THAT MUSIC BOX TO KEEP ME COMPANY?!

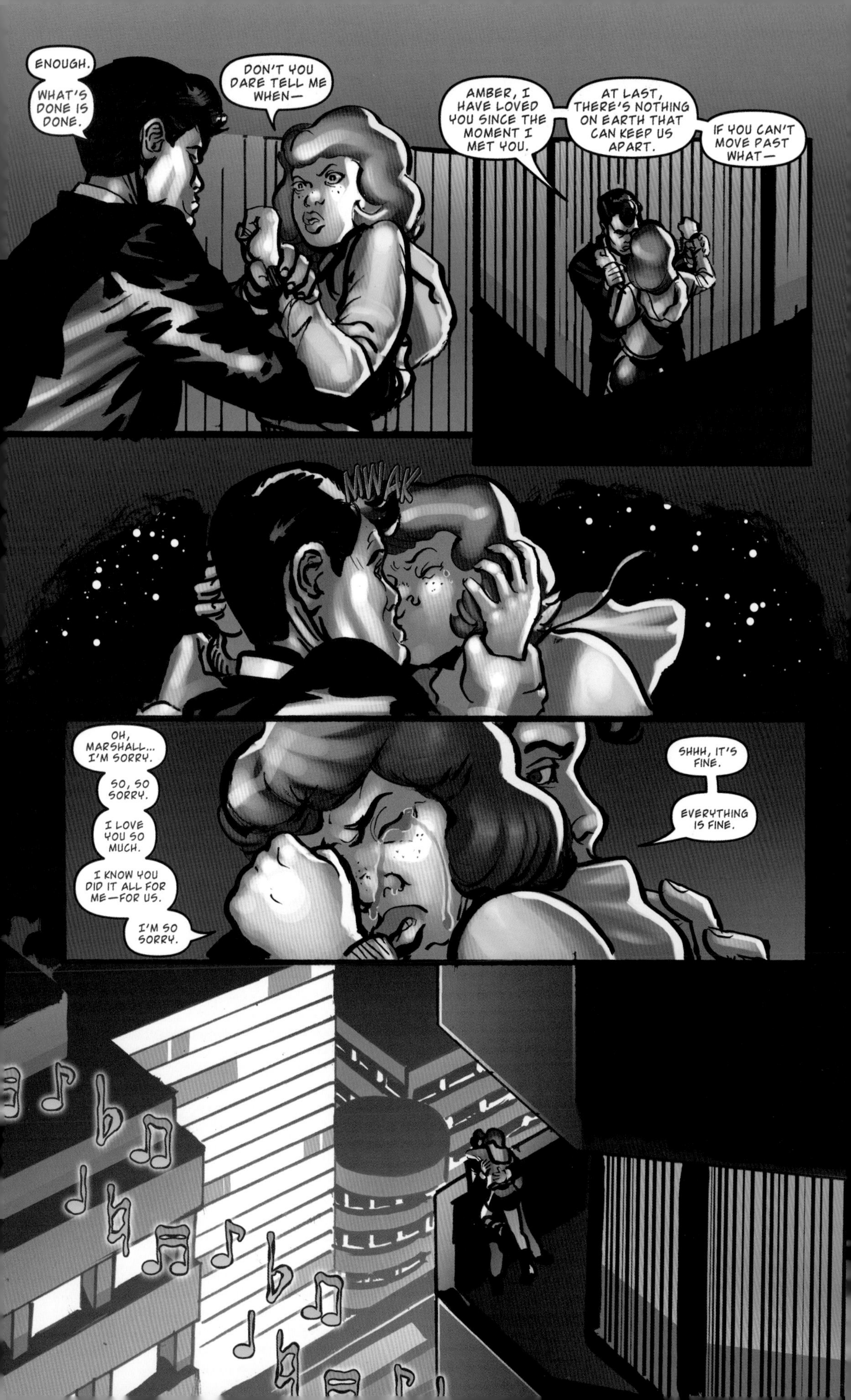
ENOUGH.
WHAT'S DONE IS DONE.
DON'T YOU DARE TELL ME WHEN—
AMBER, I HAVE LOVED YOU SINCE THE MOMENT I MET YOU.
AT LAST, THERE'S NOTHING ON EARTH THAT CAN KEEP US APART.
IF YOU CAN'T MOVE PAST WHAT—
MWAK
OH, MARSHALL... I'M SORRY.
SO, SO SORRY.
I LOVE YOU SO MUCH.
I KNOW YOU DID IT ALL FOR ME—FOR US.
I'M SO SORRY.
SHHH, IT'S FINE.
EVERYTHING IS FINE.

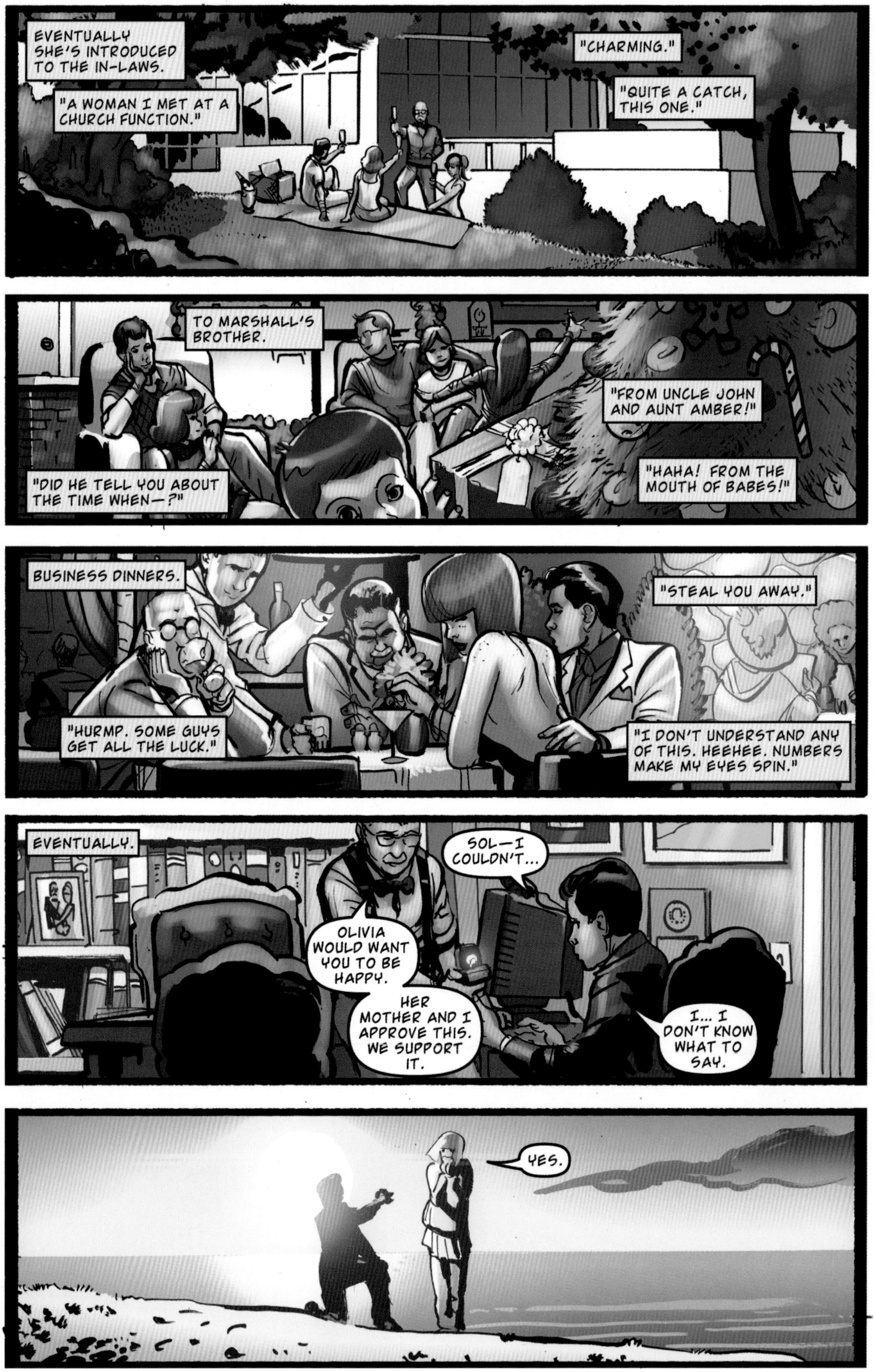
EVENTUALLY SHE'S INTRODUCED TO THE IN-LAWS.
"A WOMAN I MET AT A CHURCH FUNCTION."
"CHARMING."
"QUITE A CATCH, THIS ONE."
TO MARSHALL'S BROTHER.
"DID HE TELL YOU ABOUT THE TIME WHEN—?"
"FROM UNCLE JOHN AND AUNT AMBER!"
"HAHA! FROM THE MOUTH OF BABES!"
BUSINESS DINNERS.
"HURMP. SOME GUYS GET ALL THE LUCK."
"STEAL YOU AWAY."
"I DON'T UNDERSTAND ANY OF THIS. HEEHEE. NUMBERS MAKE MY EYES SPIN."
EVENTUALLY.
SOL—I COULDN'T...
OLIVIA WOULD WANT YOU TO BE HAPPY.
HER MOTHER AND I APPROVE THIS. WE SUPPORT IT.
I... I DON'T KNOW WHAT TO SAY.
YES.

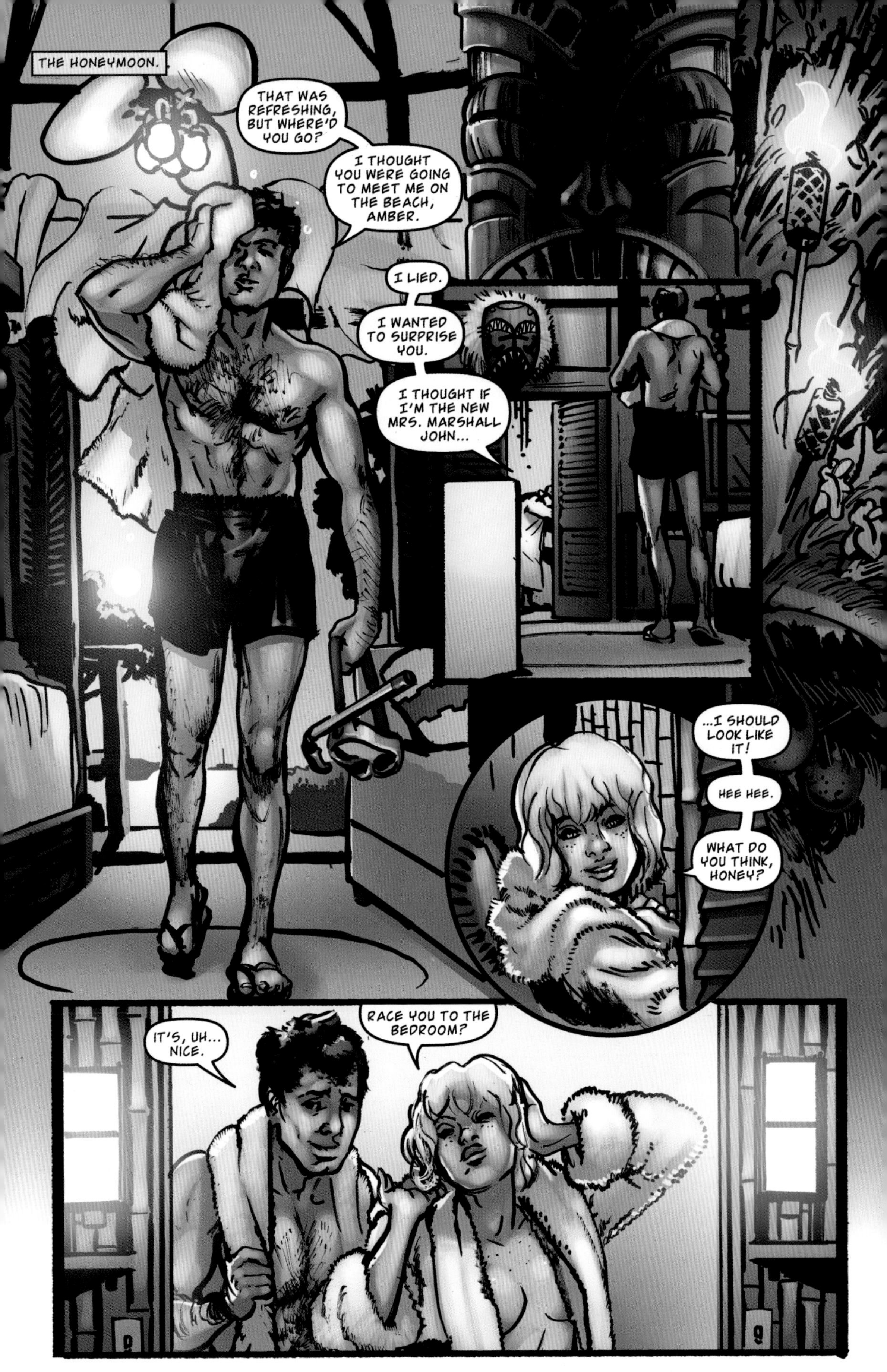
THE HONEYMOON.
THAT WAS REFRESHING, BUT WHERE'D YOU GO?
I THOUGHT YOU WERE GOING TO MEET ME ON THE BEACH, AMBER.
I LIED.
I WANTED TO SURPRISE YOU.
I THOUGHT IF I'M THE NEW MRS. MARSHALL JOHN...
...I SHOULD LOOK LIKE IT!
HEE HEE.
WHAT DO YOU THINK, HONEY?
IT'S, UH... NICE.
RACE YOU TO THE BEDROOM?

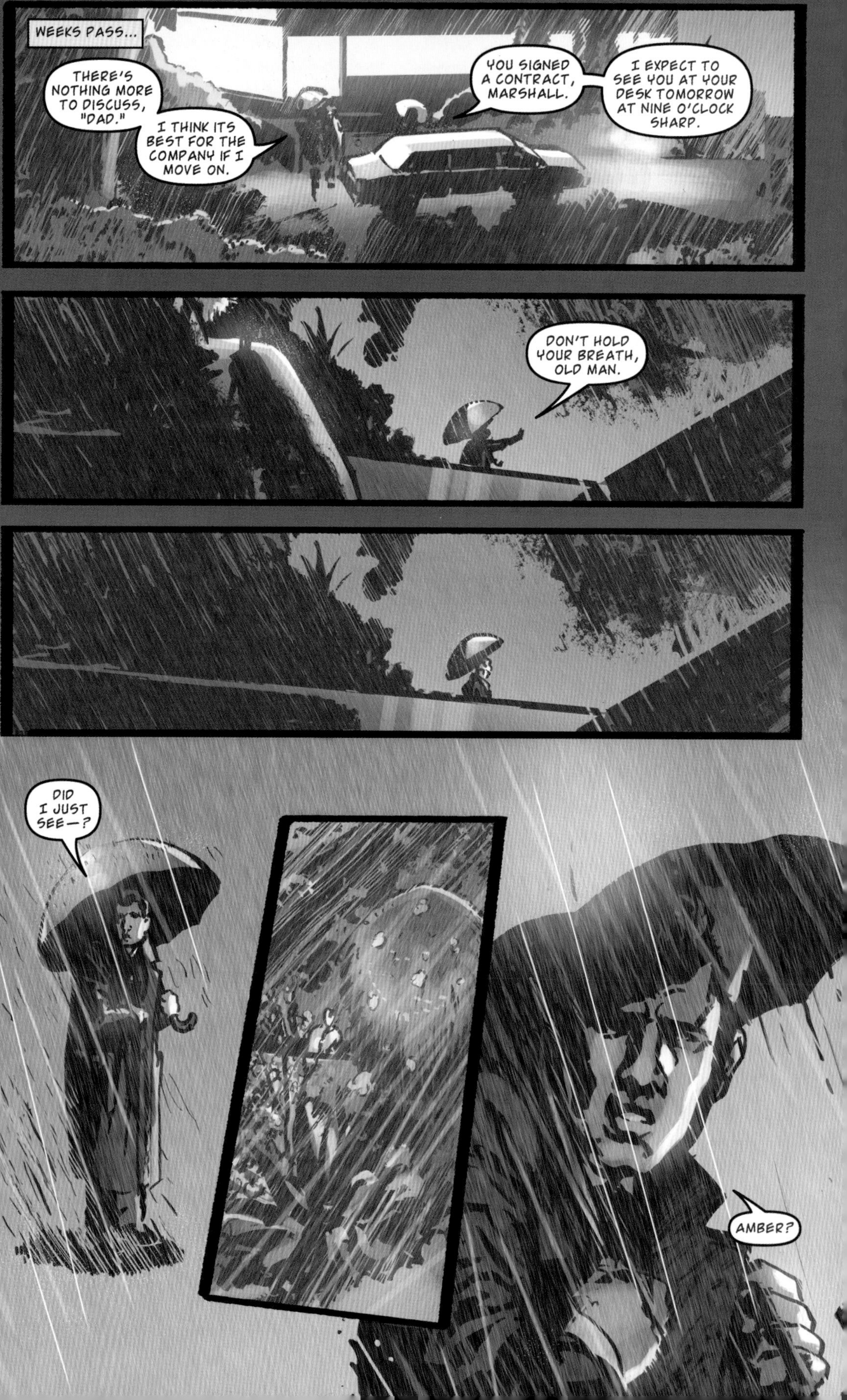
WEEKS PASS...
THERE'S NOTHING MORE TO DISCUSS, "DAD."
I THINK ITS BEST FOR THE COMPANY IF I MOVE ON.
YOU SIGNED A CONTRACT, MARSHALL.
I EXPECT TO SEE YOU AT YOUR DESK TOMORROW AT NINE O'CLOCK SHARP.
DON'T HOLD YOUR BREATH, OLD MAN.
DID I JUST SEE—?
AMBER?

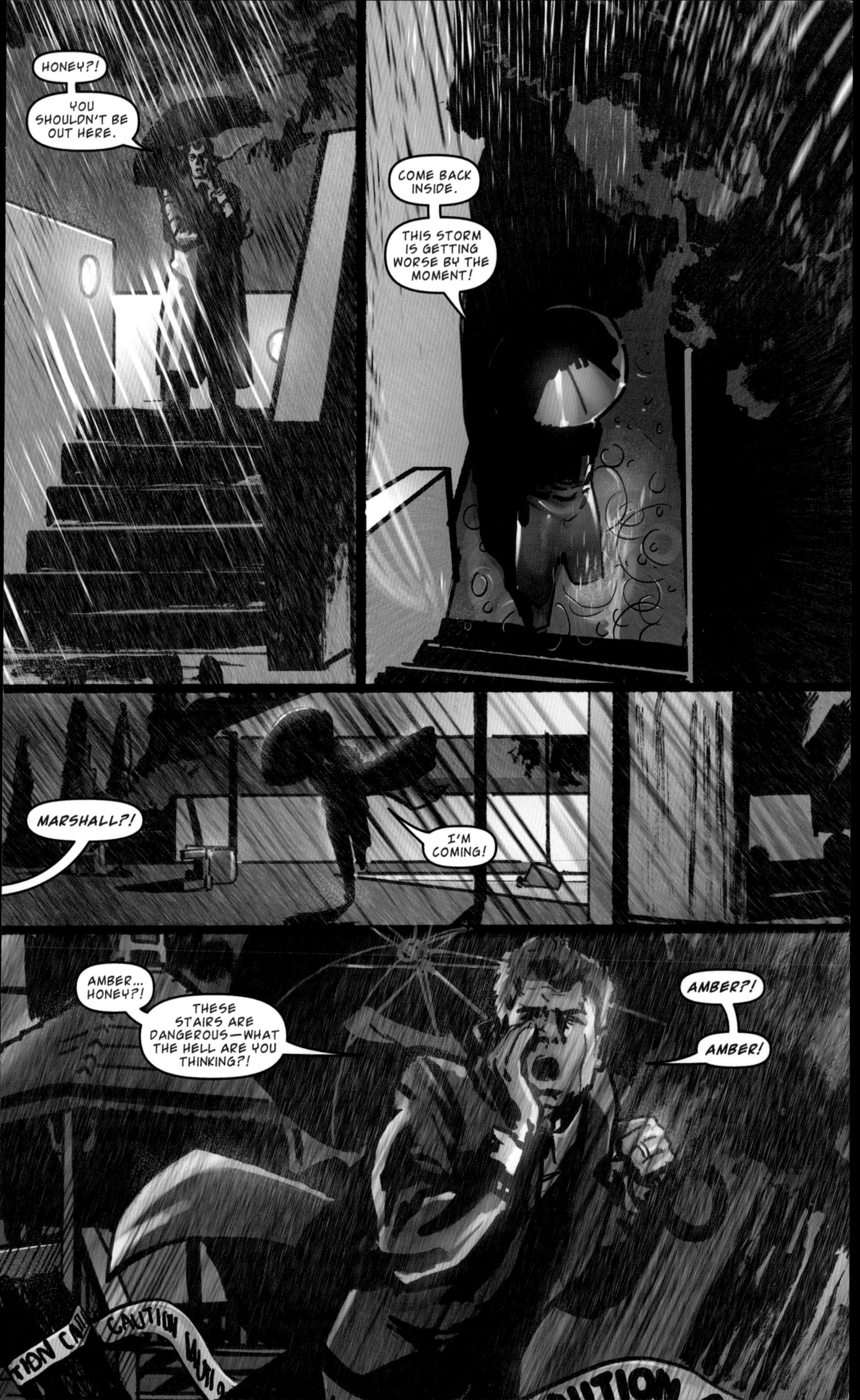
HONEY?!
YOU SHOULDN'T BE OUT HERE.
COME BACK INSIDE.
THIS STORM IS GETTING WORSE BY THE MOMENT!
MARSHALL?!
I'M COMING!
AMBER... HONEY?!
THESE STAIRS ARE DANGEROUS—WHAT THE HELL ARE YOU THINKING?!
AMBER?!
AMBER!
CAUTION
CAUTION

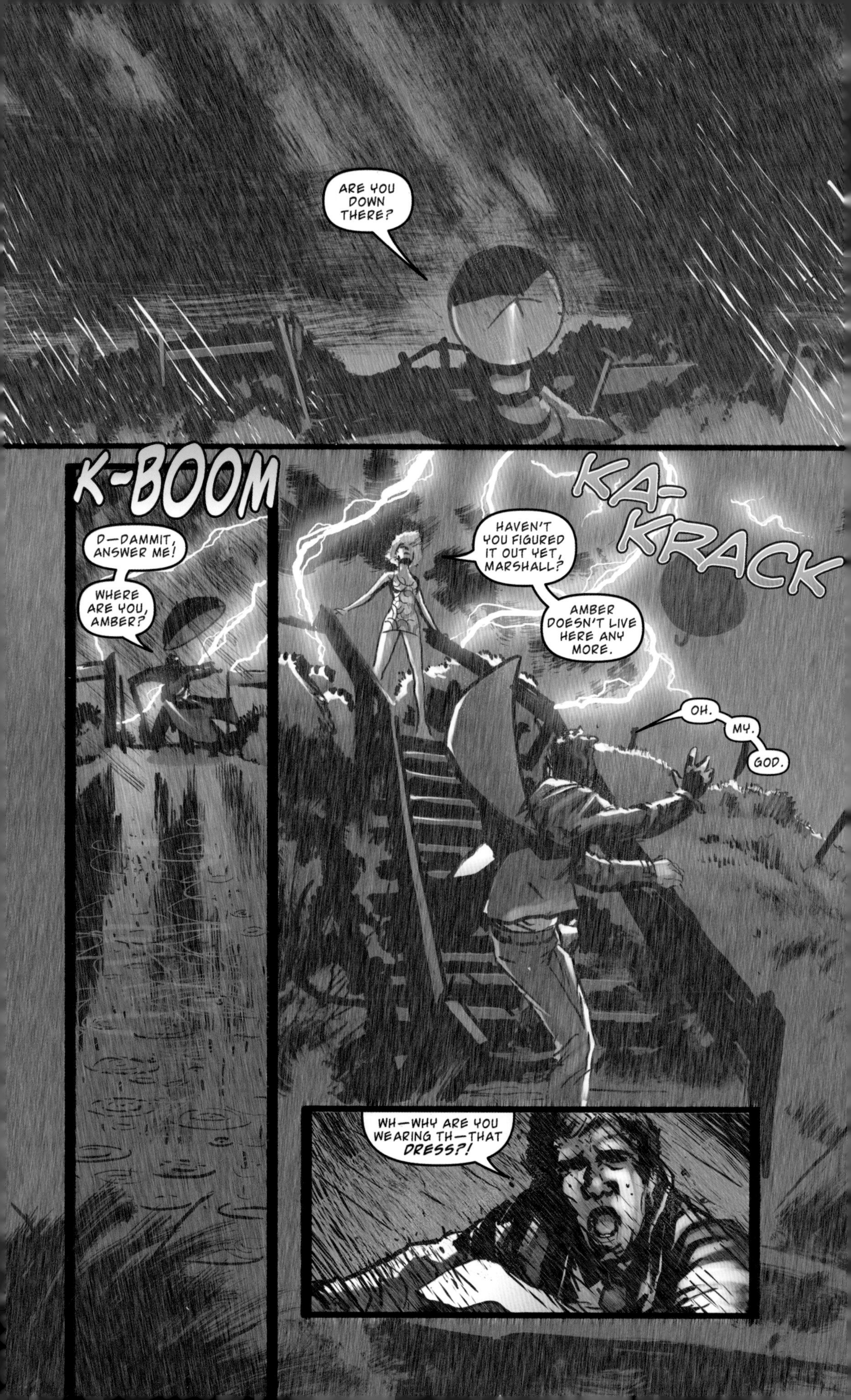
ARE YOU DOWN THERE?
K-BOOM
D—DAMMIT, ANSWER ME!
WHERE ARE YOU, AMBER?
KA-KRACK
HAVEN'T YOU FIGURED IT OUT YET, MARSHALL?
AMBER DOESN'T LIVE HERE ANY MORE.
OH. MY. GOD.
WH—WHY ARE YOU WEARING TH—THAT DRESS?!

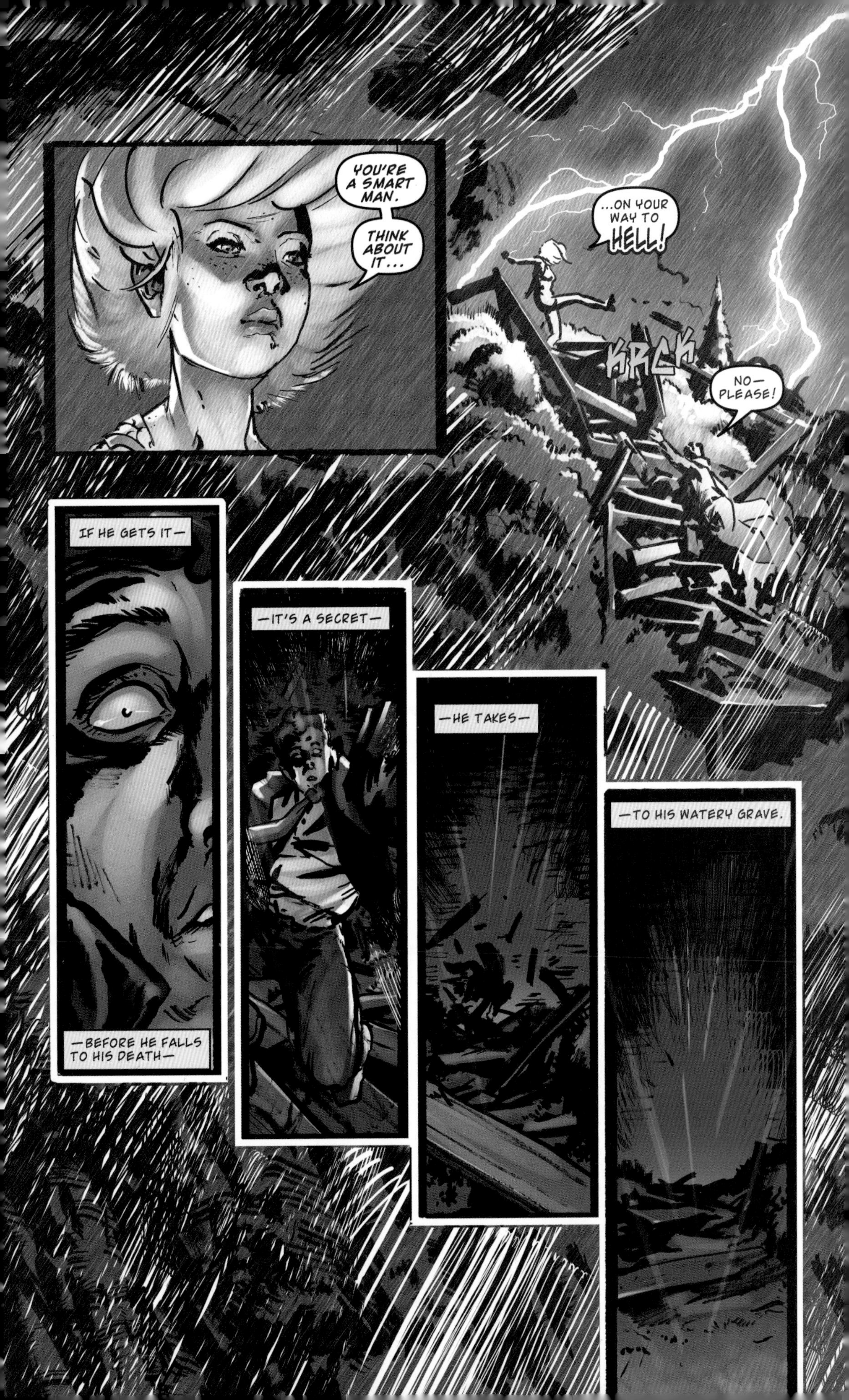
YOU'RE A SMART MAN.
THINK ABOUT IT...
...ON YOUR WAY TO HELL!
KRCK
NO— PLEASE!
IF HE GETS IT—
—BEFORE HE FALLS TO HIS DEATH—
—IT'S A SECRET—
—HE TAKES—
—TO HIS WATERY GRAVE.

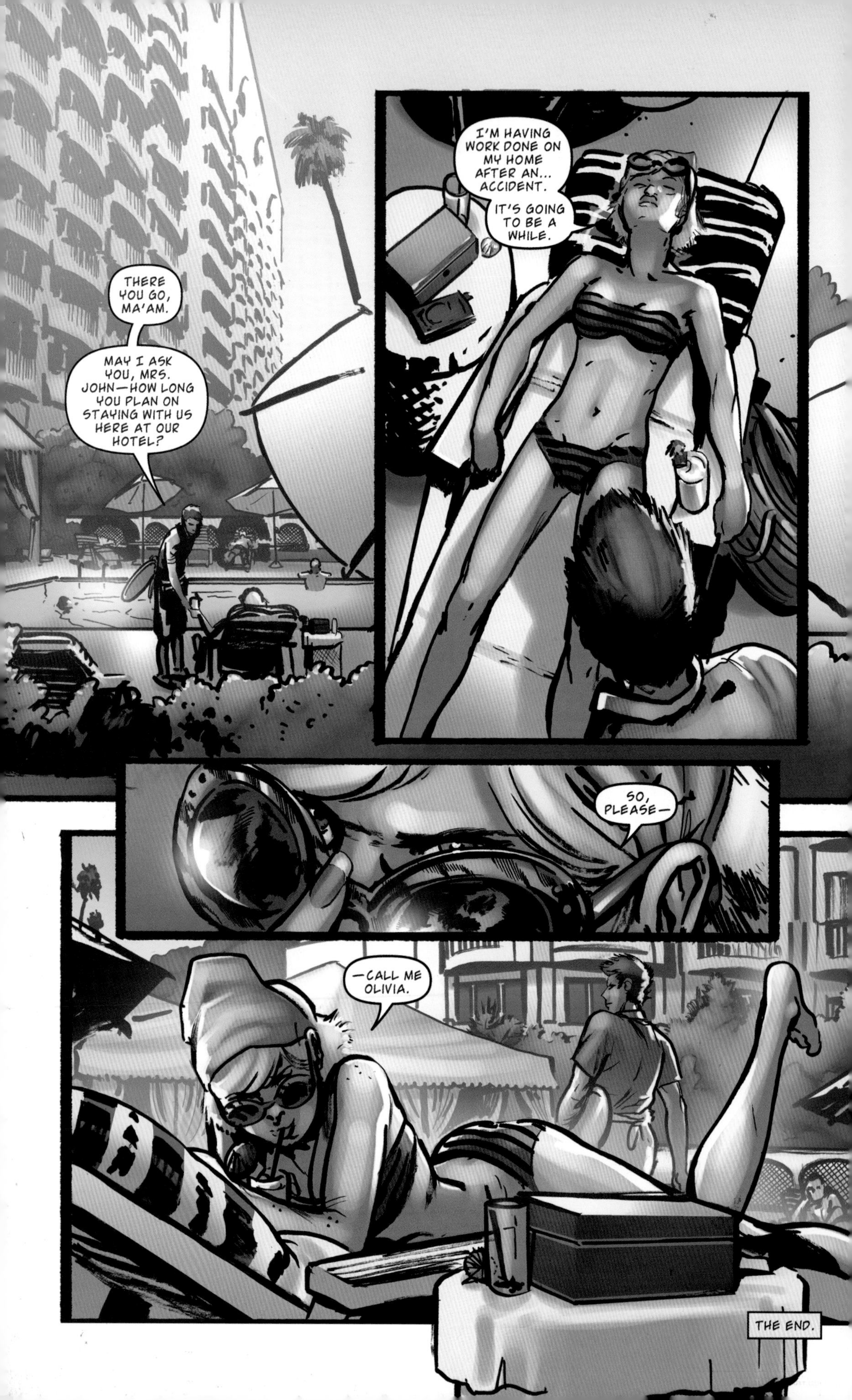
THERE YOU GO, MA'AM.
MAY I ASK YOU, MRS. JOHN—HOW LONG YOU PLAN ON STAYING WITH US HERE AT OUR HOTEL?
I'M HAVING WORK DONE ON MY HOME AFTER AN... ACCIDENT.
IT'S GOING TO BE A WHILE.
SO, PLEASE—
—CALL ME OLIVIA.
THE END.

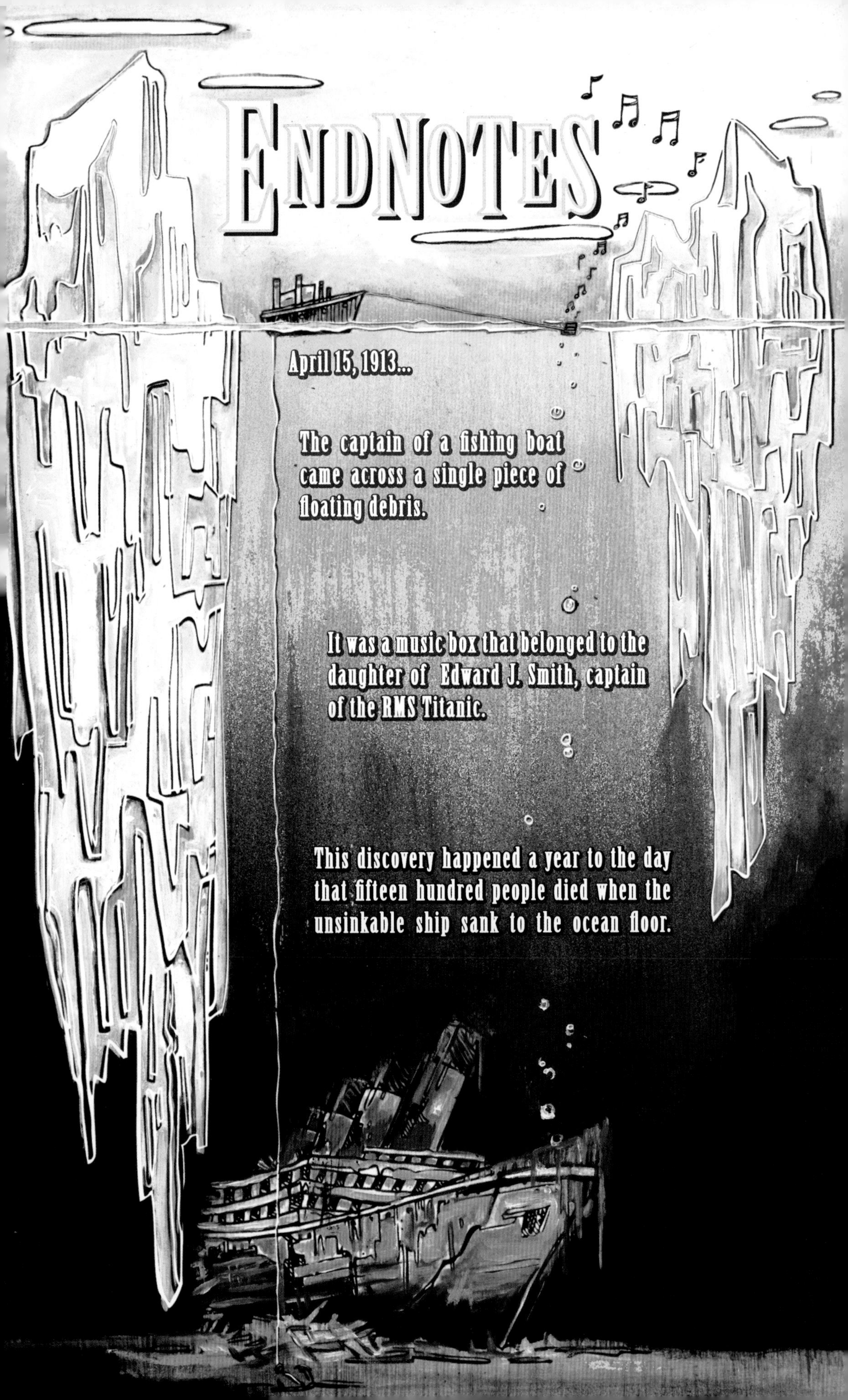
ENDNOTES
April 15, 1913...
The captain of a fishing boat came across a single piece of floating debris.
It was a music box that belonged to the daughter of Edward J. Smith, captain of the RMS Titanic.
This discovery happened a year to the day that fifteen hundred people died when the unsinkable ship sank to the ocean floor.

Chapter Three: "Nightmare at 30,000 feet!"

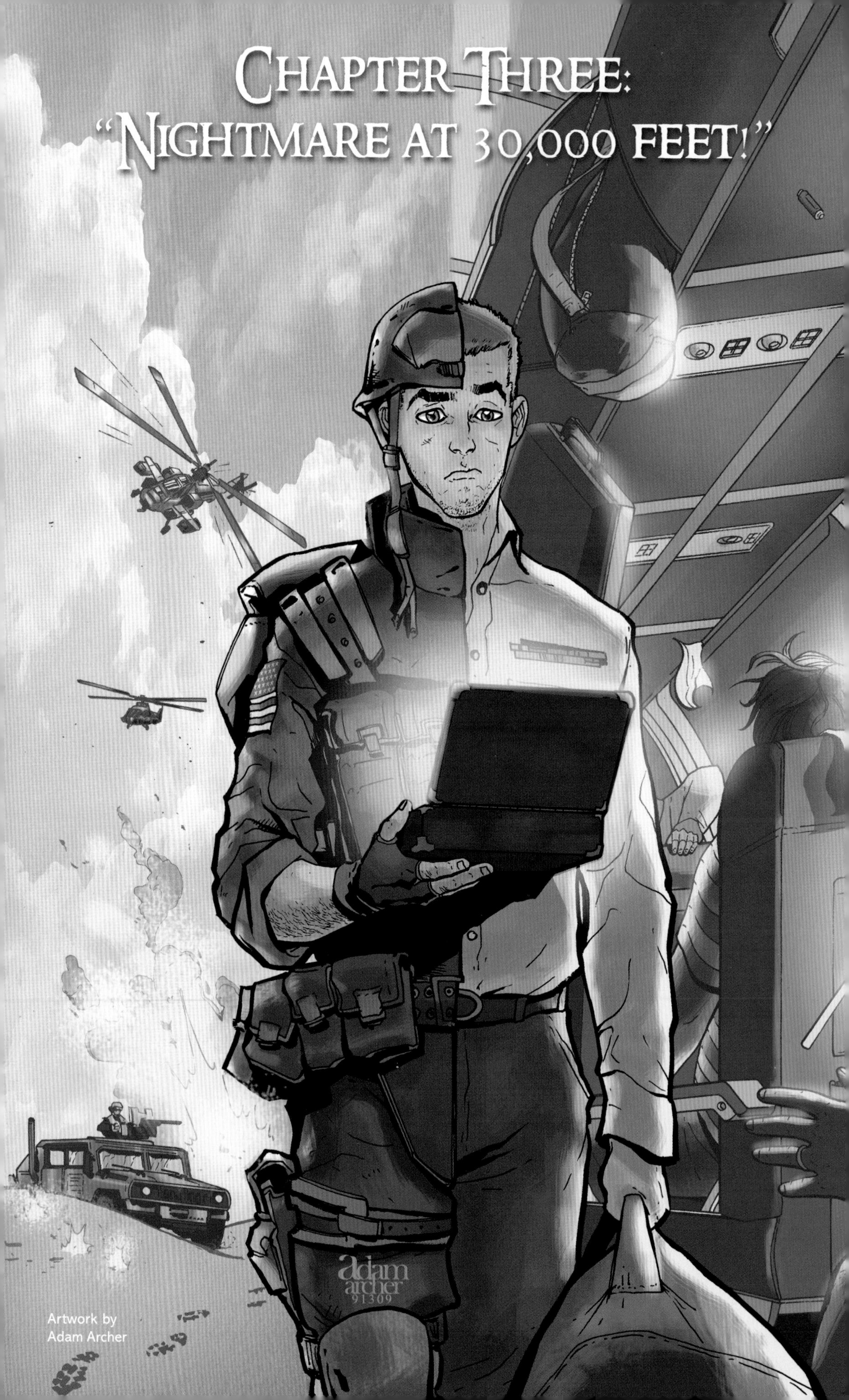
adam archer 91309

Artwork by Adam Archer

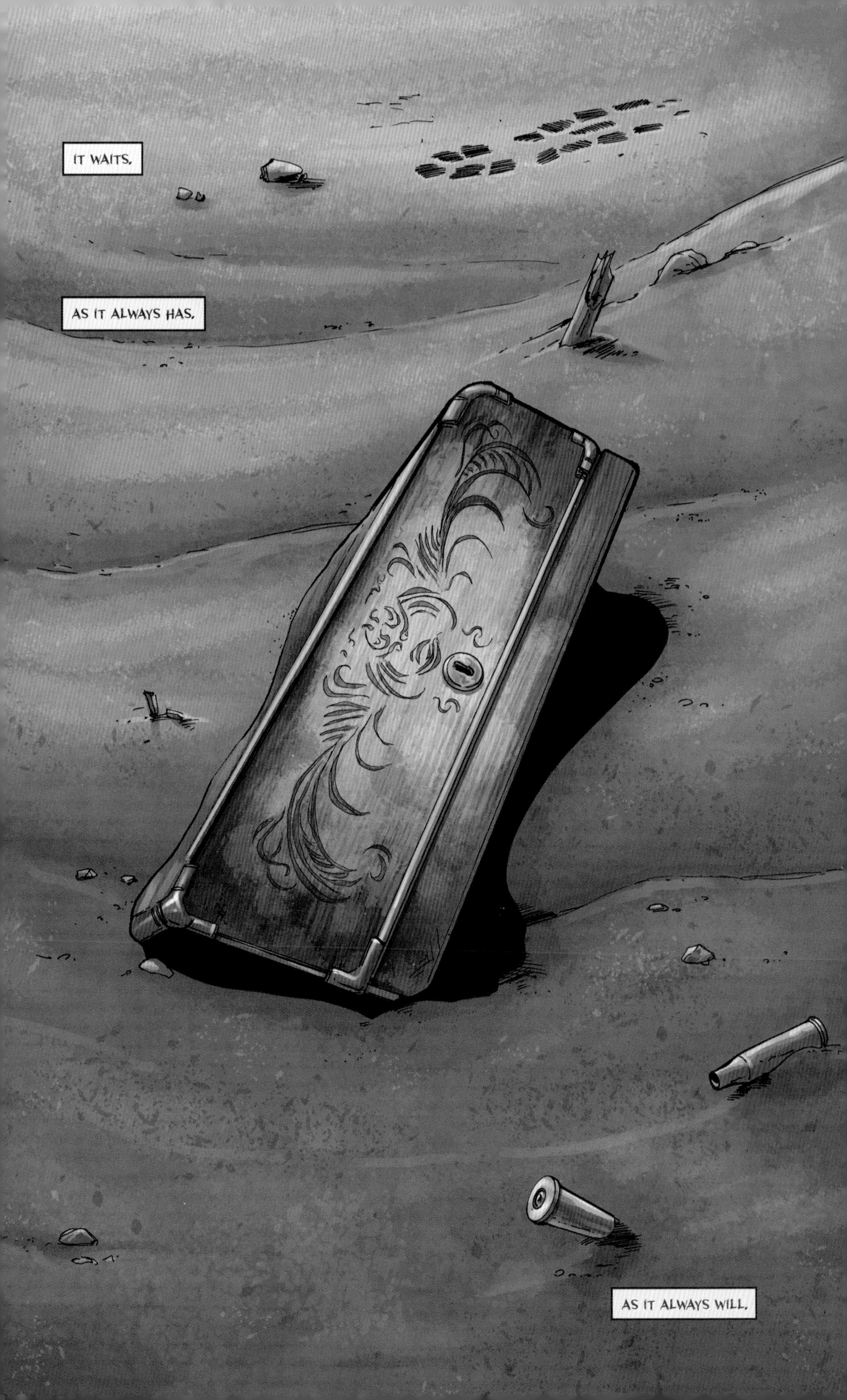
IT WAITS.
AS IT ALWAYS HAS.
AS IT ALWAYS WILL.

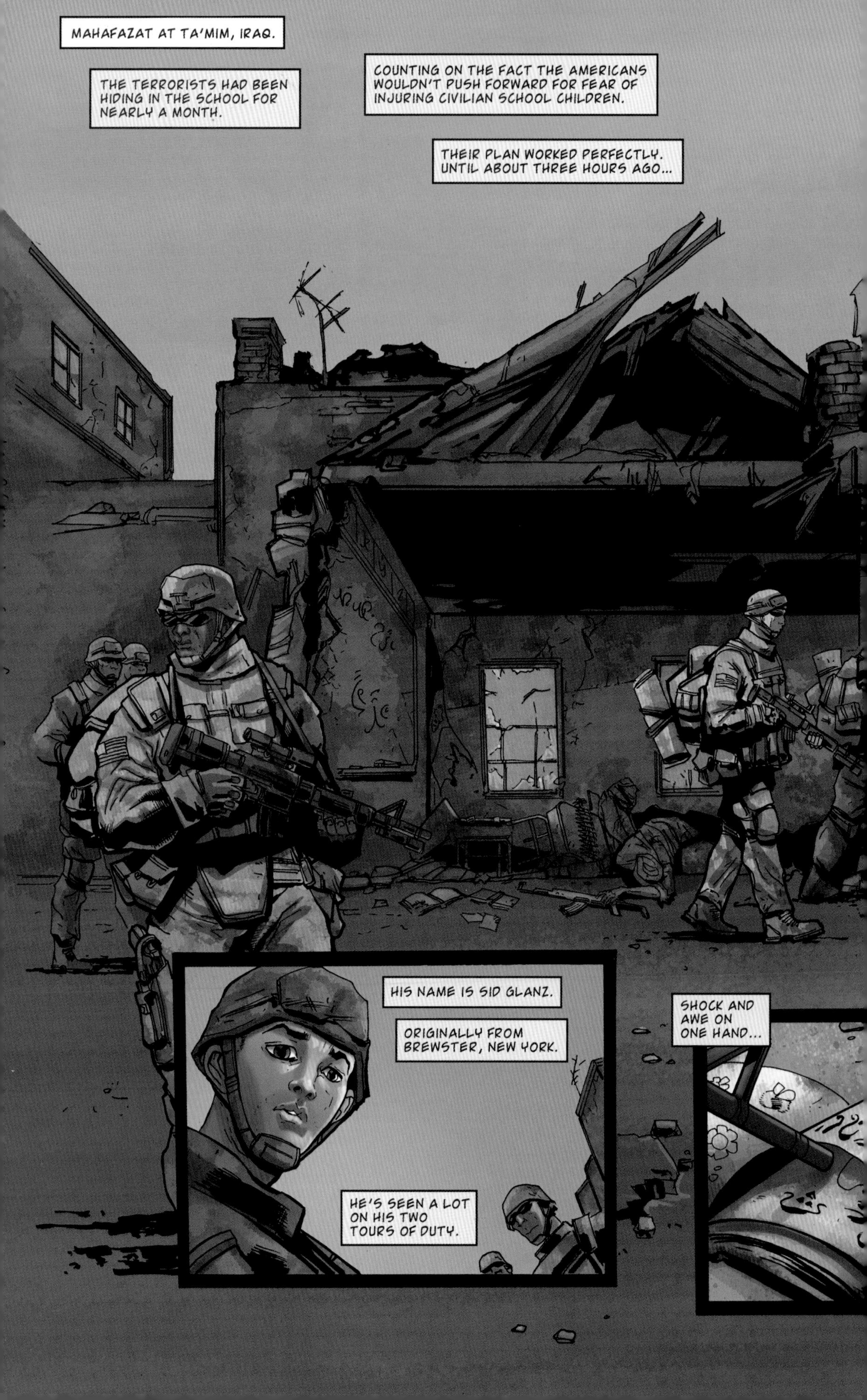
MAHAFAZAT AT TA'MIM, IRAQ.
THE TERRORISTS HAD BEEN HIDING IN THE SCHOOL FOR NEARLY A MONTH.
COUNTING ON THE FACT THE AMERICANS WOULDN'T PUSH FORWARD FOR FEAR OF INJURING CIVILIAN SCHOOL CHILDREN.
THEIR PLAN WORKED PERFECTLY. UNTIL ABOUT THREE HOURS AGO...
HIS NAME IS SID GLANZ.
ORIGINALLY FROM BREWSTER, NEW YORK.
HE'S SEEN A LOT ON HIS TWO TOURS OF DUTY.
SHOCK AND AWE ON ONE HAND...

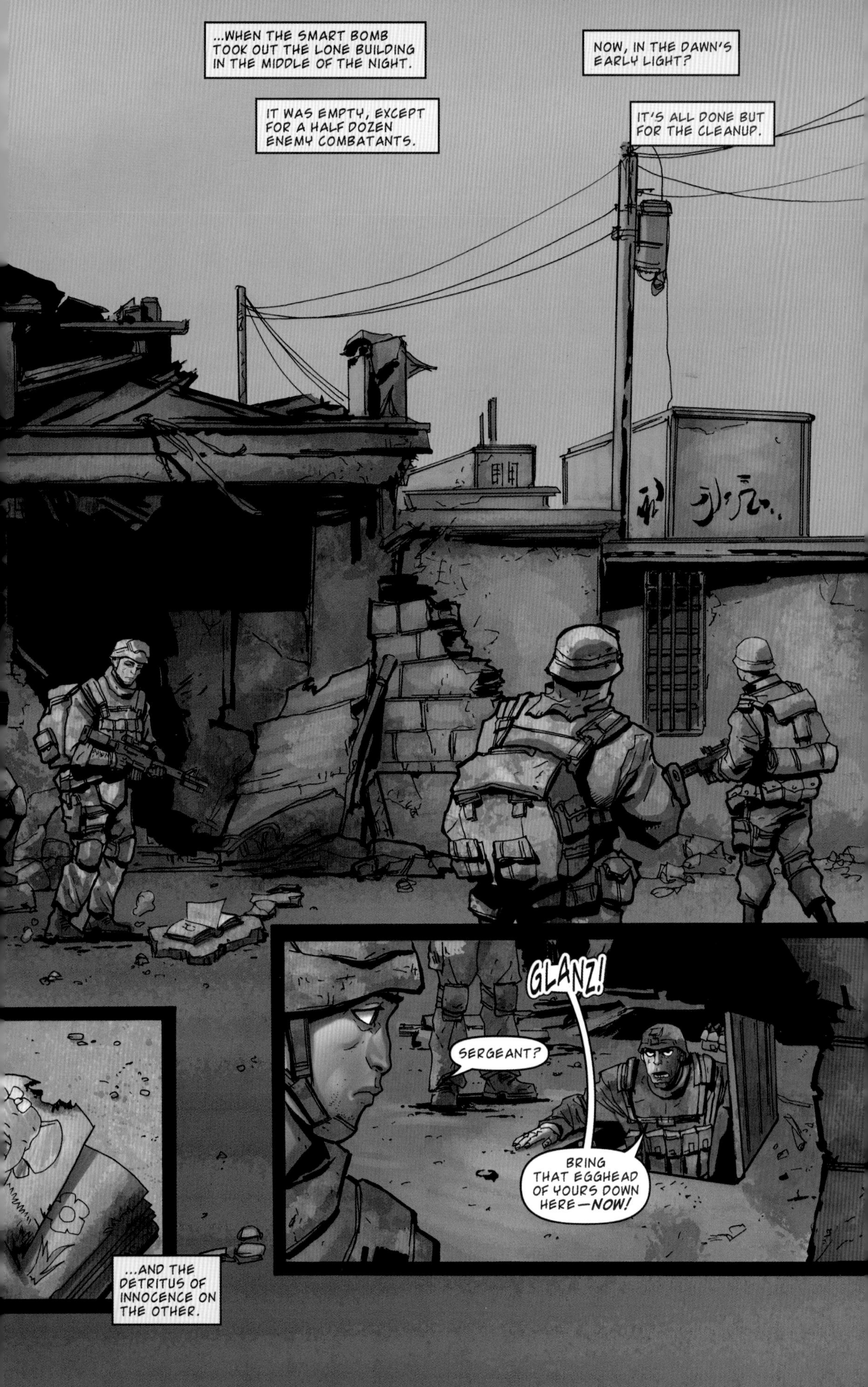
...WHEN THE SMART BOMB TOOK OUT THE LONE BUILDING IN THE MIDDLE OF THE NIGHT.
IT WAS EMPTY, EXCEPT FOR A HALF DOZEN ENEMY COMBATANTS.
NOW, IN THE DAWN'S EARLY LIGHT?
IT'S ALL DONE BUT FOR THE CLEANUP.
...AND THE DETRITUS OF INNOCENCE ON THE OTHER.
GLANZ!
SERGEANT?
BRING THAT EGGHEAD OF YOURS DOWN HERE—*NOW!*

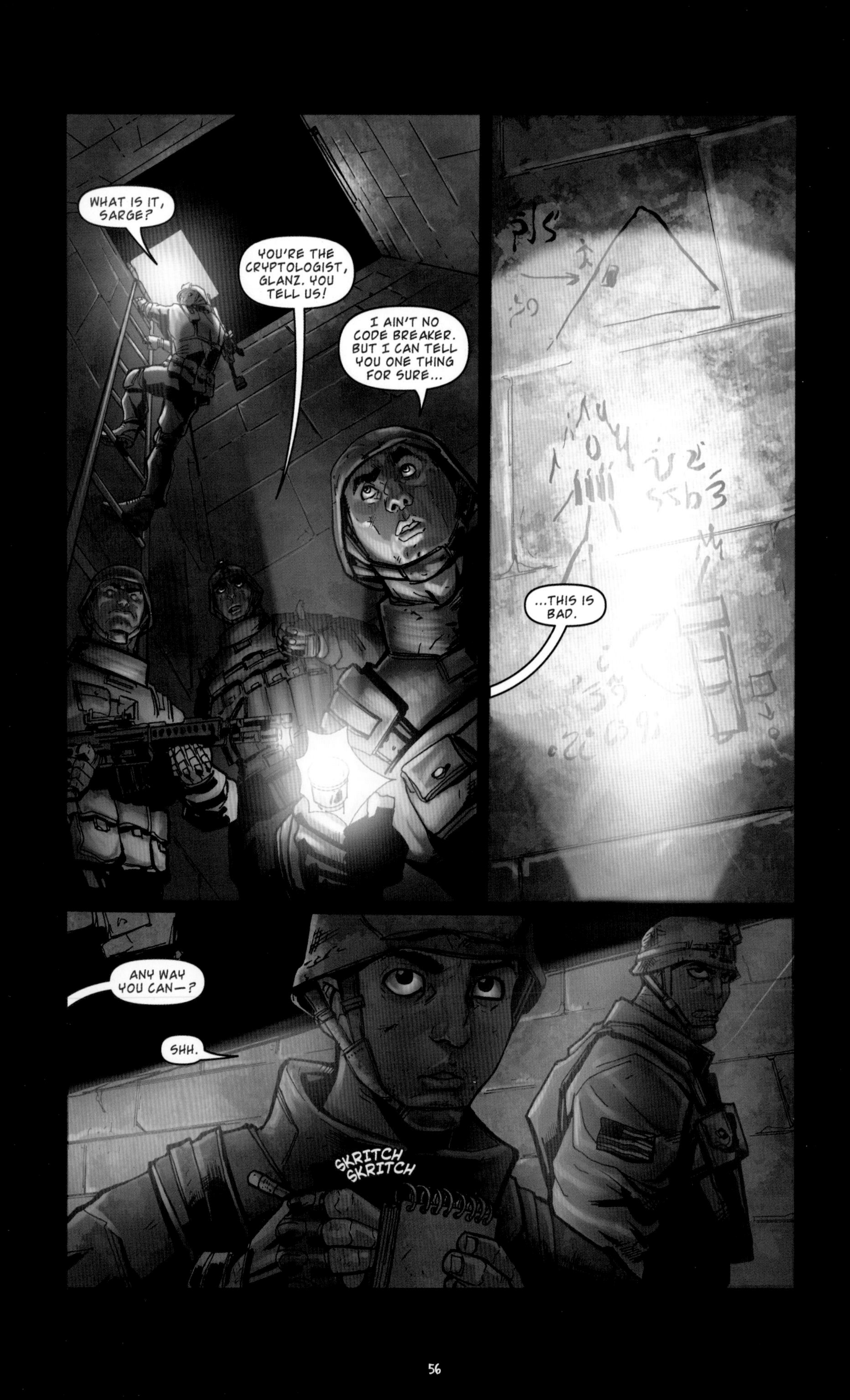
WHAT IS IT, SARGE?
YOU'RE THE CRYPTOLOGIST, GLANZ. YOU TELL US!
I AIN'T NO CODE BREAKER. BUT I CAN TELL YOU ONE THING FOR SURE...
...THIS IS BAD.
ANY WAY YOU CAN—?
SHH.
SKRITCH SKRITCH

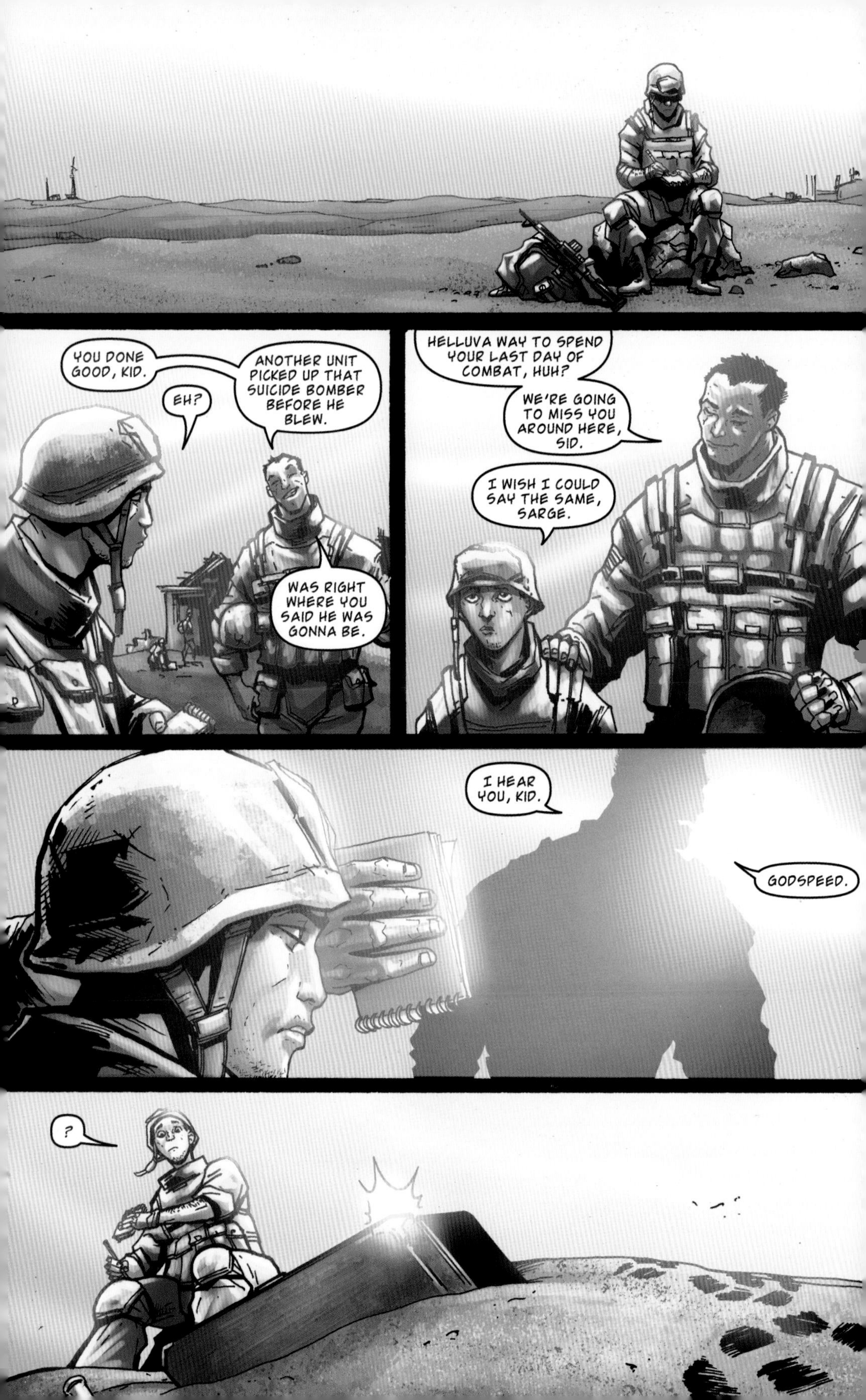
YOU DONE GOOD, KID.
EH?
ANOTHER UNIT PICKED UP THAT SUICIDE BOMBER BEFORE HE BLEW.
WAS RIGHT WHERE YOU SAID HE WAS GONNA BE.
HELLUVA WAY TO SPEND YOUR LAST DAY OF COMBAT, HUH?
WE'RE GOING TO MISS YOU AROUND HERE, SID.
I WISH I COULD SAY THE SAME, SARGE.
I HEAR YOU, KID.
GODSPEED.
?

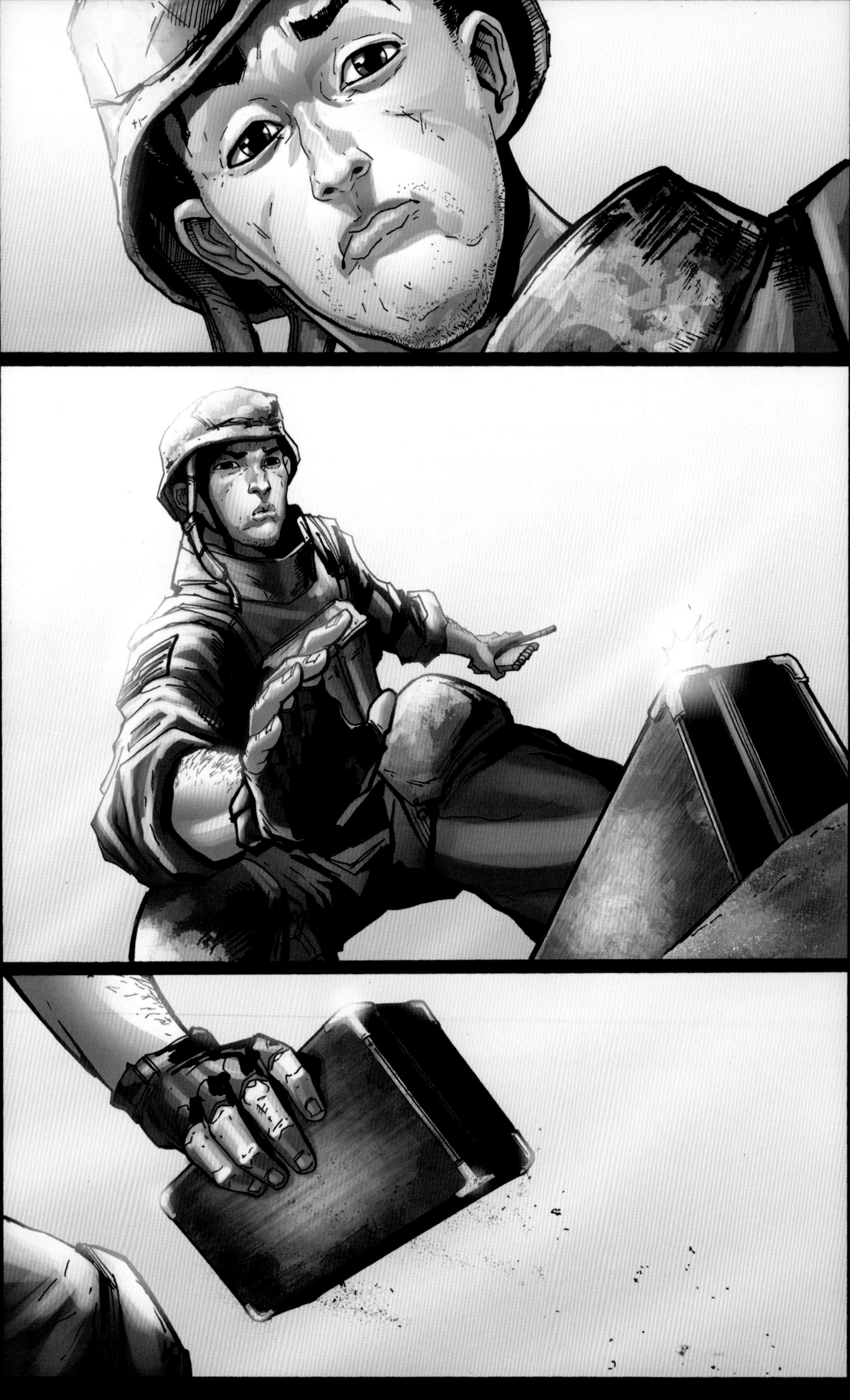

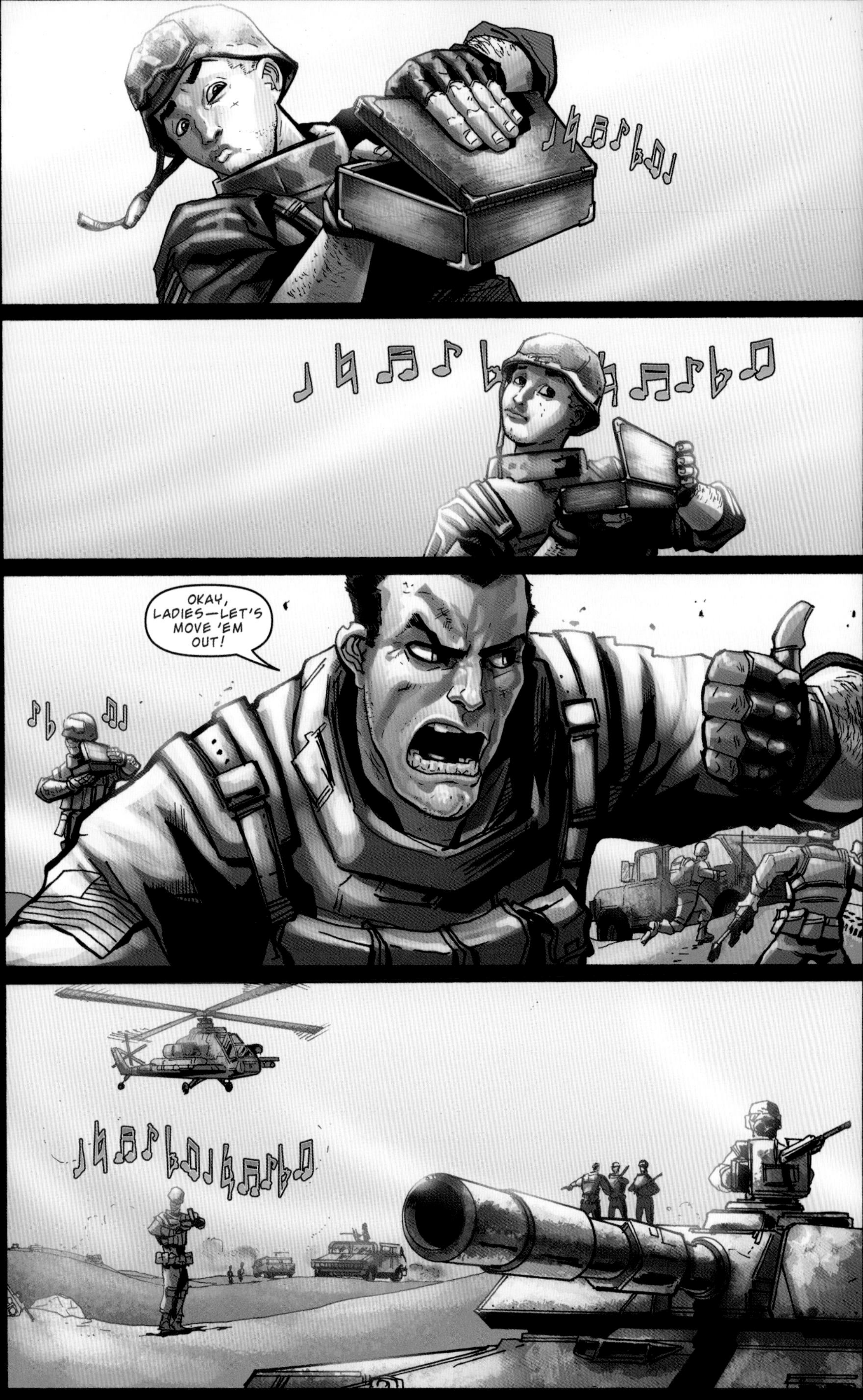
OKAY, LADIES—LET'S MOVE 'EM OUT!

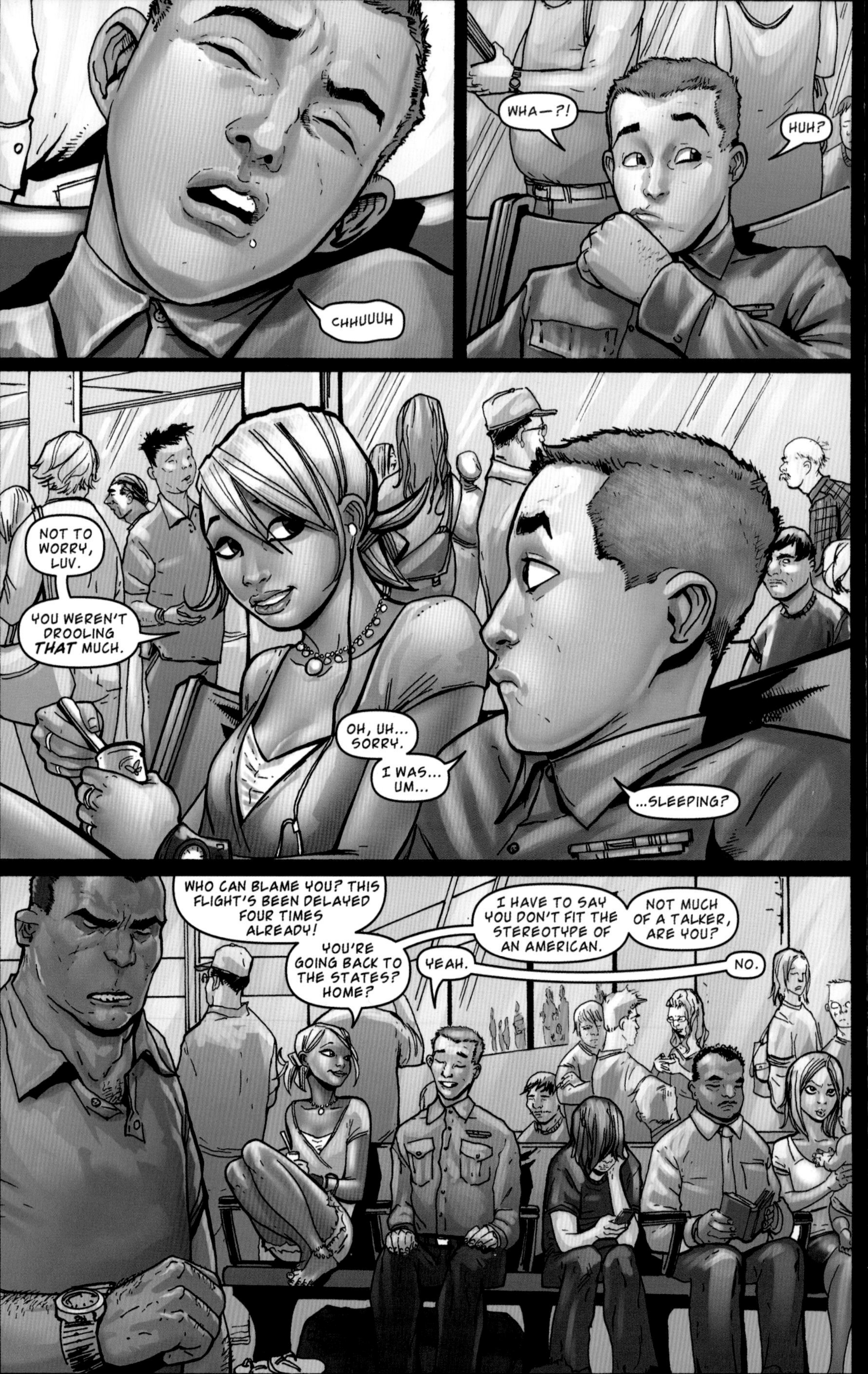
CHHUUUH
WHA—?!
HUH?
NOT TO WORRY, LUV.
YOU WEREN'T DROOLING *THAT* MUCH.
OH, UH... SORRY.
I WAS... UM...
...SLEEPING?
WHO CAN BLAME YOU? THIS FLIGHT'S BEEN DELAYED FOUR TIMES ALREADY!
YOU'RE GOING BACK TO THE STATES? HOME?
YEAH.
I HAVE TO SAY YOU DON'T FIT THE STEREOTYPE OF AN AMERICAN.
NOT MUCH OF A TALKER, ARE YOU?
NO.

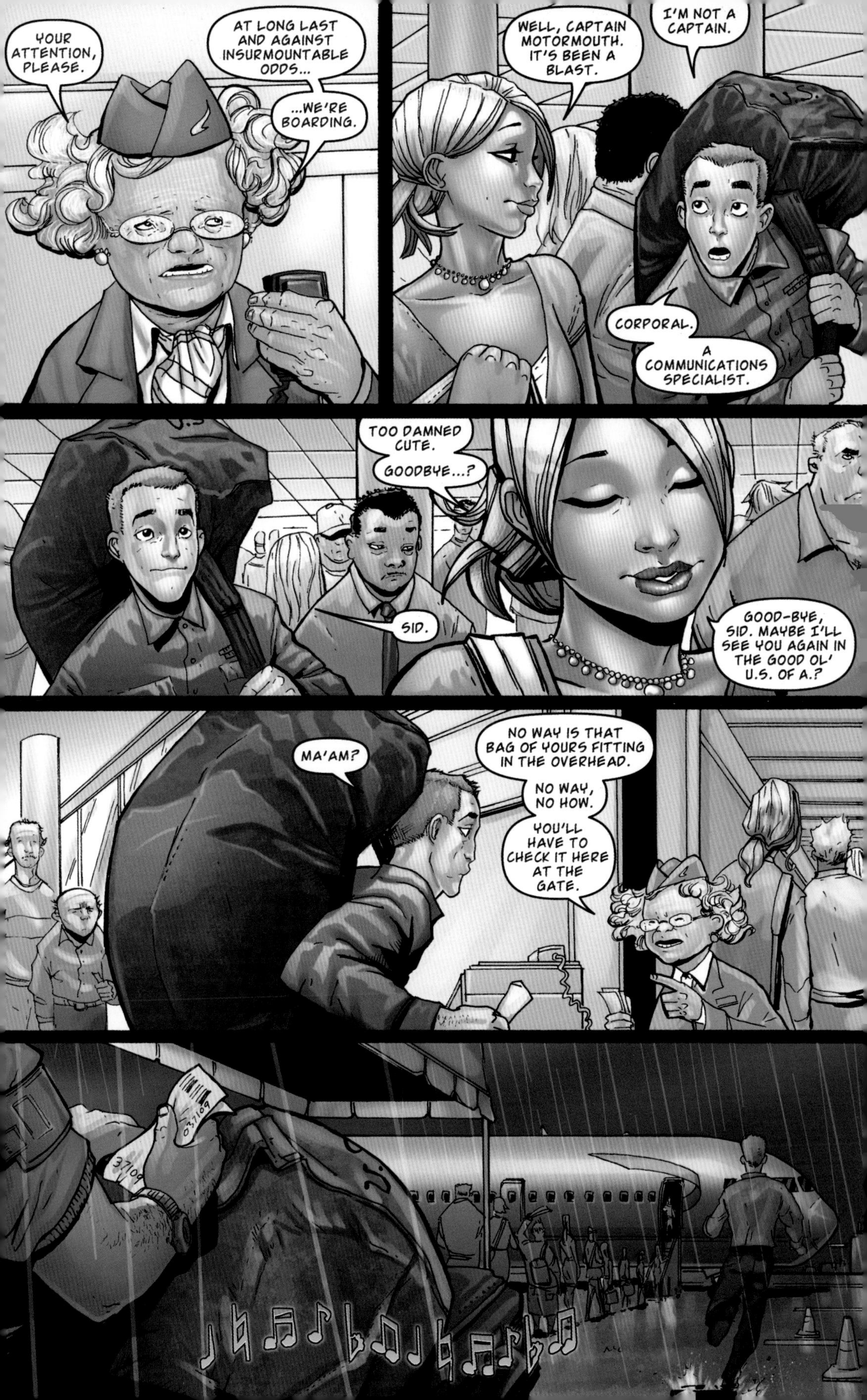
YOUR ATTENTION, PLEASE.
AT LONG LAST AND AGAINST INSURMOUNTABLE ODDS...
...WE'RE BOARDING.
WELL, CAPTAIN MOTORMOUTH. IT'S BEEN A BLAST.
I'M NOT A CAPTAIN.
CORPORAL.
A COMMUNICATIONS SPECIALIST.
TOO DAMNED CUTE.
GOODBYE...?
SID.
GOOD-BYE, SID. MAYBE I'LL SEE YOU AGAIN IN THE GOOD OL' U.S. OF A.?
MA'AM?
NO WAY IS THAT BAG OF YOURS FITTING IN THE OVERHEAD.
NO WAY, NO HOW.
YOU'LL HAVE TO CHECK IT HERE AT THE GATE.

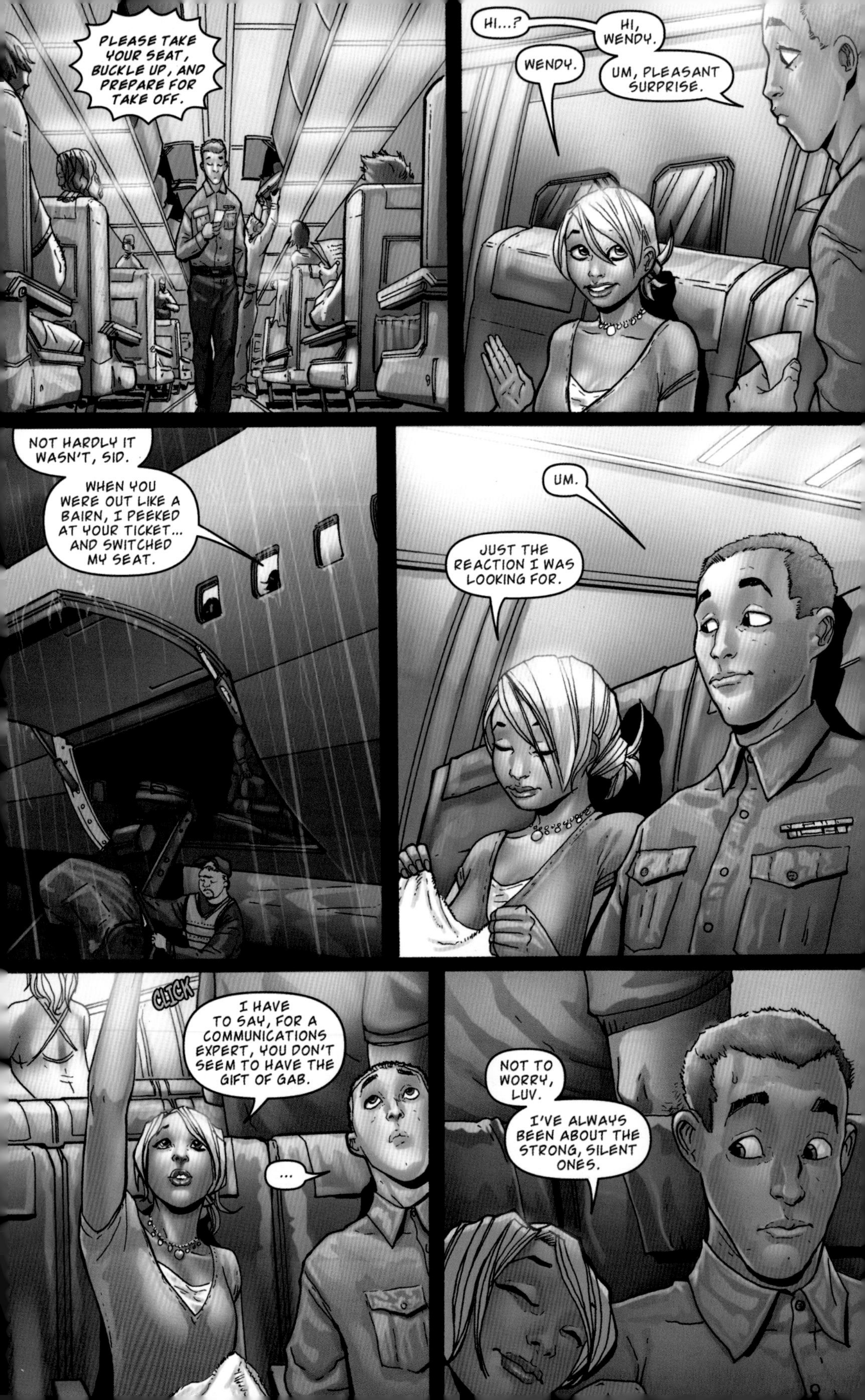
PLEASE TAKE YOUR SEAT, BUCKLE UP, AND PREPARE FOR TAKE OFF.
HI...?
HI, WENDY.
WENDY.
UM, PLEASANT SURPRISE.
NOT HARDLY IT WASN'T, SID.
WHEN YOU WERE OUT LIKE A BAIRN, I PEEKED AT YOUR TICKET... AND SWITCHED MY SEAT.
UM.
JUST THE REACTION I WAS LOOKING FOR.
CLICK
I HAVE TO SAY, FOR A COMMUNICATIONS EXPERT, YOU DON'T SEEM TO HAVE THE GIFT OF GAB.
...
NOT TO WORRY, LUV.
I'VE ALWAYS BEEN ABOUT THE STRONG, SILENT ONES.

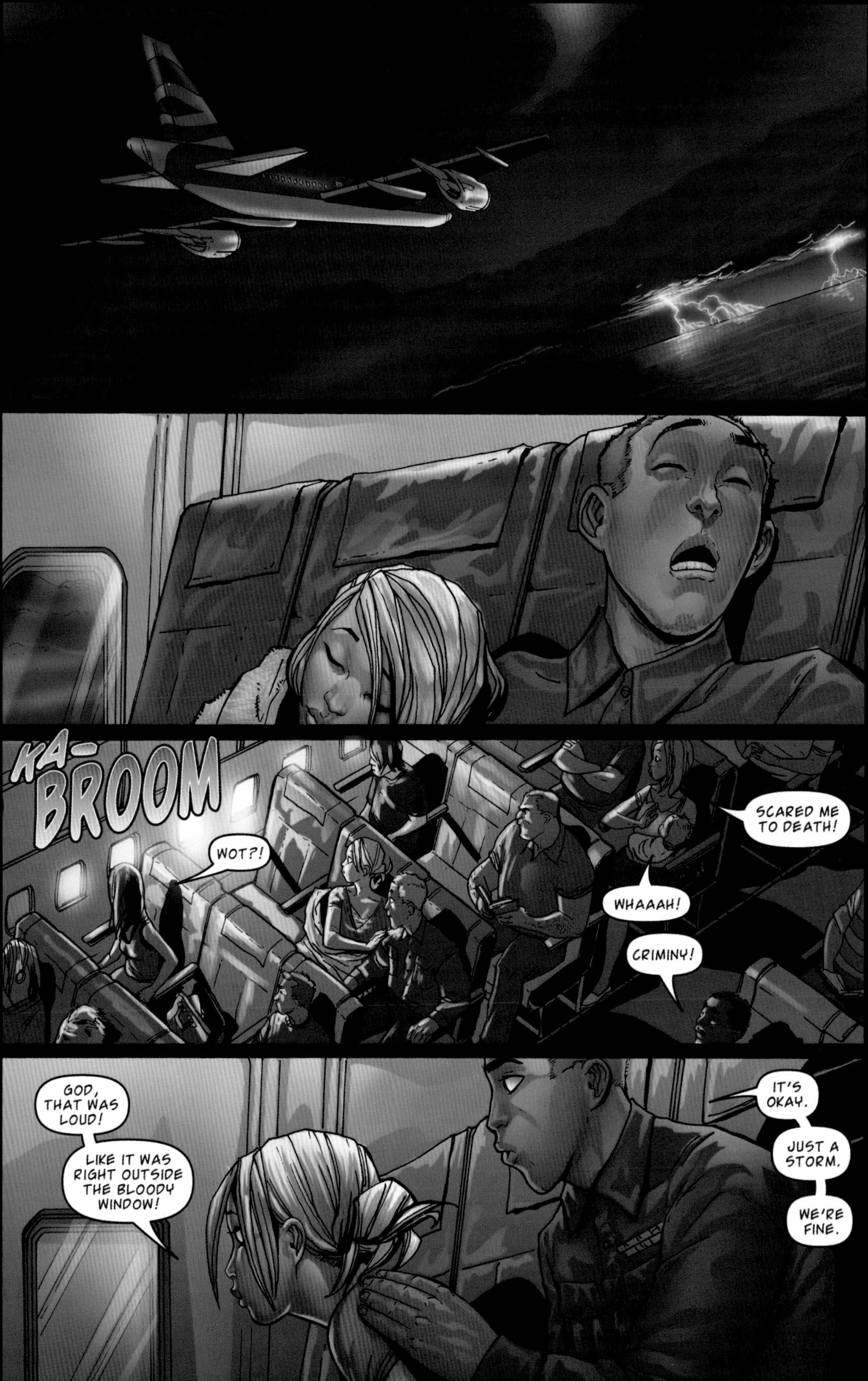
KA-BROOM
WOT?!
SCARED ME TO DEATH!
WHAAAH!
CRIMINY!
GOD, THAT WAS LOUD!
LIKE IT WAS RIGHT OUTSIDE THE BLOODY WINDOW!
IT'S OKAY.
JUST A STORM.
WE'RE FINE.

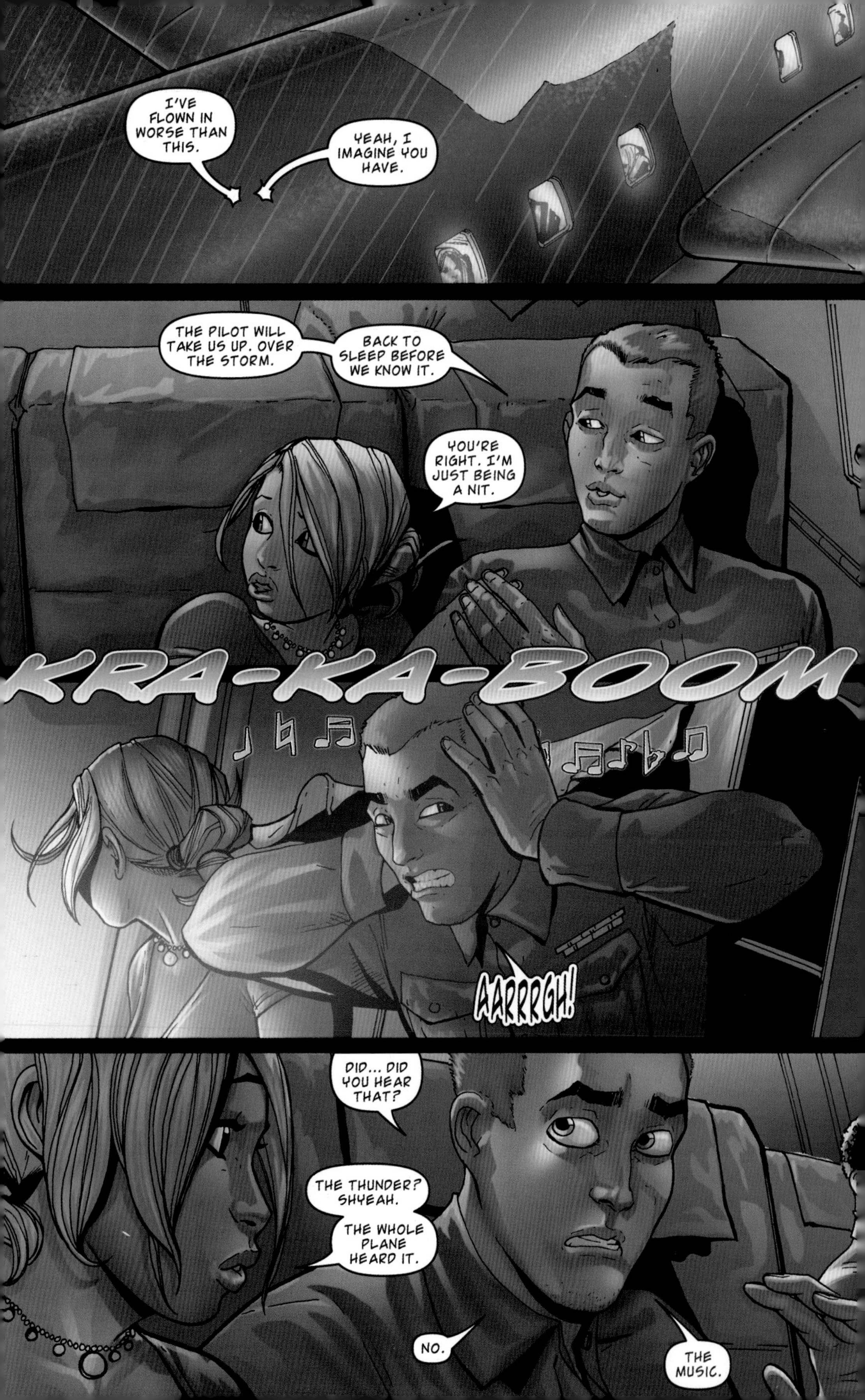
I'VE FLOWN IN WORSE THAN THIS.
YEAH, I IMAGINE YOU HAVE.
THE PILOT WILL TAKE US UP. OVER THE STORM.
BACK TO SLEEP BEFORE WE KNOW IT.
YOU'RE RIGHT. I'M JUST BEING A NIT.
KRA-KA-BOOM
AARRRGH!
DID... DID YOU HEAR THAT?
THE THUNDER? SHYEAH.
THE WHOLE PLANE HEARD IT.
NO.
THE MUSIC.

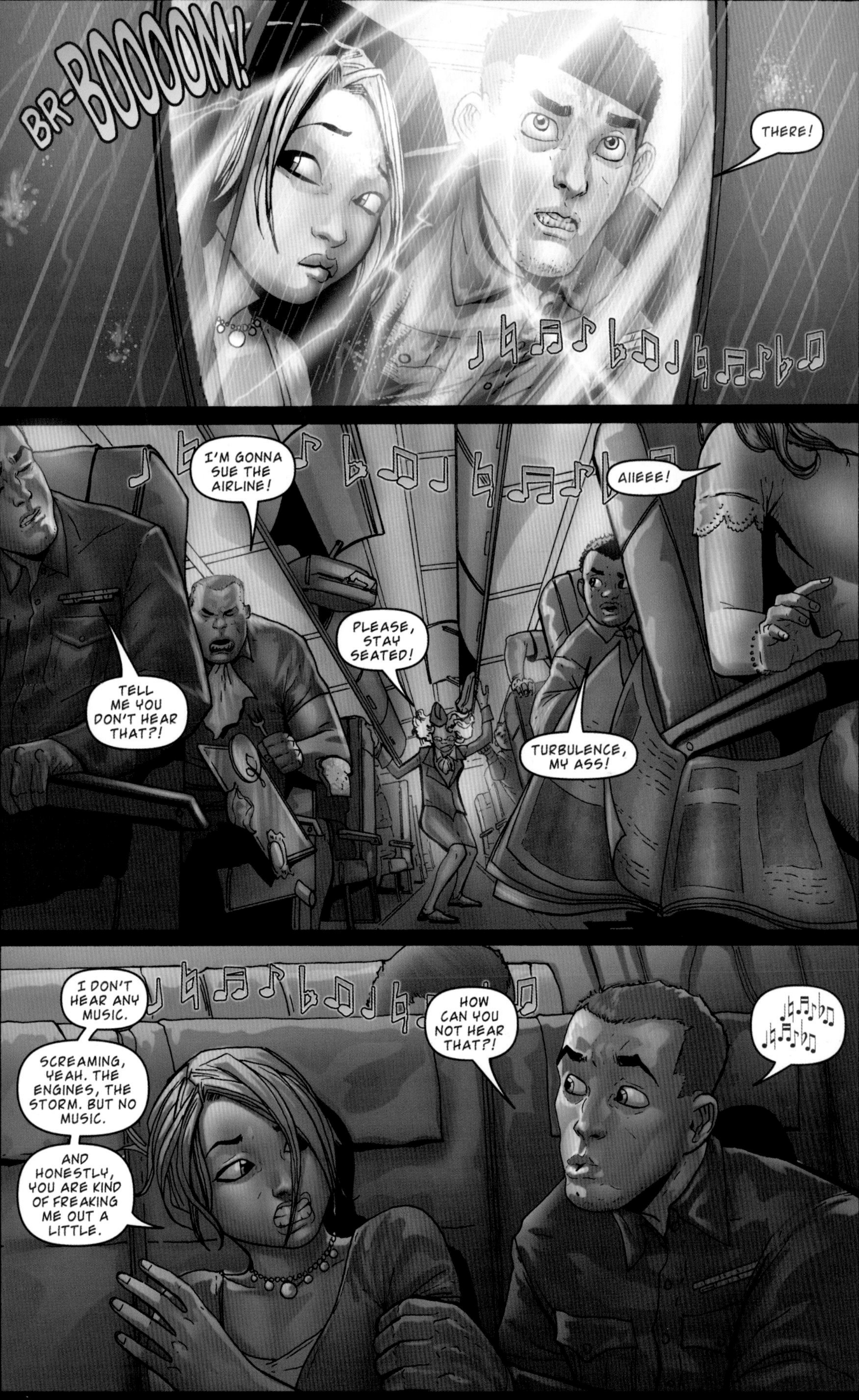
BR-BOOOOM!
THERE!
I'M GONNA SUE THE AIRLINE!
AIIEEE!
PLEASE, STAY SEATED!
TELL ME YOU DON'T HEAR THAT?!
TURBULENCE, MY ASS!
I DON'T HEAR ANY MUSIC.
SCREAMING, YEAH. THE ENGINES, THE STORM. BUT NO MUSIC.
AND HONESTLY, YOU ARE KIND OF FREAKING ME OUT A LITTLE.
HOW CAN YOU NOT HEAR THAT?!

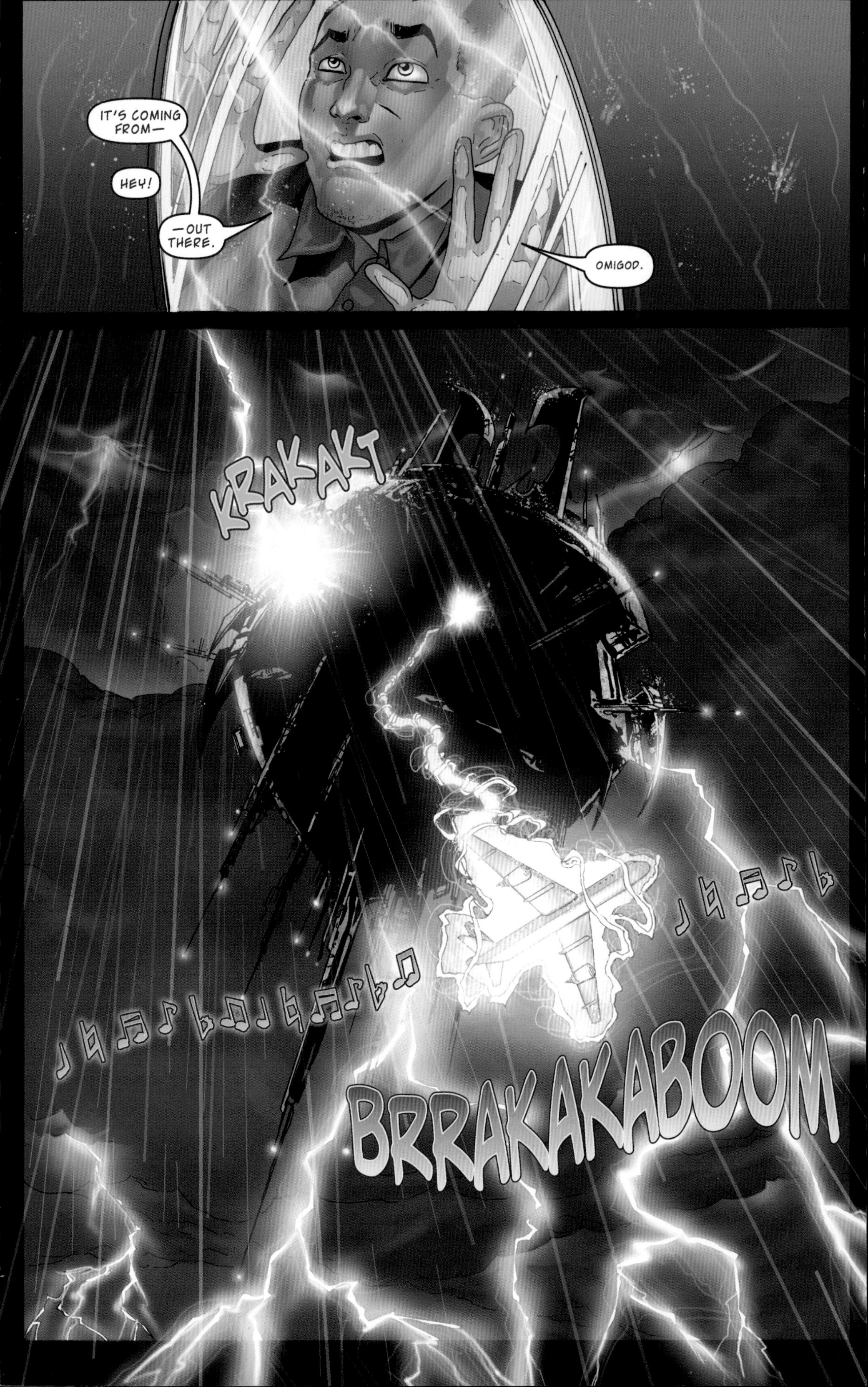
IT'S COMING FROM—
HEY!
—OUT THERE.
OMIGOD.
KRAKAKT
BRRAKAKABOOM

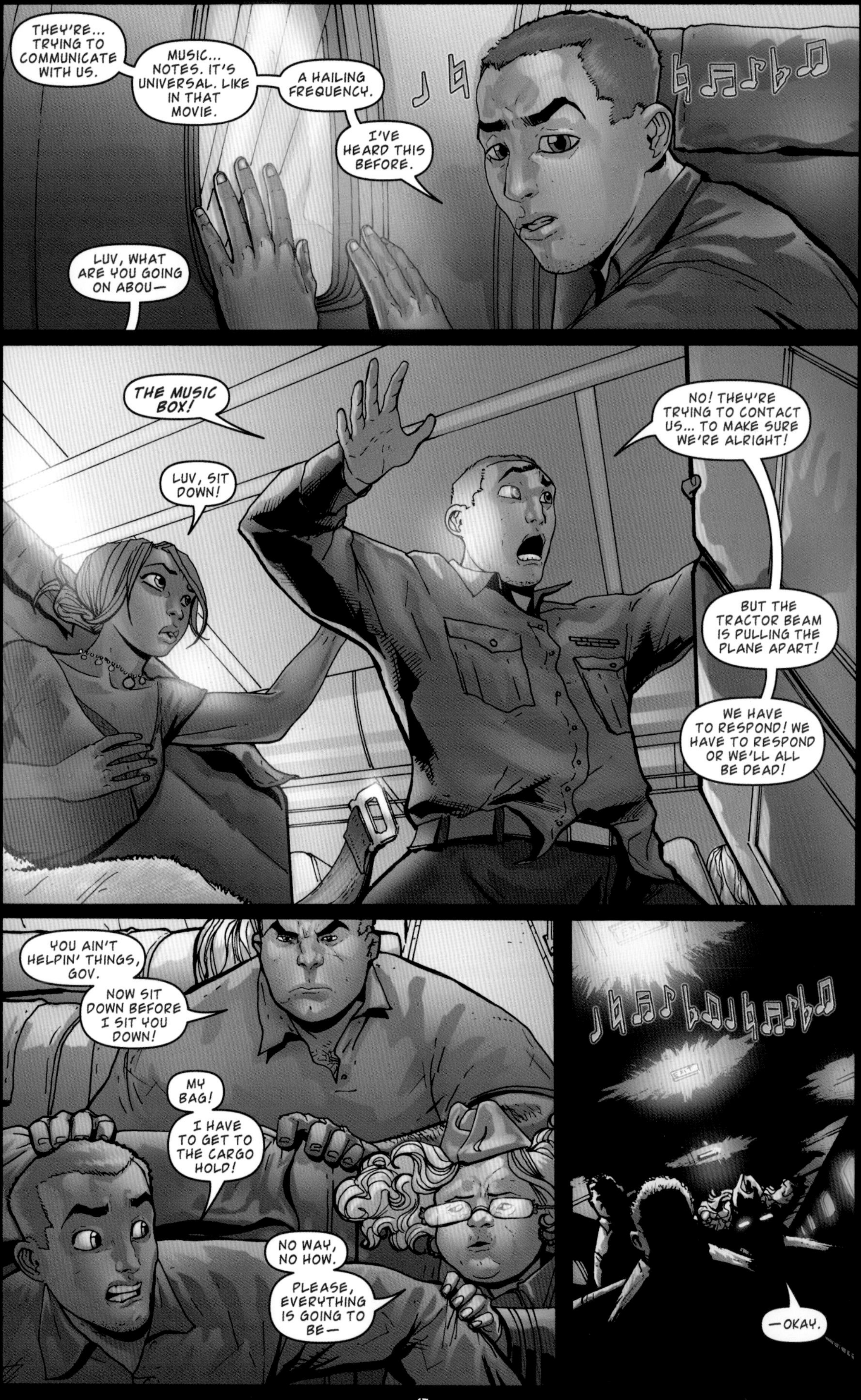
THEY'RE... TRYING TO COMMUNICATE WITH US.
MUSIC... NOTES. IT'S UNIVERSAL. LIKE IN THAT MOVIE.
A HAILING FREQUENCY.
I'VE HEARD THIS BEFORE.
LUV, WHAT ARE YOU GOING ON ABOU—
THE MUSIC BOX!
LUV, SIT DOWN!
NO! THEY'RE TRYING TO CONTACT US... TO MAKE SURE WE'RE ALRIGHT!
BUT THE TRACTOR BEAM IS PULLING THE PLANE APART!
WE HAVE TO RESPOND! WE HAVE TO RESPOND OR WE'LL ALL BE DEAD!
YOU AIN'T HELPIN' THINGS, GOV.
NOW SIT DOWN BEFORE I SIT YOU DOWN!
MY BAG!
I HAVE TO GET TO THE CARGO HOLD!
NO WAY, NO HOW.
PLEASE, EVERYTHING IS GOING TO BE—
—OKAY.

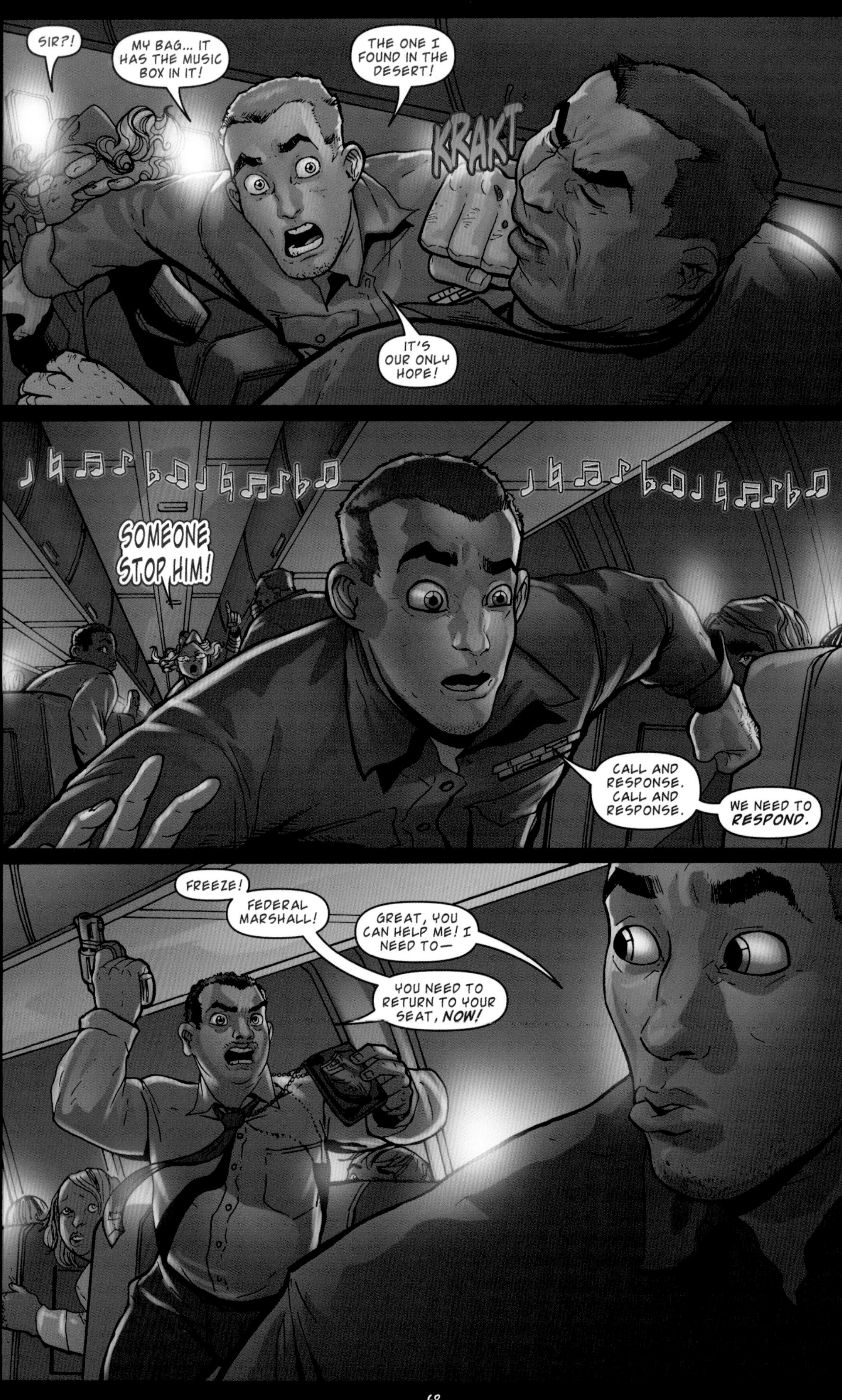
SIR?!
MY BAG... IT HAS THE MUSIC BOX IN IT!
THE ONE I FOUND IN THE DESERT!
KRAKT
IT'S OUR ONLY HOPE!
SOMEONE STOP HIM!
CALL AND RESPONSE. CALL AND RESPONSE.
WE NEED TO **RESPOND.**
FREEZE!
FEDERAL MARSHALL!
GREAT, YOU CAN HELP ME! I NEED TO—
YOU NEED TO RETURN TO YOUR SEAT, **NOW!**

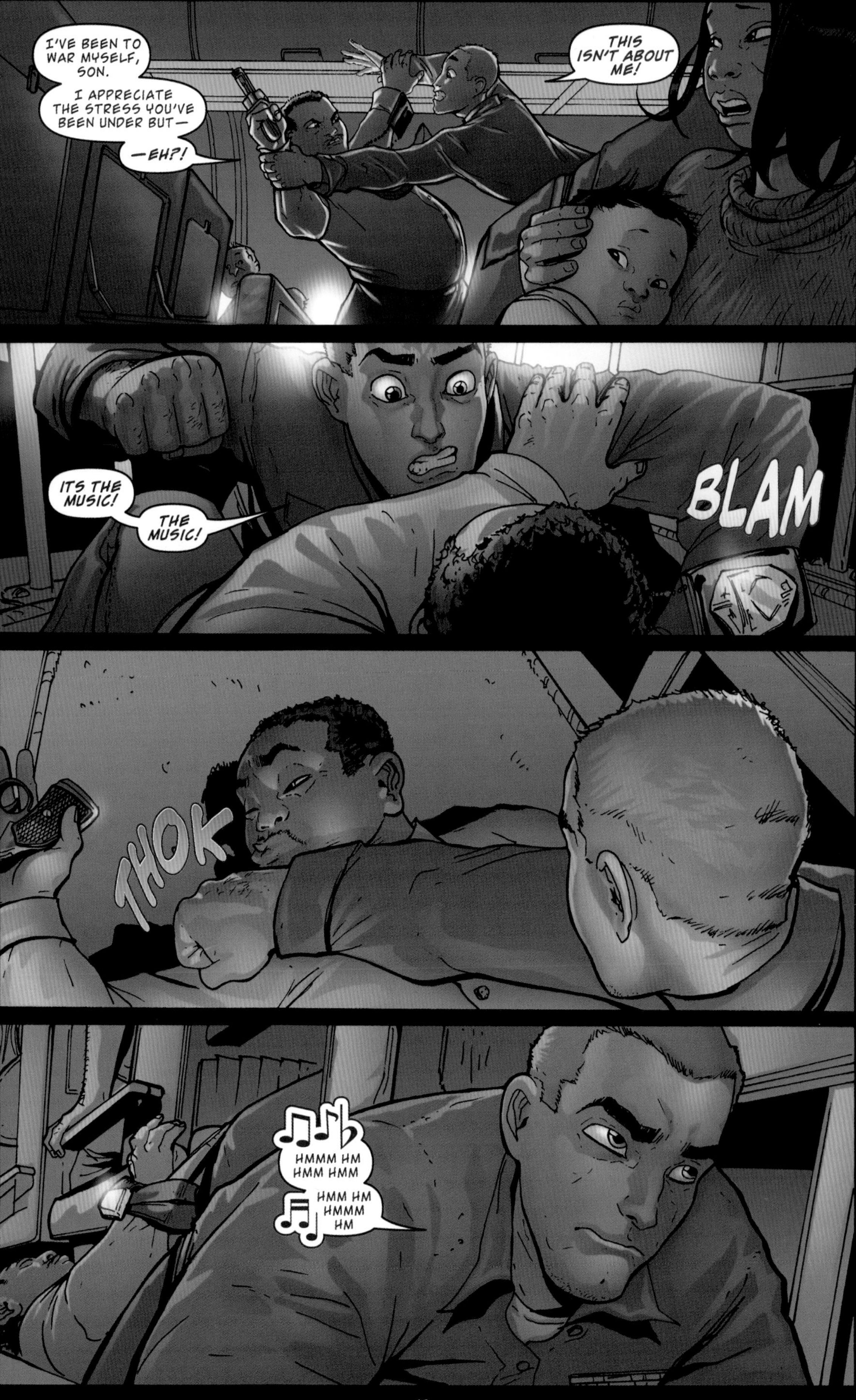
I'VE BEEN TO WAR MYSELF, SON.
I APPRECIATE THE STRESS YOU'VE BEEN UNDER BUT—
—EH?!
THIS ISN'T ABOUT ME!
ITS THE MUSIC!
THE MUSIC!
BLAM
THOK
HMMM HM HMM HMM
HMM HM HMMM HM

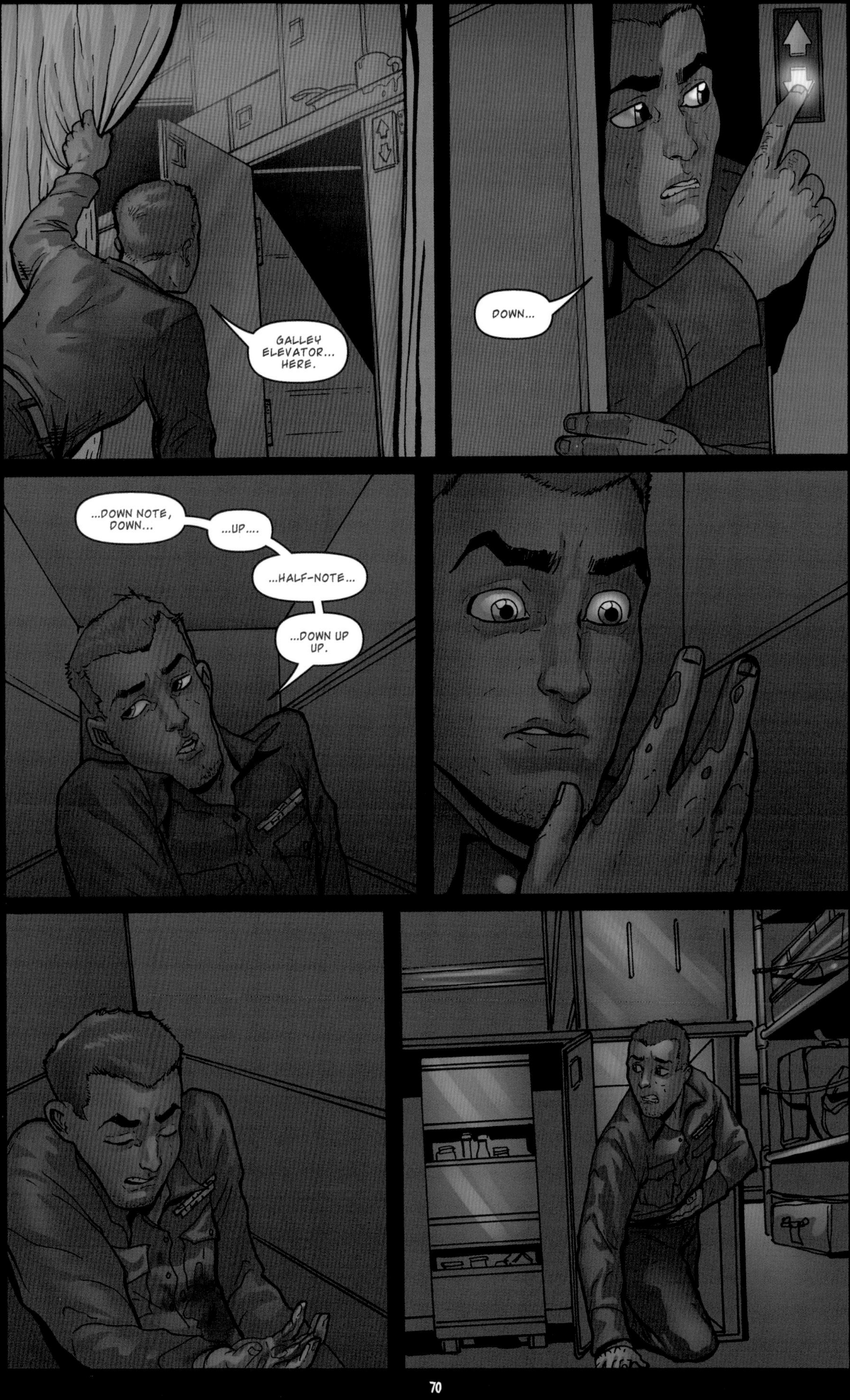
GALLEY ELEVATOR... HERE.
DOWN...
...DOWN NOTE, DOWN...
...UP....
...HALF-NOTE...
...DOWN UP UP.

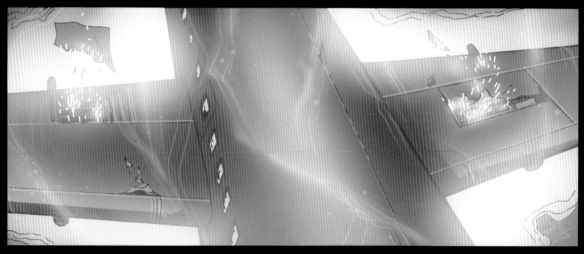

WHERE...?

THERE!

C'MON... C'MON!

HUNHH...

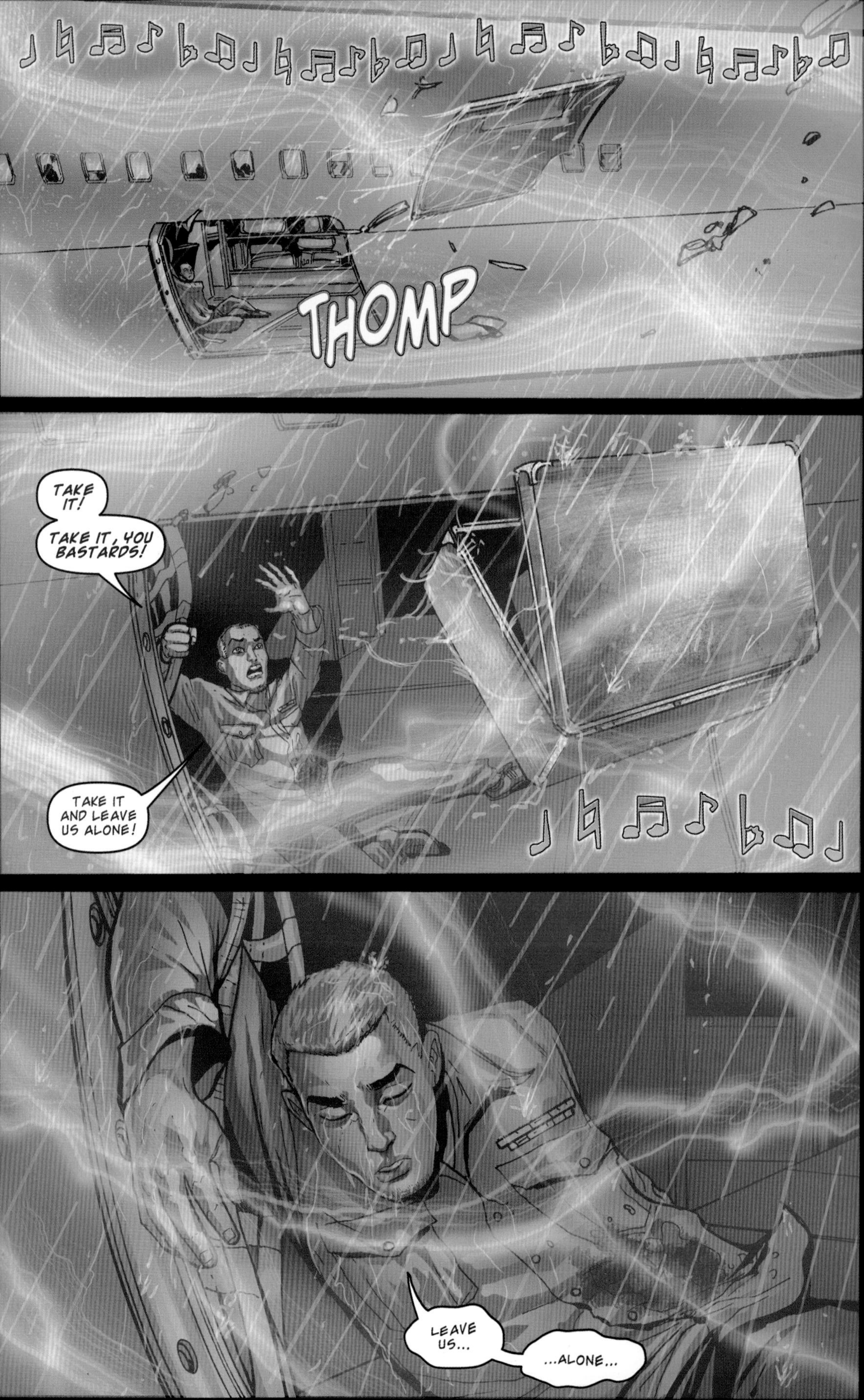
THOMP
TAKE IT!
TAKE IT, YOU BASTARDS!
TAKE IT AND LEAVE US ALONE!
LEAVE US...
...ALONE...

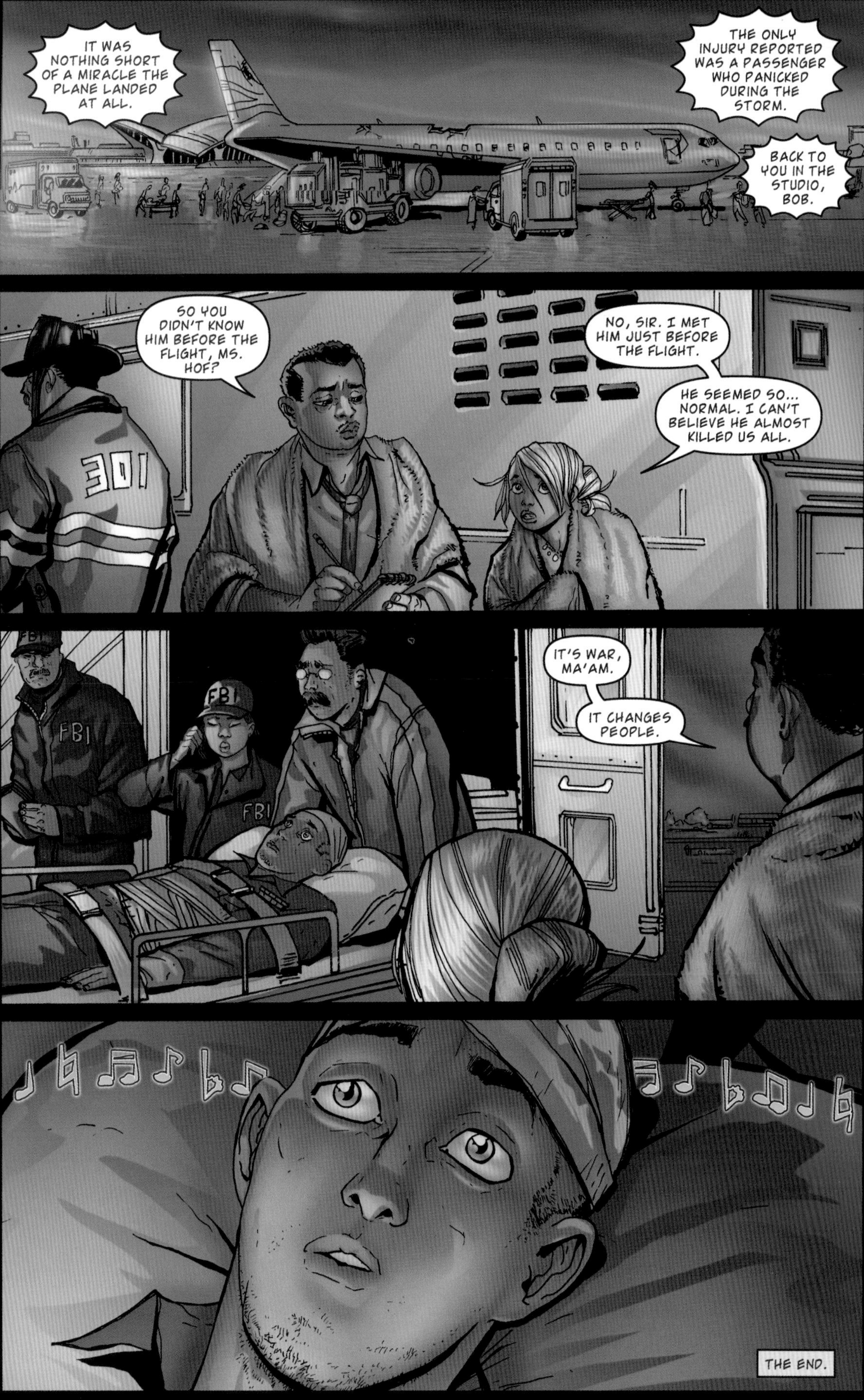
IT WAS NOTHING SHORT OF A MIRACLE THE PLANE LANDED AT ALL.
THE ONLY INJURY REPORTED WAS A PASSENGER WHO PANICKED DURING THE STORM.
BACK TO YOU IN THE STUDIO, BOB.
SO YOU DIDN'T KNOW HIM BEFORE THE FLIGHT, MS. HOF?
NO, SIR. I MET HIM JUST BEFORE THE FLIGHT.
HE SEEMED SO... NORMAL. I CAN'T BELIEVE HE ALMOST KILLED US ALL.
IT'S WAR, MA'AM.
IT CHANGES PEOPLE.
THE END.

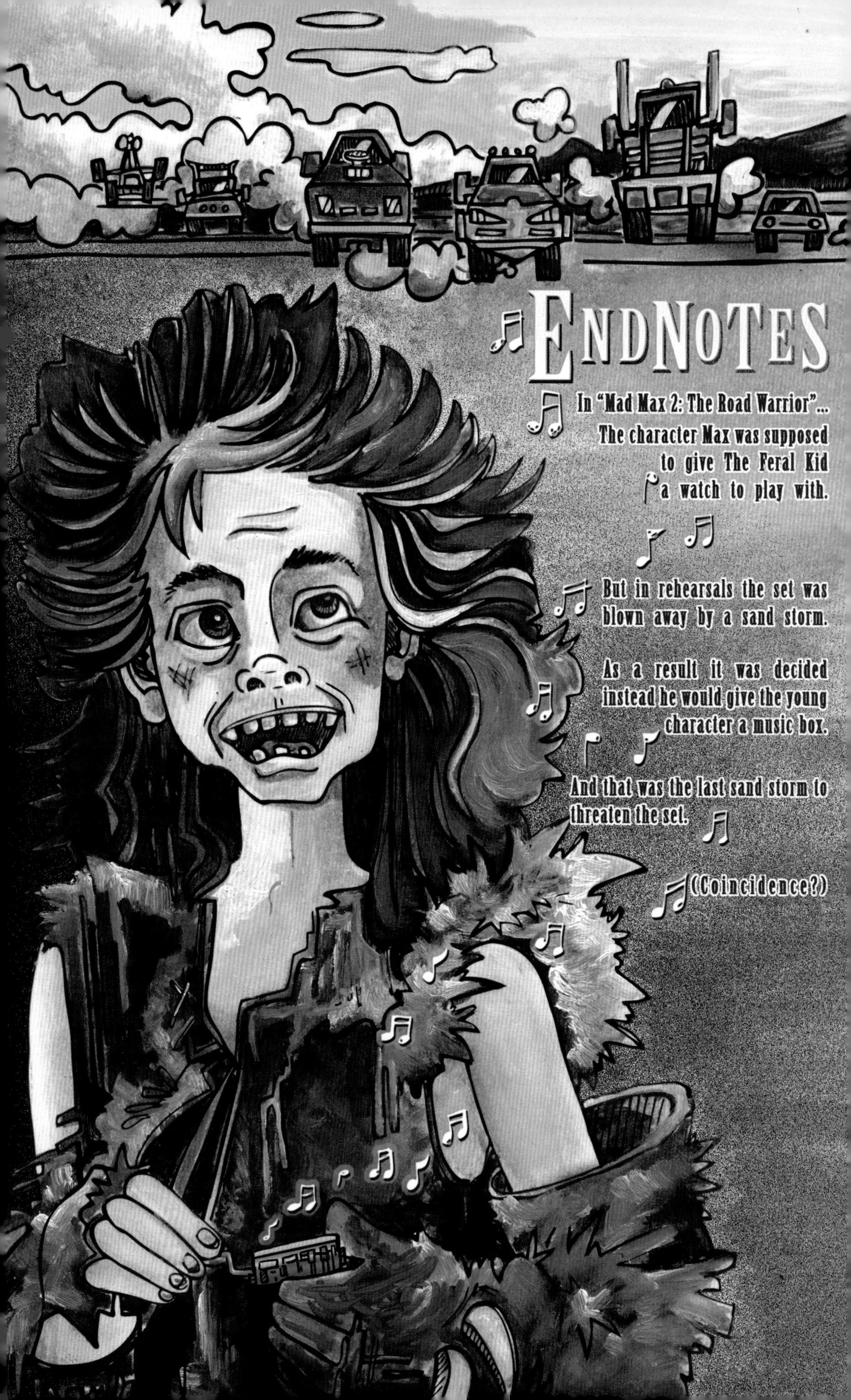
EndNotes
In "Mad Max 2: The Road Warrior"...
The character Max was supposed to give The Feral Kid a watch to play with.
But in rehearsals the set was blown away by a sand storm.
As a result it was decided instead he would give the young character a music box.
And that was the last sand storm to threaten the set.
(Coincidence?)

Chapter Four: "The Flapper"

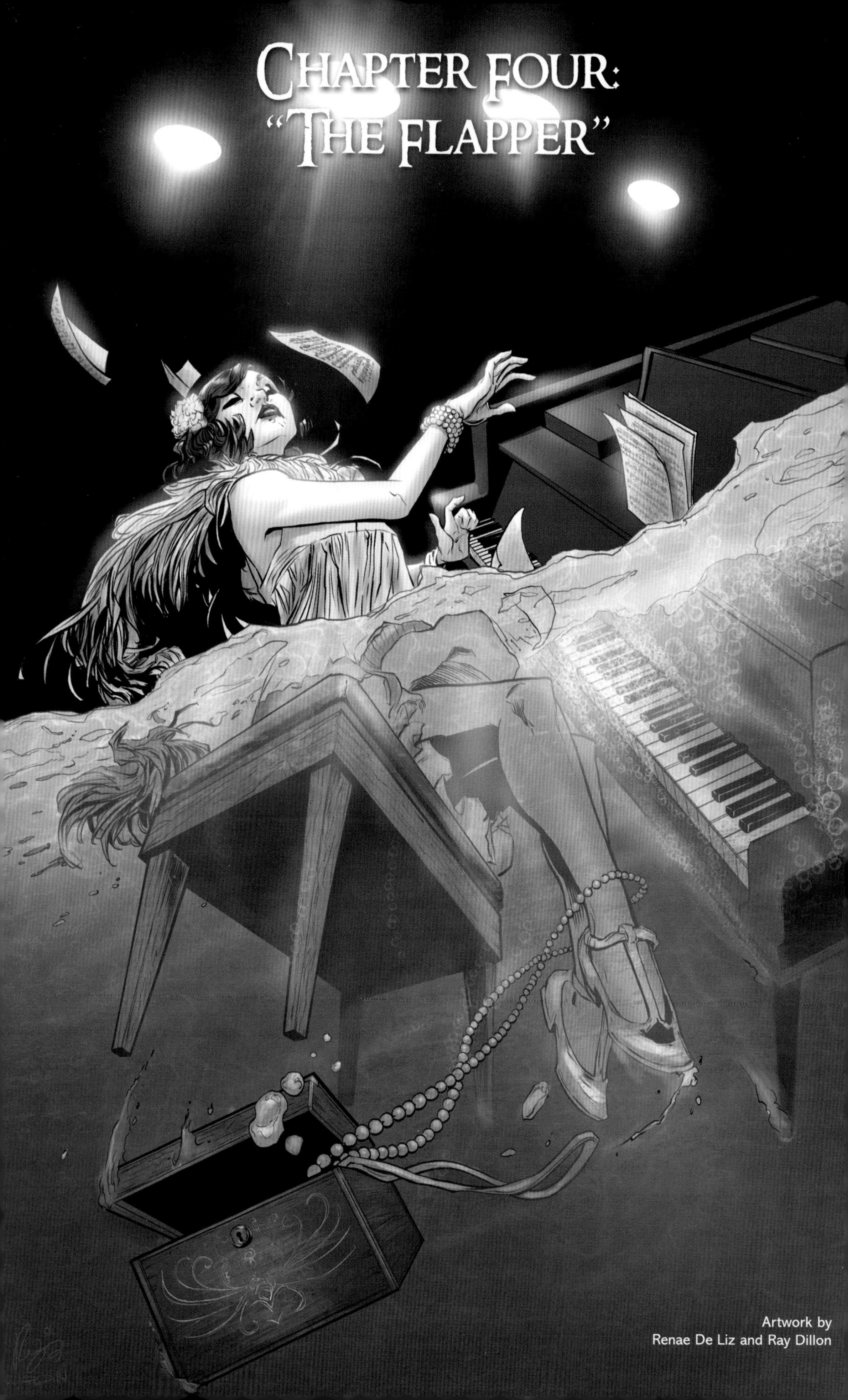

Artwork by
Renae De Liz and Ray Dillon

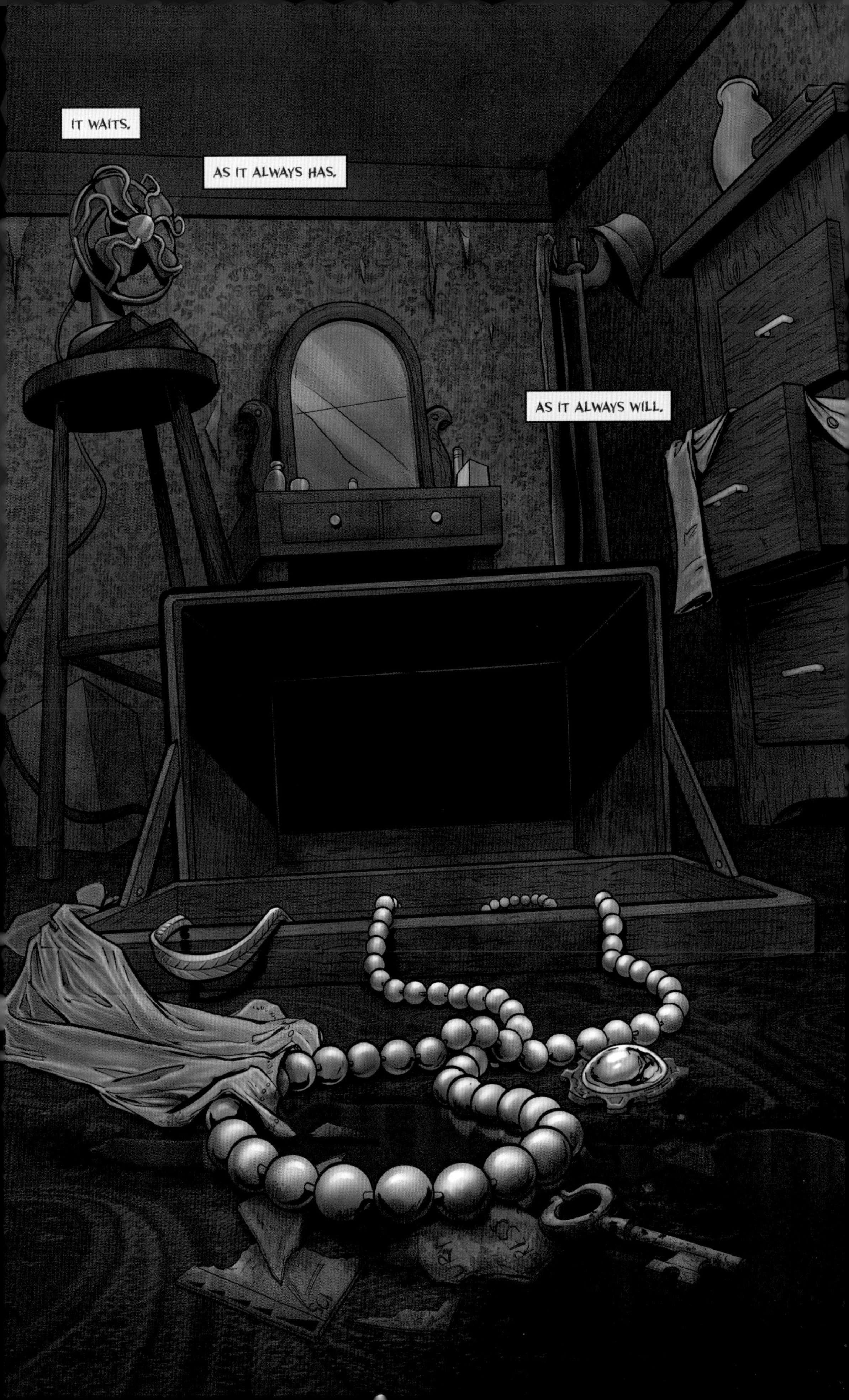
IT WAITS.
AS IT ALWAYS HAS.
AS IT ALWAYS WILL.

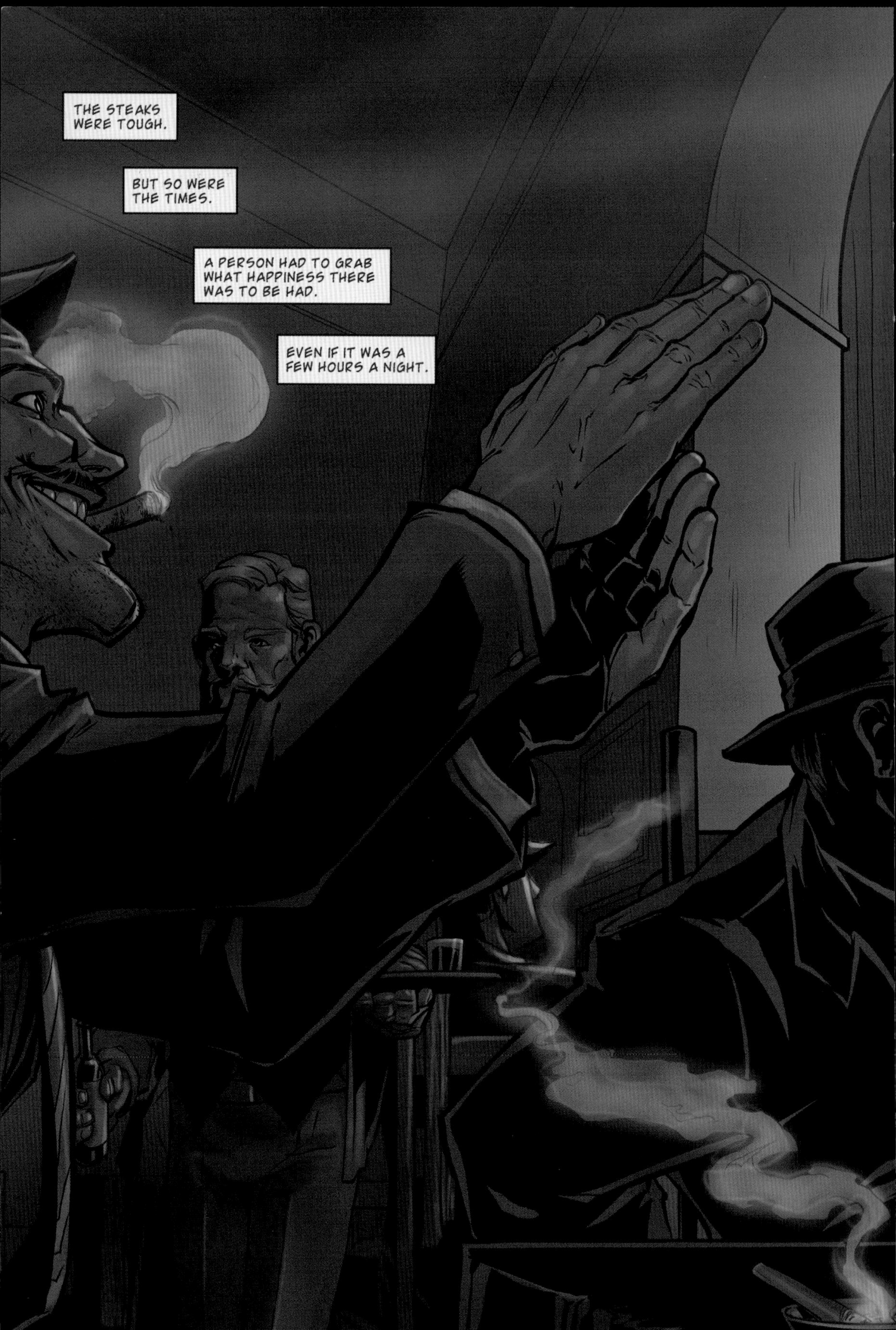
THE STEAKS WERE TOUGH.
BUT SO WERE THE TIMES.
A PERSON HAD TO GRAB WHAT HAPPINESS THERE WAS TO BE HAD.
EVEN IF IT WAS A FEW HOURS A NIGHT.

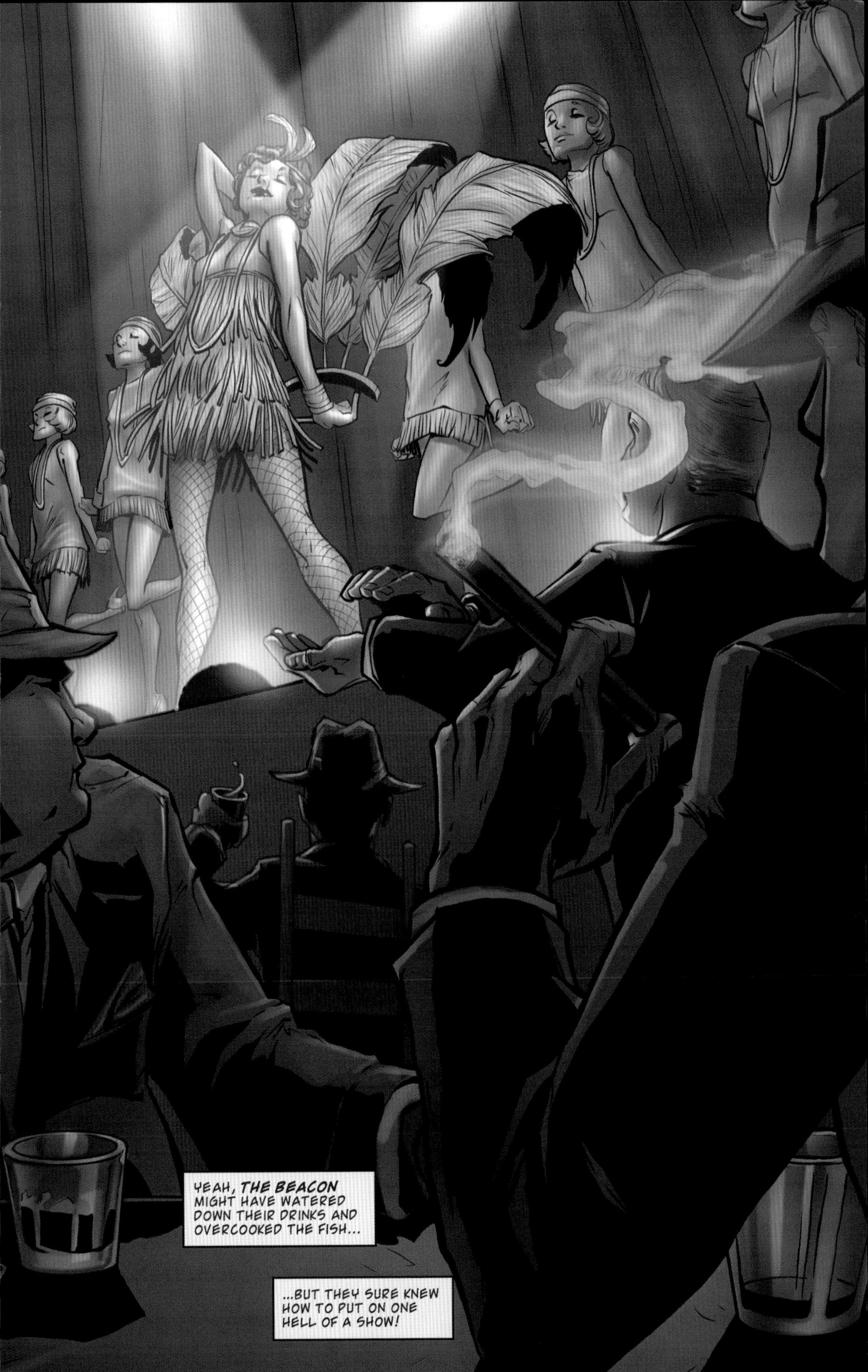
YEAH, THE BEACON MIGHT HAVE WATERED DOWN THEIR DRINKS AND OVERCOOKED THE FISH...
...BUT THEY SURE KNEW HOW TO PUT ON ONE HELL OF A SHOW!

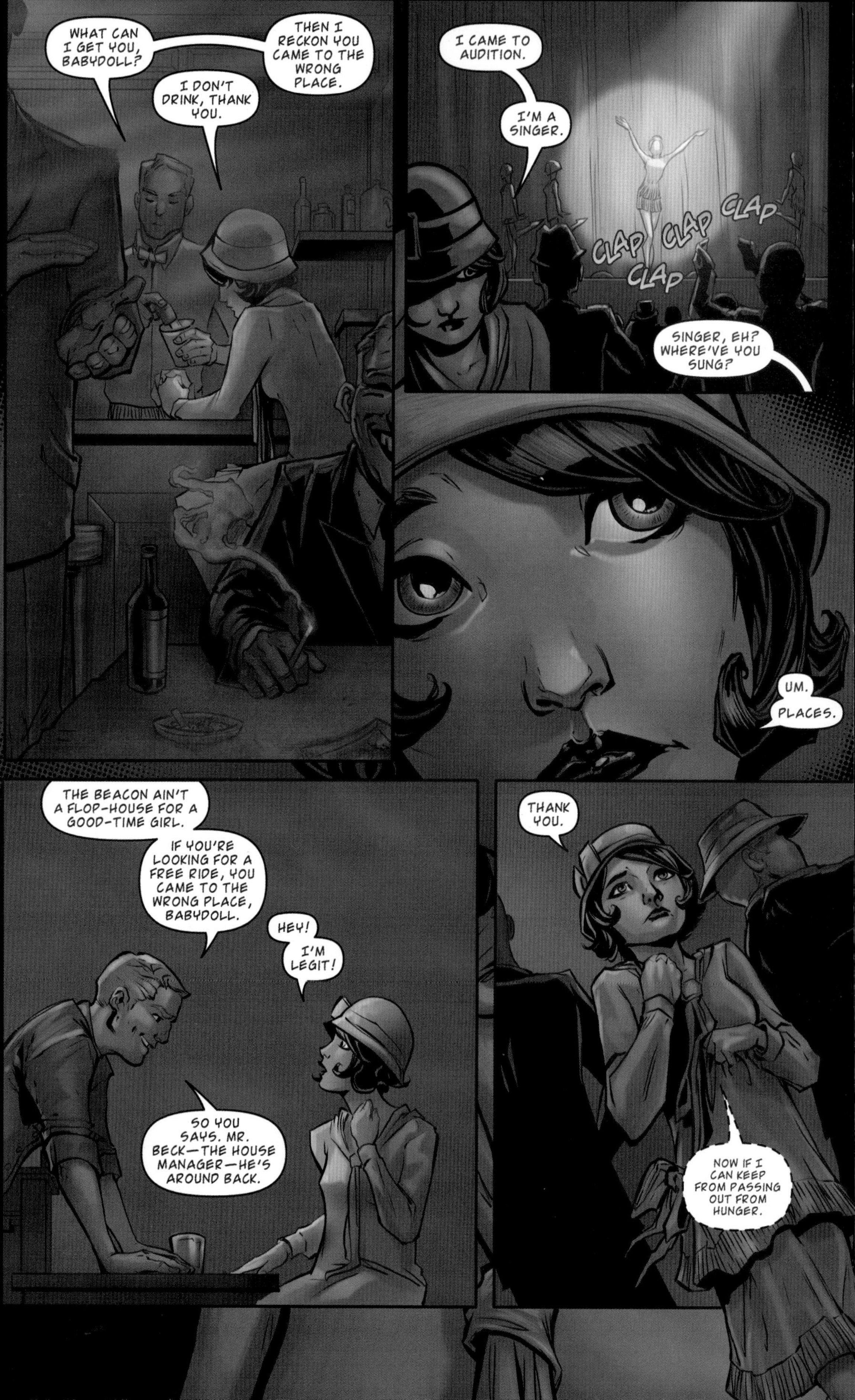
WHAT CAN I GET YOU, BABYDOLL?
I DON'T DRINK, THANK YOU.
THEN I RECKON YOU CAME TO THE WRONG PLACE.
I CAME TO AUDITION.
I'M A SINGER.
CLAP CLAP CLAP
CLAP CLAP
SINGER, EH? WHERE'VE YOU SUNG?
UM.
PLACES.
THE BEACON AIN'T A FLOP-HOUSE FOR A GOOD-TIME GIRL.
IF YOU'RE LOOKING FOR A FREE RIDE, YOU CAME TO THE WRONG PLACE, BABYDOLL.
HEY!
I'M LEGIT!
SO YOU SAYS. MR. BECK—THE HOUSE MANAGER—HE'S AROUND BACK.
THANK YOU.
NOW IF I CAN KEEP FROM PASSING OUT FROM HUNGER.

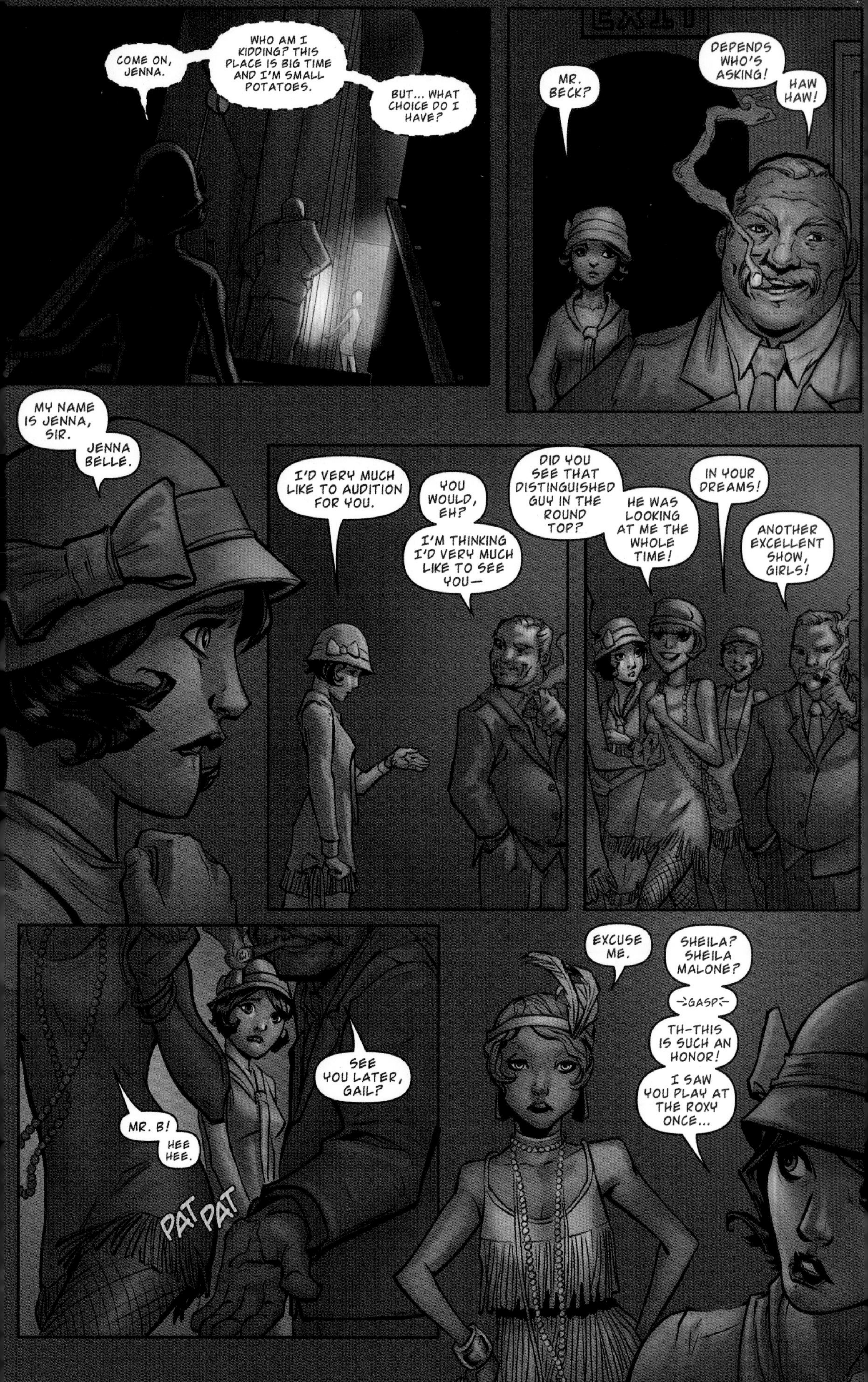
COME ON, JENNA.
WHO AM I KIDDING? THIS PLACE IS BIG TIME AND I'M SMALL POTATOES.
BUT... WHAT CHOICE DO I HAVE?
MR. BECK?
DEPENDS WHO'S ASKING!
HAW HAW!
MY NAME IS JENNA, SIR.
JENNA BELLE.
I'D VERY MUCH LIKE TO AUDITION FOR YOU.
YOU WOULD, EH?
I'M THINKING I'D VERY MUCH LIKE TO SEE YOU—
DID YOU SEE THAT DISTINGUISHED GUY IN THE ROUND TOP?
HE WAS LOOKING AT ME THE WHOLE TIME!
IN YOUR DREAMS!
ANOTHER EXCELLENT SHOW, GIRLS!
SEE YOU LATER, GAIL?
MR. B!
HEE HEE.
PAT PAT
EXCUSE ME.
SHEILA? SHEILA MALONE?
GASP
TH-THIS IS SUCH AN HONOR!
I SAW YOU PLAY AT THE ROXY ONCE...

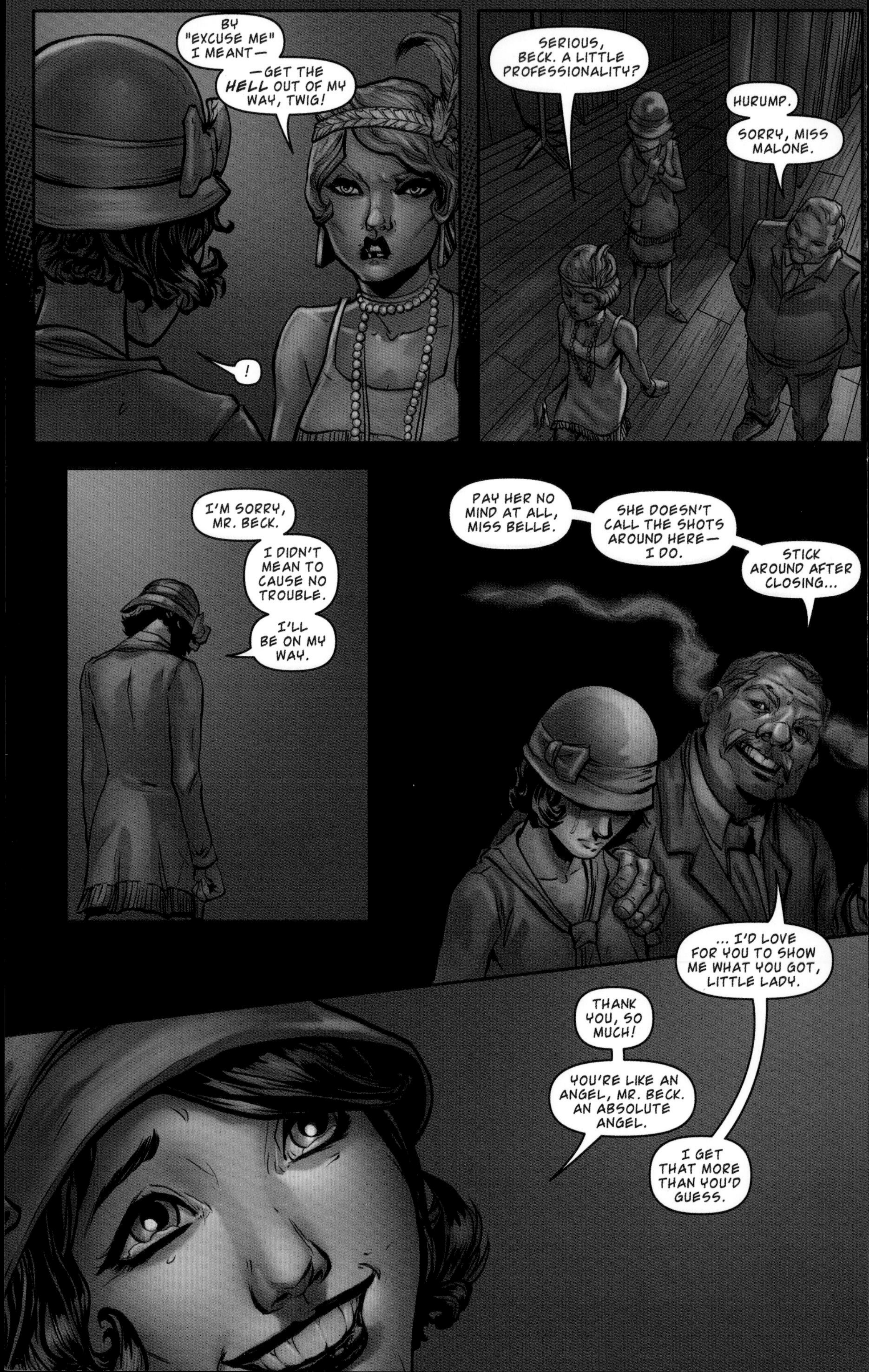
BY "EXCUSE ME" I MEANT—
—GET THE **HELL** OUT OF MY WAY, TWIG!
!
SERIOUS, BECK. A LITTLE PROFESSIONALITY?
HURUMP.
SORRY, MISS MALONE.
I'M SORRY, MR. BECK.
I DIDN'T MEAN TO CAUSE NO TROUBLE.
I'LL BE ON MY WAY.
PAY HER NO MIND AT ALL, MISS BELLE.
SHE DOESN'T CALL THE SHOTS AROUND HERE— I DO.
STICK AROUND AFTER CLOSING...
... I'D LOVE FOR YOU TO SHOW ME WHAT YOU GOT, LITTLE LADY.
THANK YOU, SO MUCH!
YOU'RE LIKE AN ANGEL, MR. BECK. AN ABSOLUTE ANGEL.
I GET THAT MORE THAN YOU'D GUESS.

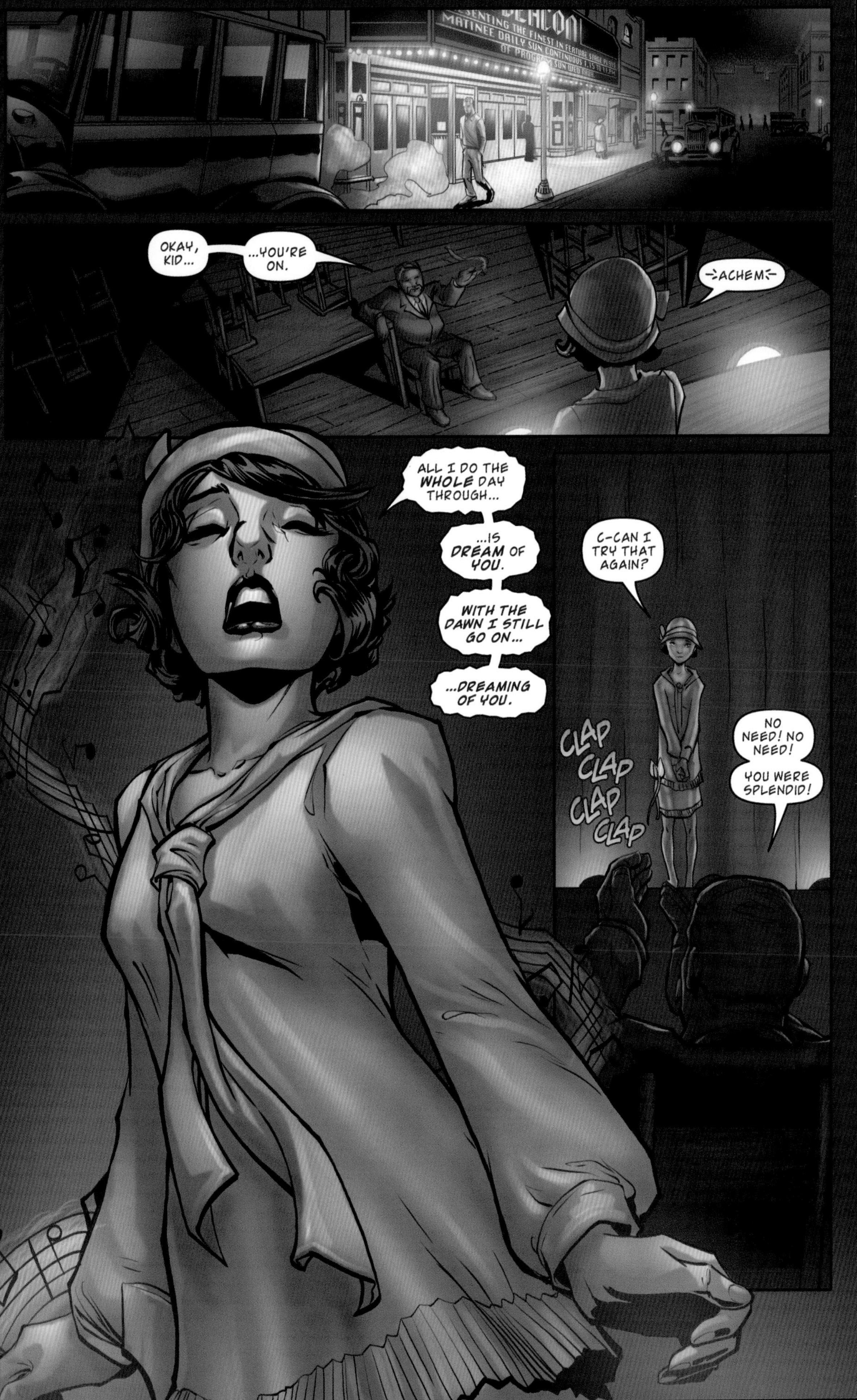
OKAY, KID...
...YOU'RE ON.
ACHEM
ALL I DO THE WHOLE DAY THROUGH...
...IS DREAM OF YOU.
WITH THE DAWN I STILL GO ON...
...DREAMING OF YOU.
C-CAN I TRY THAT AGAIN?
CLAP CLAP CLAP CLAP
NO NEED! NO NEED!
YOU WERE SPLENDID!

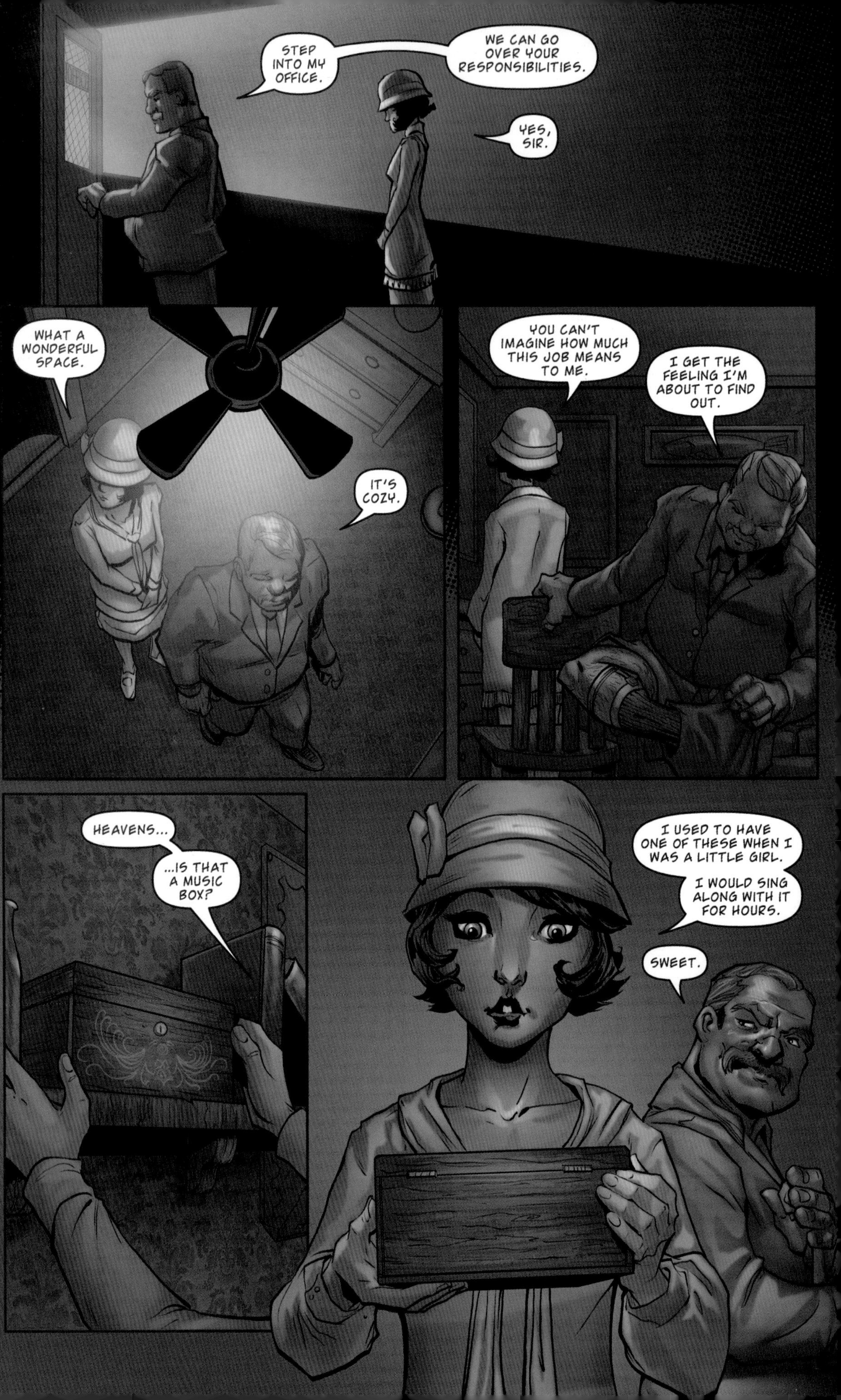
STEP INTO MY OFFICE.
WE CAN GO OVER YOUR RESPONSIBILITIES.
YES, SIR.
WHAT A WONDERFUL SPACE.
IT'S COZY.
YOU CAN'T IMAGINE HOW MUCH THIS JOB MEANS TO ME.
I GET THE FEELING I'M ABOUT TO FIND OUT.
HEAVENS...
...IS THAT A MUSIC BOX?
I USED TO HAVE ONE OF THESE WHEN I WAS A LITTLE GIRL.
I WOULD SING ALONG WITH IT FOR HOURS.
SWEET.

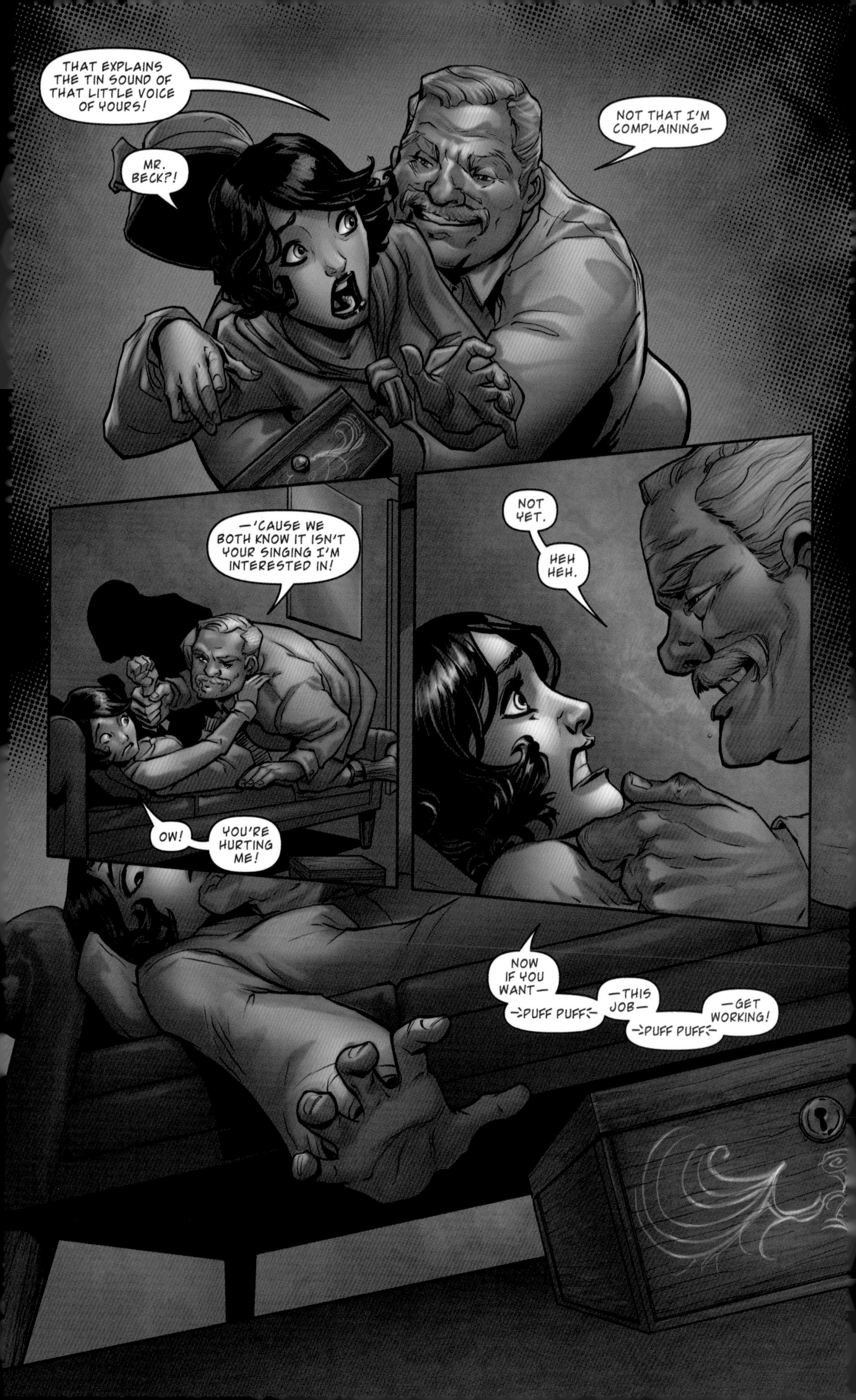
THAT EXPLAINS THE TIN SOUND OF THAT LITTLE VOICE OF YOURS!
MR. BECK?!
NOT THAT I'M COMPLAINING—
—'CAUSE WE BOTH KNOW IT ISN'T YOUR SINGING I'M INTERESTED IN!
OW!
YOU'RE HURTING ME!
NOT YET.
HEH HEH.
NOW IF YOU WANT—
—PUFF PUFF—
—THIS JOB—
—PUFF PUFF—
—GET WORKING!

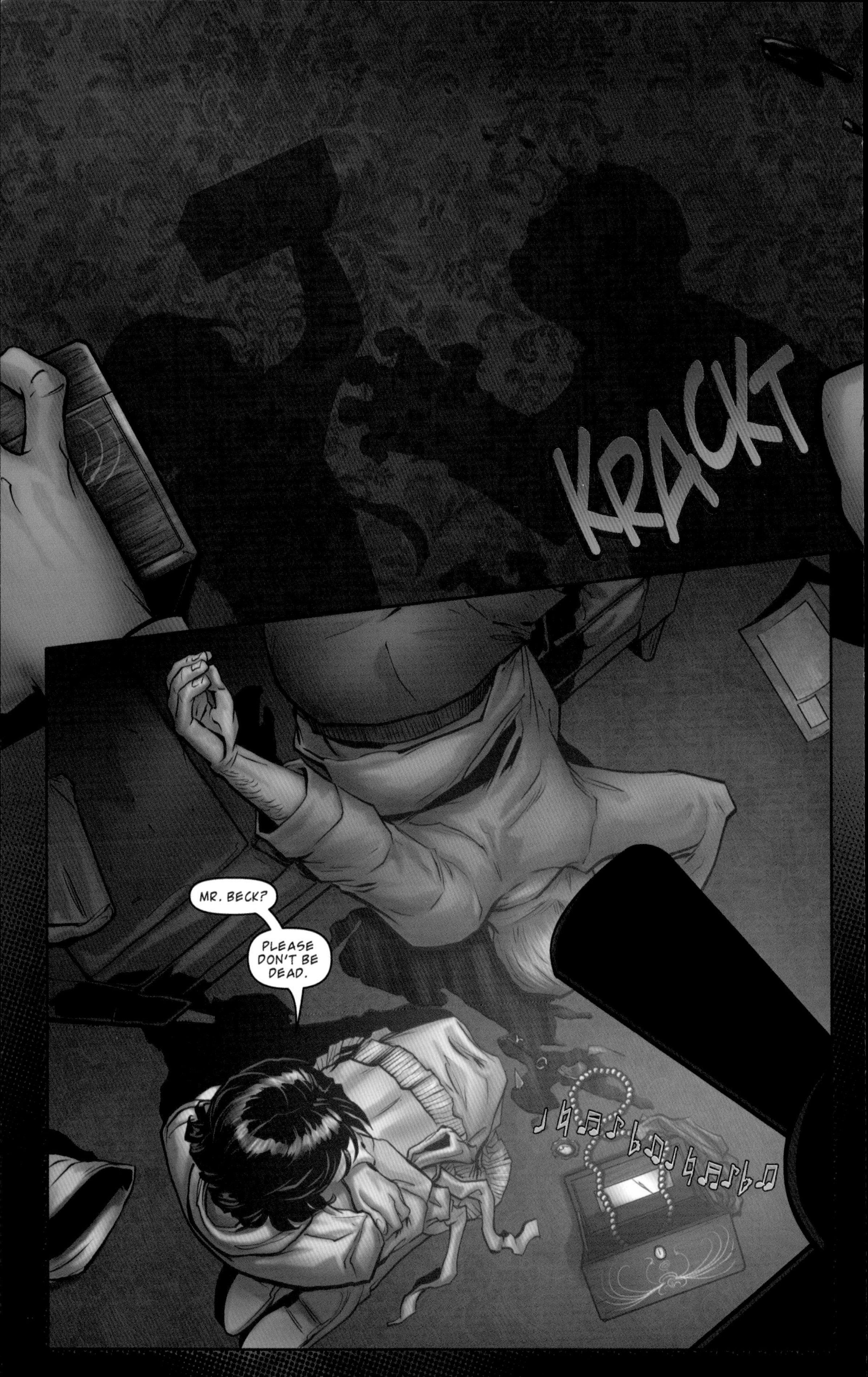
KRACKT
MR. BECK?
PLEASE DON'T BE DEAD.

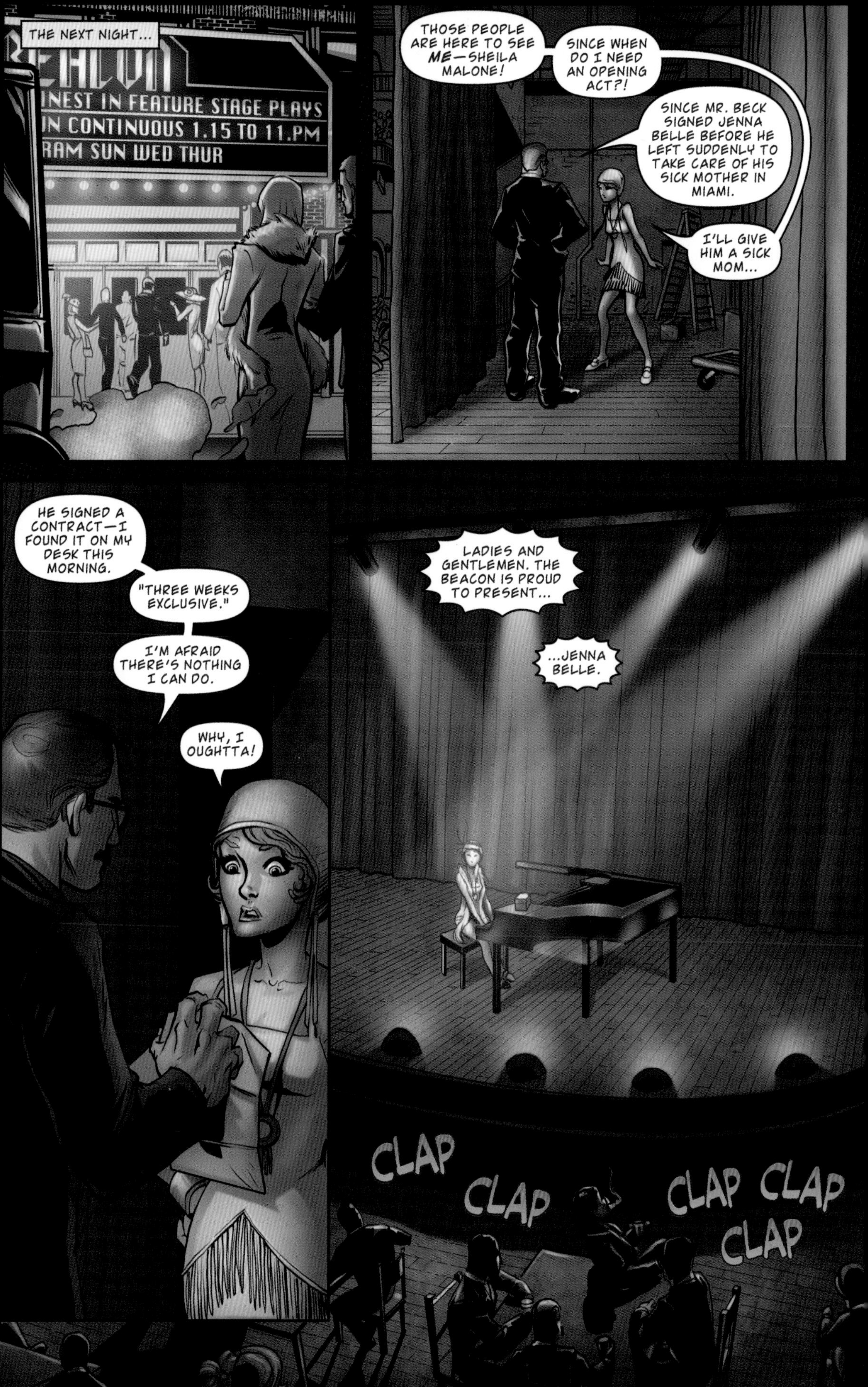
THE NEXT NIGHT...
BEACON
FINEST IN FEATURE STAGE PLAYS
RUN CONTINUOUS 1.15 TO 11.PM
RAM SUN WED THUR
THOSE PEOPLE ARE HERE TO SEE ME—SHEILA MALONE!
SINCE WHEN DO I NEED AN OPENING ACT?!
SINCE MR. BECK SIGNED JENNA BELLE BEFORE HE LEFT SUDDENLY TO TAKE CARE OF HIS SICK MOTHER IN MIAMI.
I'LL GIVE HIM A SICK MOM...
HE SIGNED A CONTRACT—I FOUND IT ON MY DESK THIS MORNING.
"THREE WEEKS EXCLUSIVE."
I'M AFRAID THERE'S NOTHING I CAN DO.
WHY, I OUGHTTA!
LADIES AND GENTLEMEN. THE BEACON IS PROUD TO PRESENT...
...JENNA BELLE.
CLAP
CLAP
CLAP CLAP
CLAP

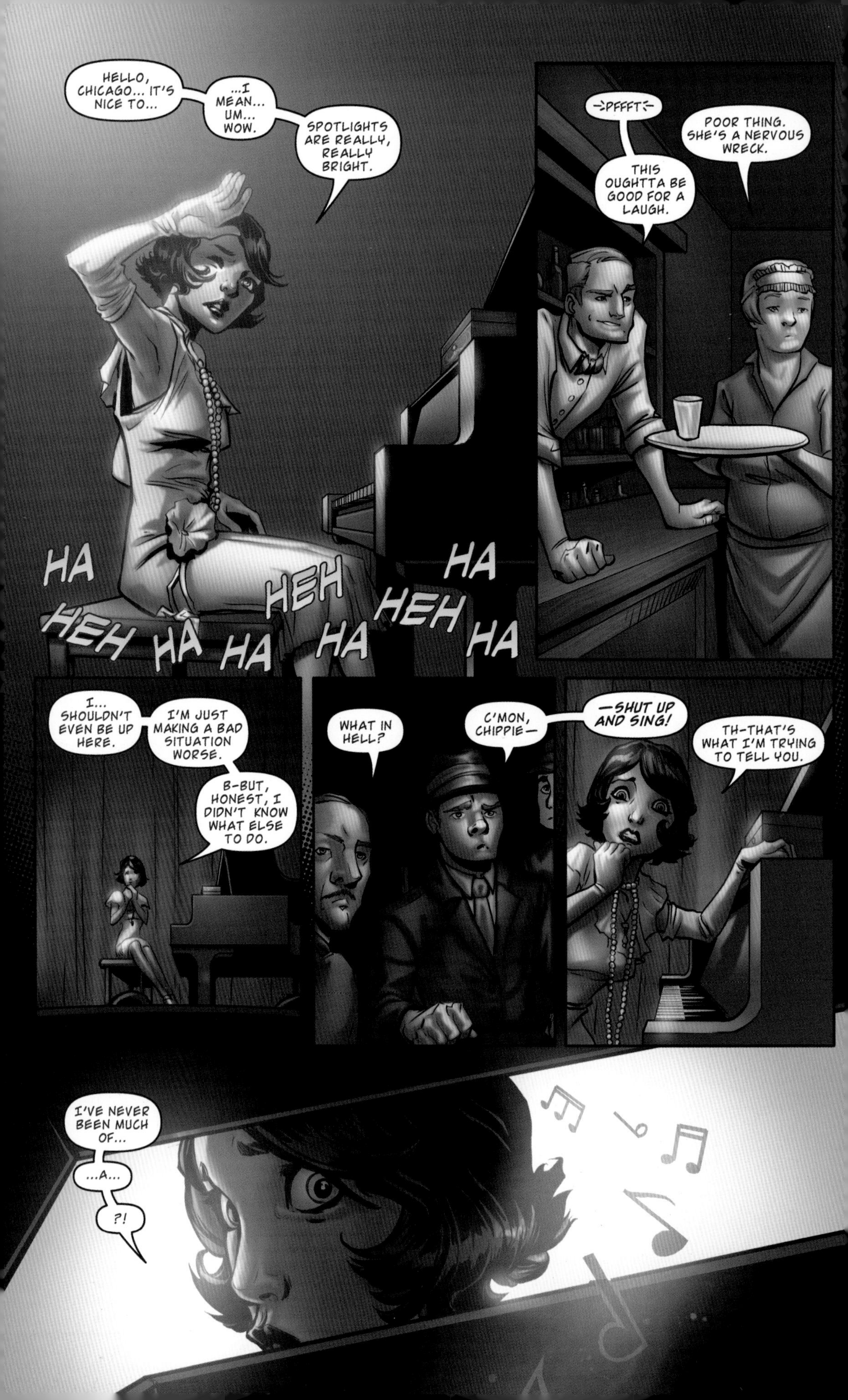
HELLO, CHICAGO... IT'S NICE TO...
...I MEAN... UM... WOW.
SPOTLIGHTS ARE REALLY, REALLY BRIGHT.
-PFFFT-
THIS OUGHTTA BE GOOD FOR A LAUGH.
POOR THING. SHE'S A NERVOUS WRECK.
HA HEH HA HA HEH HA HEH HA HA
I... SHOULDN'T EVEN BE UP HERE.
I'M JUST MAKING A BAD SITUATION WORSE.
B-BUT, HONEST, I DIDN'T KNOW WHAT ELSE TO DO.
WHAT IN HELL?
C'MON, CHIPPIE—
—SHUT UP AND SING!
TH-THAT'S WHAT I'M TRYING TO TELL YOU.
I'VE NEVER BEEN MUCH OF...
...A...
?!

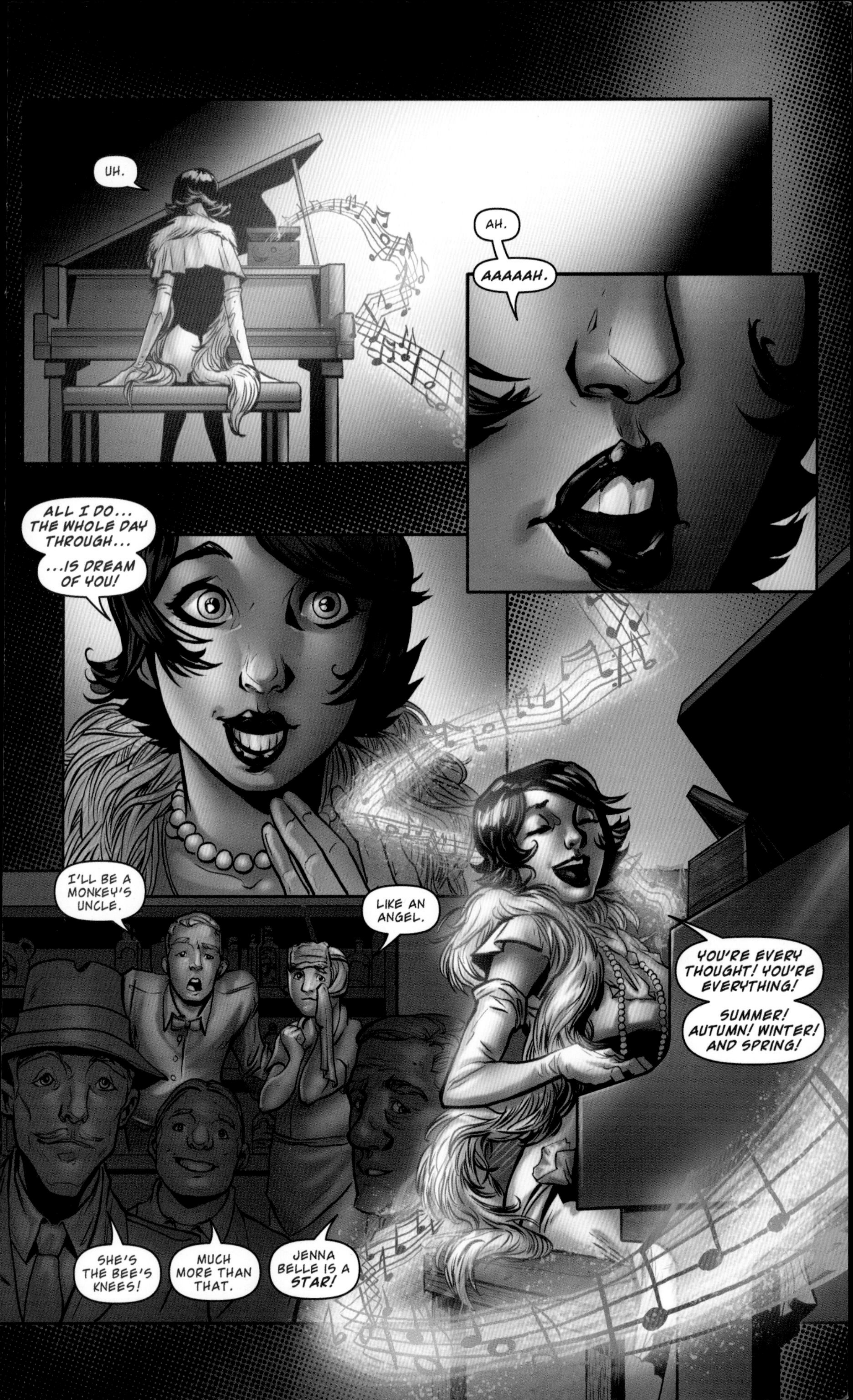
UH.
AH.
AAAAAH.
ALL I DO... THE WHOLE DAY THROUGH...
...IS DREAM OF YOU!
I'LL BE A MONKEY'S UNCLE.
LIKE AN ANGEL.
YOU'RE EVERY THOUGHT! YOU'RE EVERYTHING!
SUMMER! AUTUMN! WINTER! AND SPRING!
SHE'S THE BEE'S KNEES!
MUCH MORE THAN THAT.
JENNA BELLE IS A STAR!

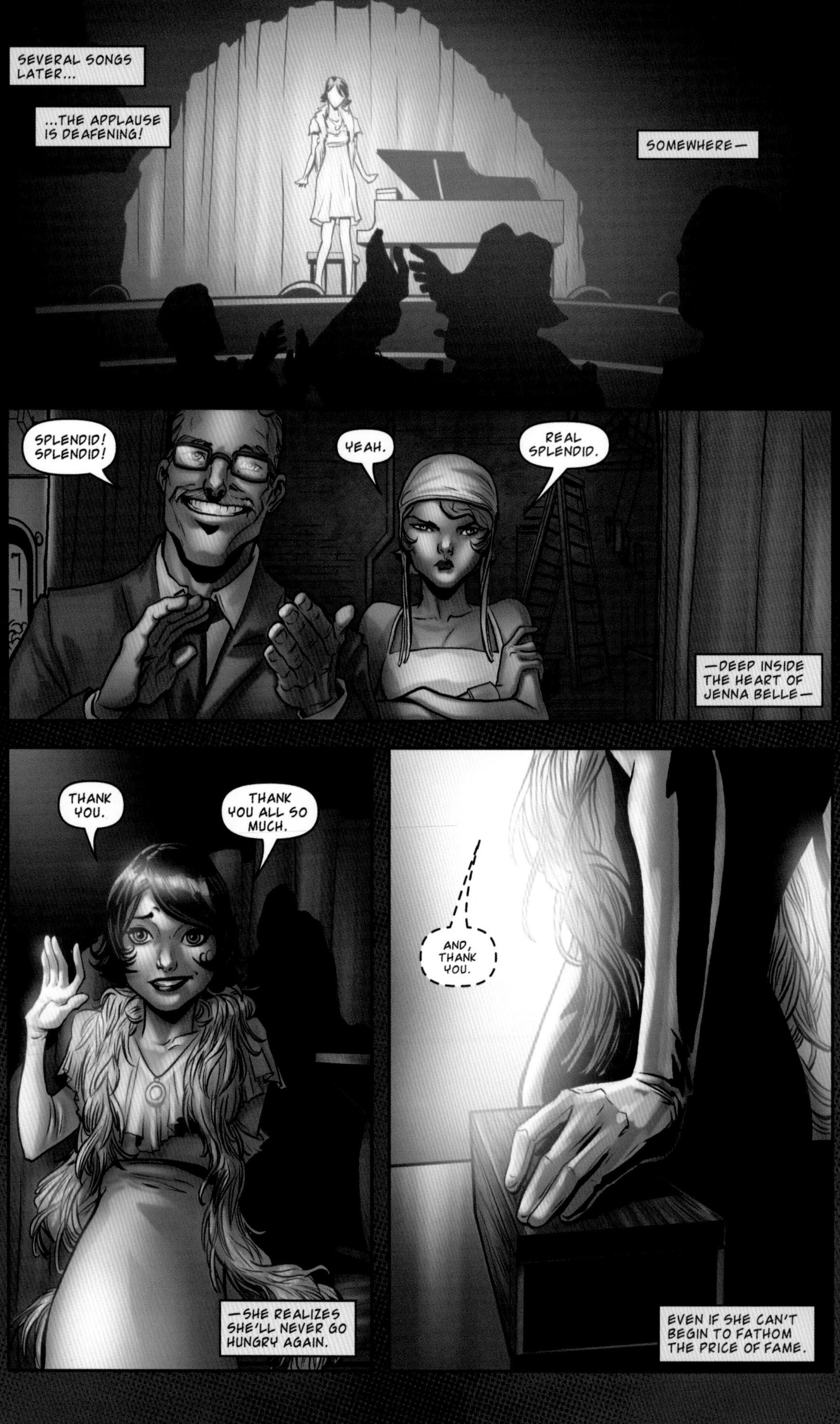
SEVERAL SONGS LATER...
...THE APPLAUSE IS DEAFENING!
SOMEWHERE—
SPLENDID! SPLENDID!
YEAH.
REAL SPLENDID.
—DEEP INSIDE THE HEART OF JENNA BELLE—
THANK YOU.
THANK YOU ALL SO MUCH.
—SHE REALIZES SHE'LL NEVER GO HUNGRY AGAIN.
AND, THANK YOU.
EVEN IF SHE CAN'T BEGIN TO FATHOM THE PRICE OF FAME.

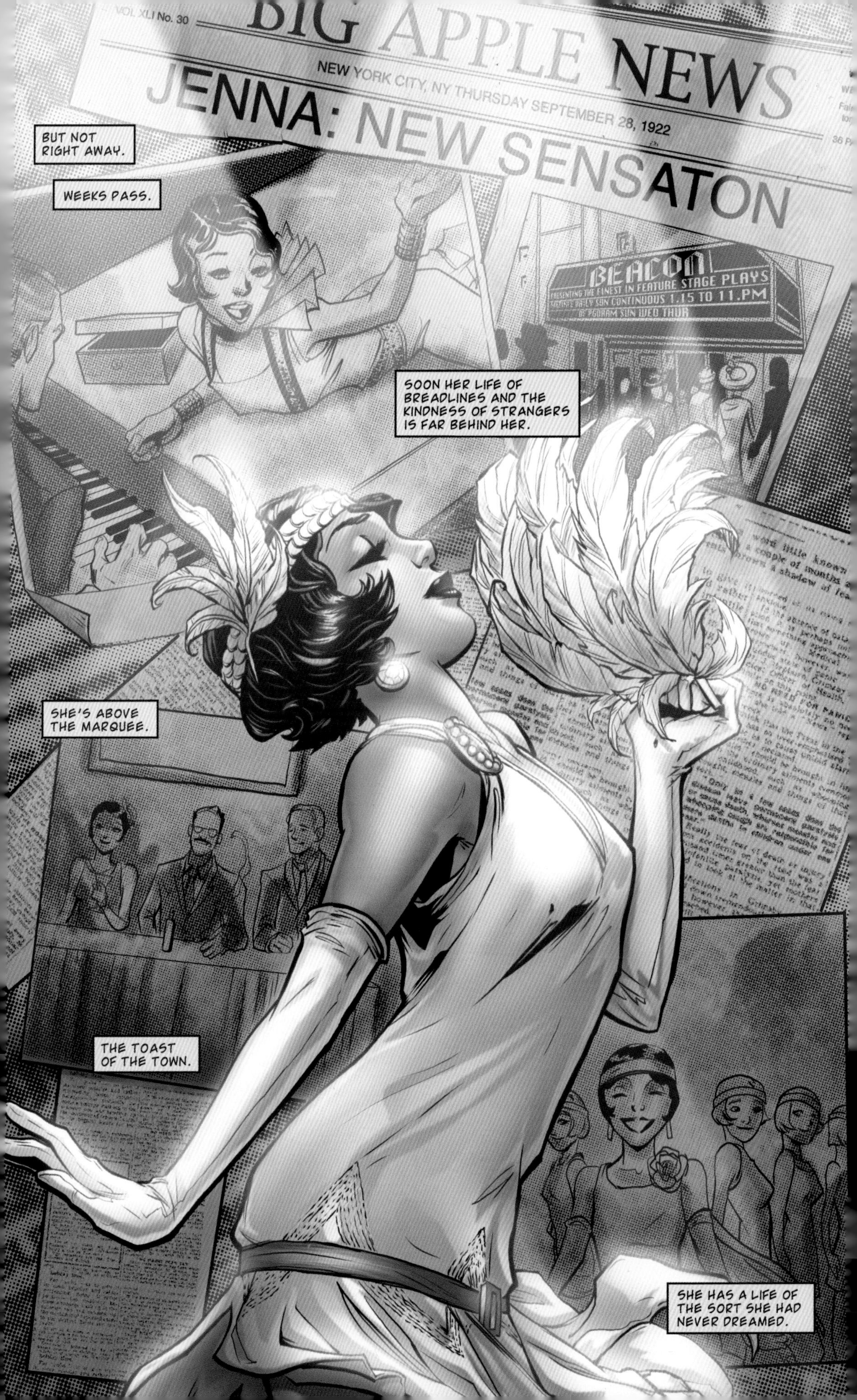
VOL XLI No. 30
BIG APPLE NEWS
NEW YORK CITY, NY THURSDAY SEPTEMBER 28, 1922
JENNA: NEW SENSATON
BUT NOT RIGHT AWAY.
WEEKS PASS.
BEACON
PRESENTING THE FINEST IN FEATURE STAGE PLAYS
SOON HER LIFE OF BREADLINES AND THE KINDNESS OF STRANGERS IS FAR BEHIND HER.
SHE'S ABOVE THE MARQUEE.
THE TOAST OF THE TOWN.
SHE HAS A LIFE OF THE SORT SHE HAD NEVER DREAMED.

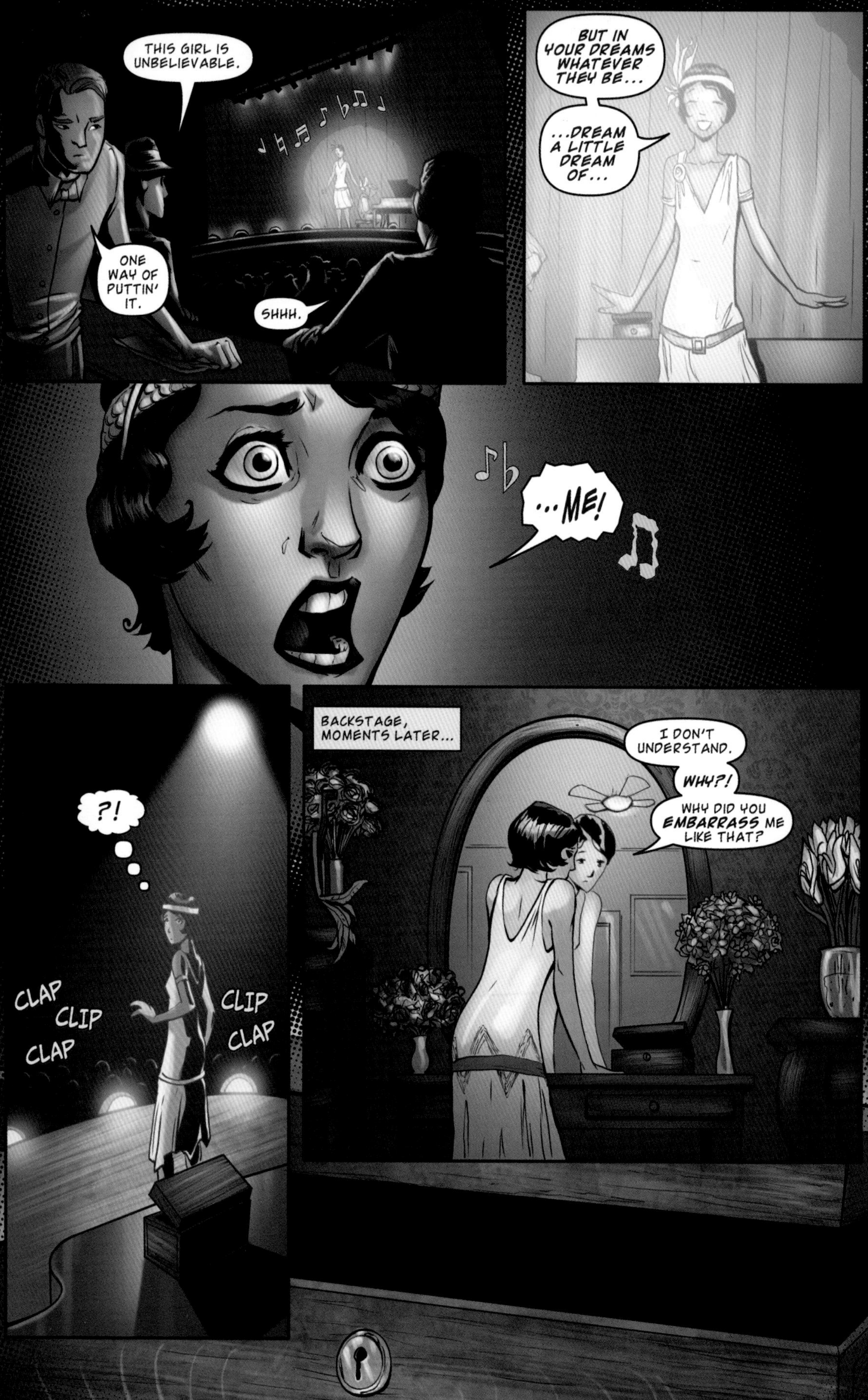
THIS GIRL IS UNBELIEVABLE.
ONE WAY OF PUTTIN' IT.
SHHH.
BUT IN YOUR DREAMS WHATEVER THEY BE...
...DREAM A LITTLE DREAM OF...
...ME!
?!
CLAP
CLIP
CLAP
CLIP
CLAP
BACKSTAGE, MOMENTS LATER...
I DON'T UNDERSTAND.
WHY?!
WHY DID YOU EMBARRASS ME LIKE THAT?

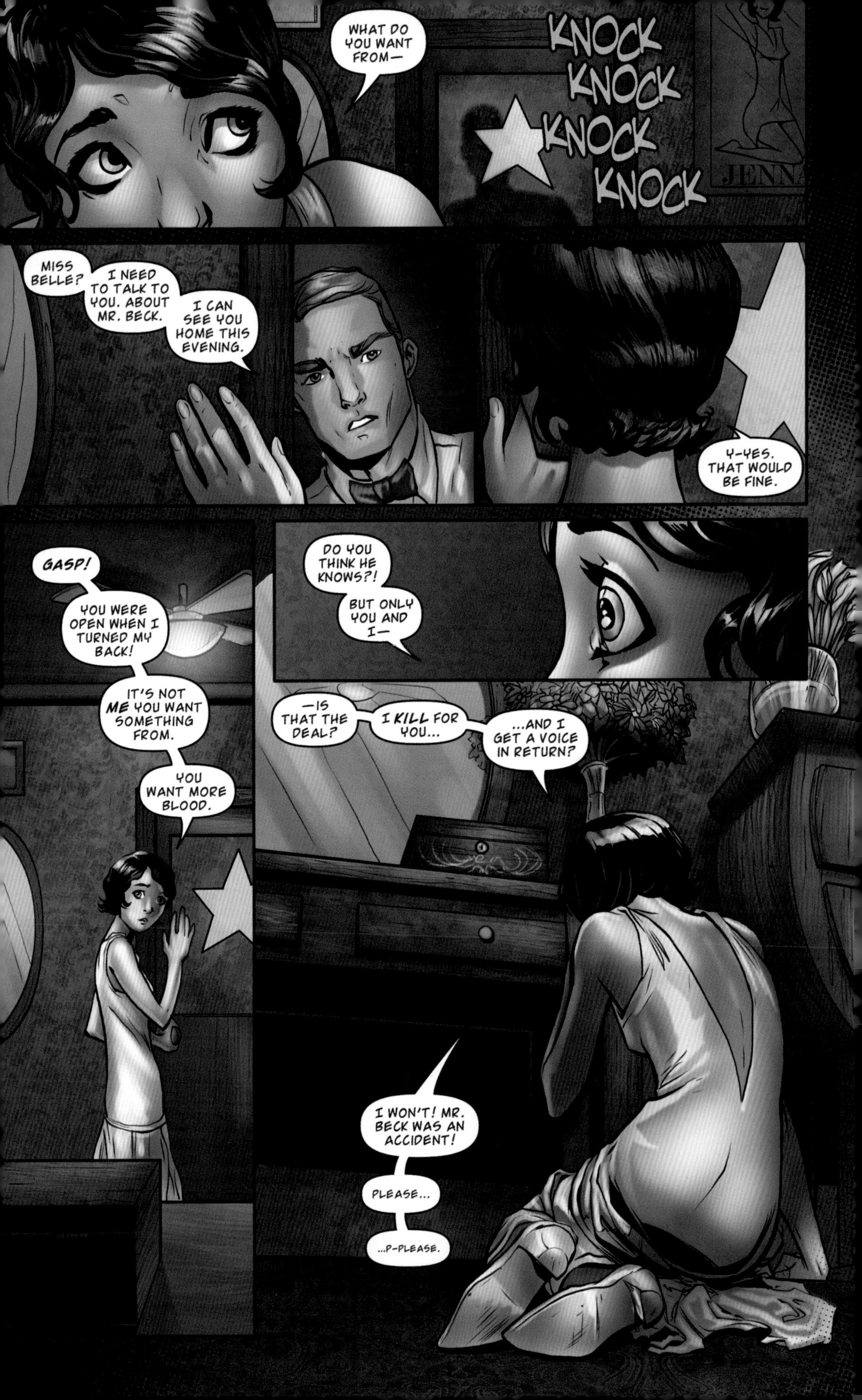

WHAT DO YOU WANT FROM—
KNOCK KNOCK KNOCK KNOCK
JENNA
MISS BELLE?
I NEED TO TALK TO YOU. ABOUT MR. BECK.
I CAN SEE YOU HOME THIS EVENING.
Y-YES. THAT WOULD BE FINE.
GASP!
YOU WERE OPEN WHEN I TURNED MY BACK!
IT'S NOT ME YOU WANT SOMETHING FROM.
YOU WANT MORE BLOOD.
DO YOU THINK HE KNOWS?!
BUT ONLY YOU AND I—
—IS THAT THE DEAL?
I KILL FOR YOU...
...AND I GET A VOICE IN RETURN?
I WON'T! MR. BECK WAS AN ACCIDENT!
PLEASE...
...P-PLEASE.

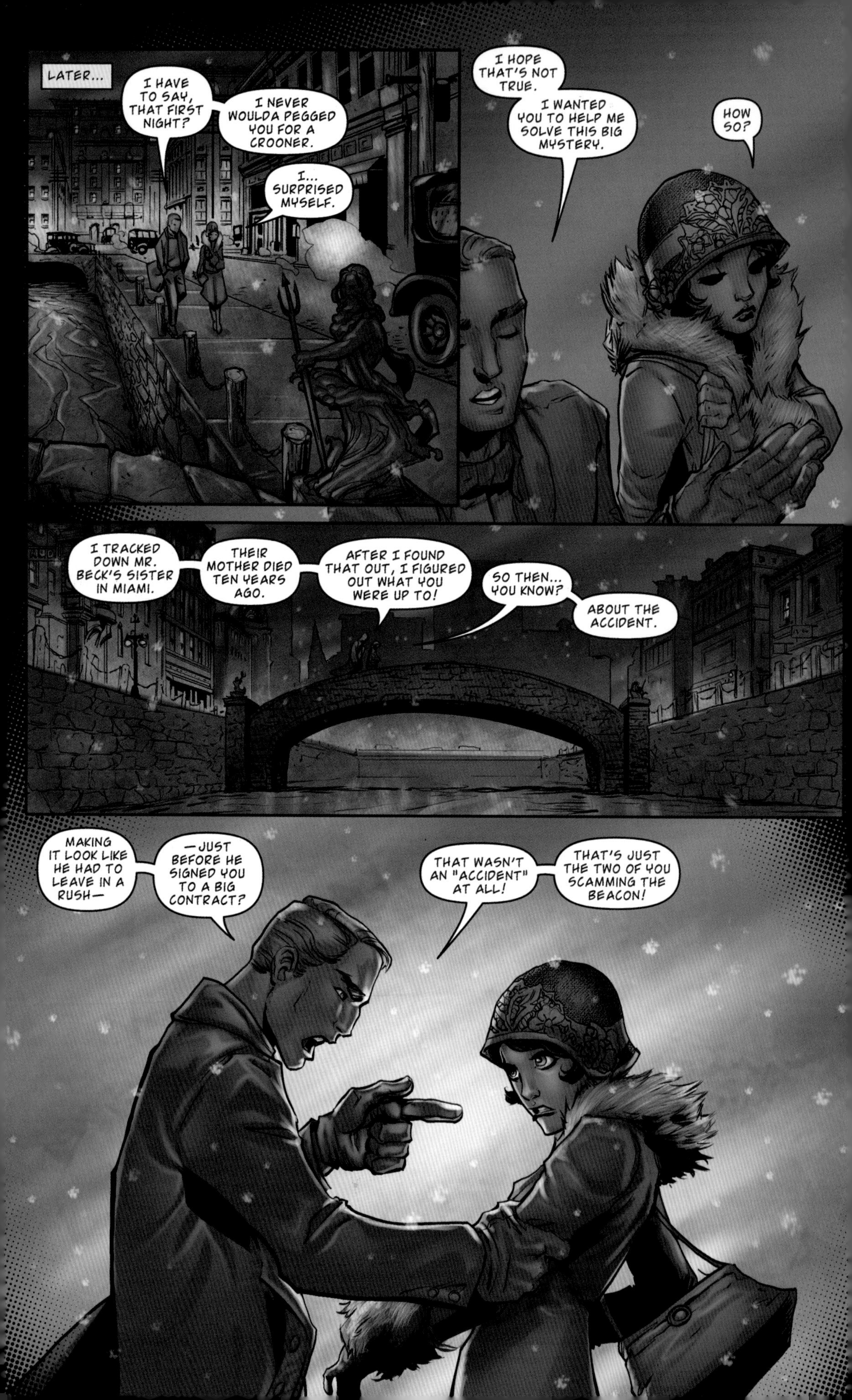
LATER...
I HAVE TO SAY, THAT FIRST NIGHT?
I NEVER WOULDA PEGGED YOU FOR A CROONER.
I... SURPRISED MYSELF.
I HOPE THAT'S NOT TRUE.
I WANTED YOU TO HELP ME SOLVE THIS BIG MYSTERY.
HOW SO?
I TRACKED DOWN MR. BECK'S SISTER IN MIAMI.
THEIR MOTHER DIED TEN YEARS AGO.
AFTER I FOUND THAT OUT, I FIGURED OUT WHAT YOU WERE UP TO!
SO THEN... YOU KNOW?
ABOUT THE ACCIDENT.
MAKING IT LOOK LIKE HE HAD TO LEAVE IN A RUSH—
—JUST BEFORE HE SIGNED YOU TO A BIG CONTRACT?
THAT WASN'T AN "ACCIDENT" AT ALL!
THAT'S JUST THE TWO OF YOU SCAMMING THE BEACON!

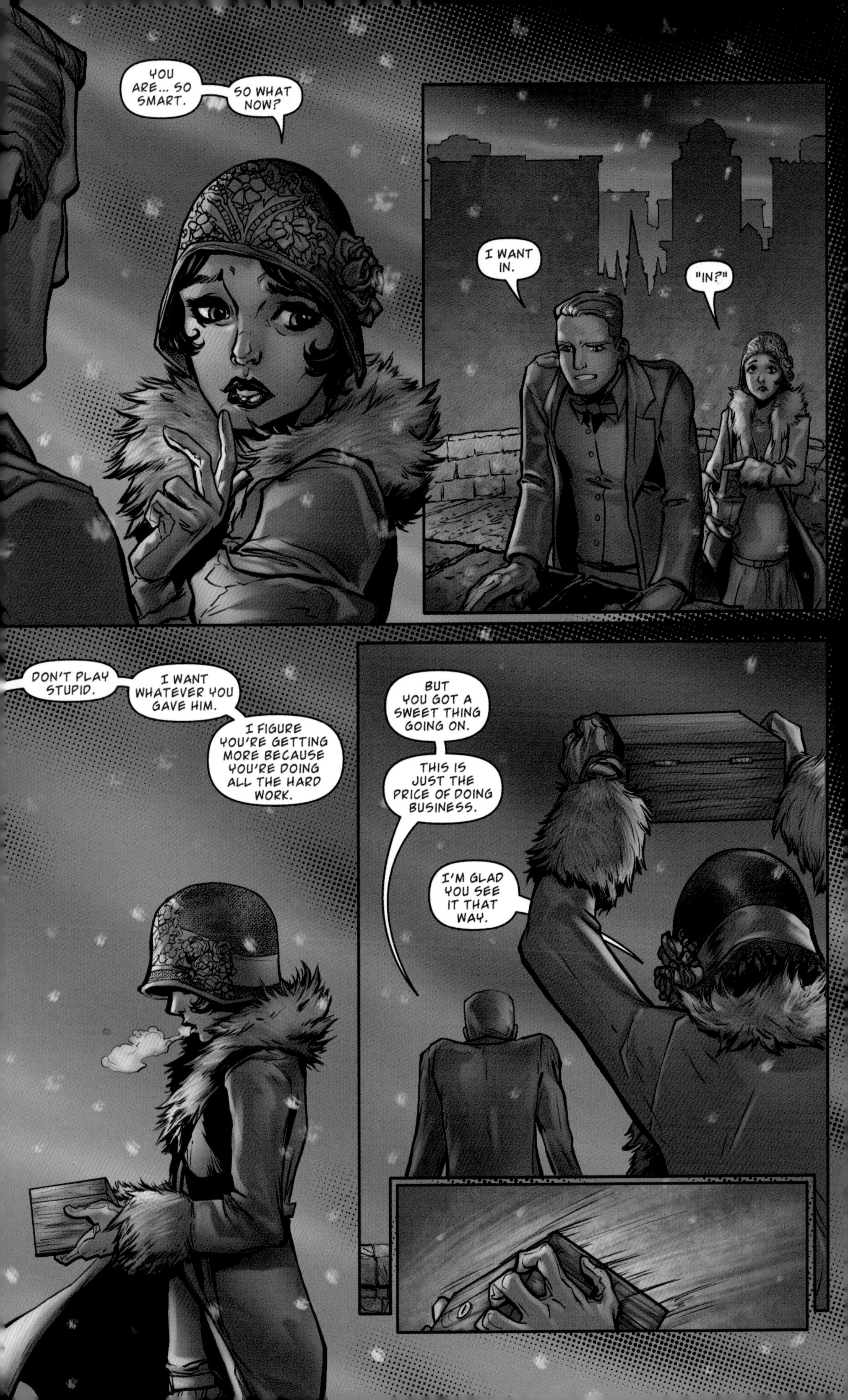
YOU ARE... SO SMART.
SO WHAT NOW?
I WANT IN.
"IN?"
DON'T PLAY STUPID.
I WANT WHATEVER YOU GAVE HIM.
I FIGURE YOU'RE GETTING MORE BECAUSE YOU'RE DOING ALL THE HARD WORK.
BUT YOU GOT A SWEET THING GOING ON.
THIS IS JUST THE PRICE OF DOING BUSINESS.
I'M GLAD YOU SEE IT THAT WAY.

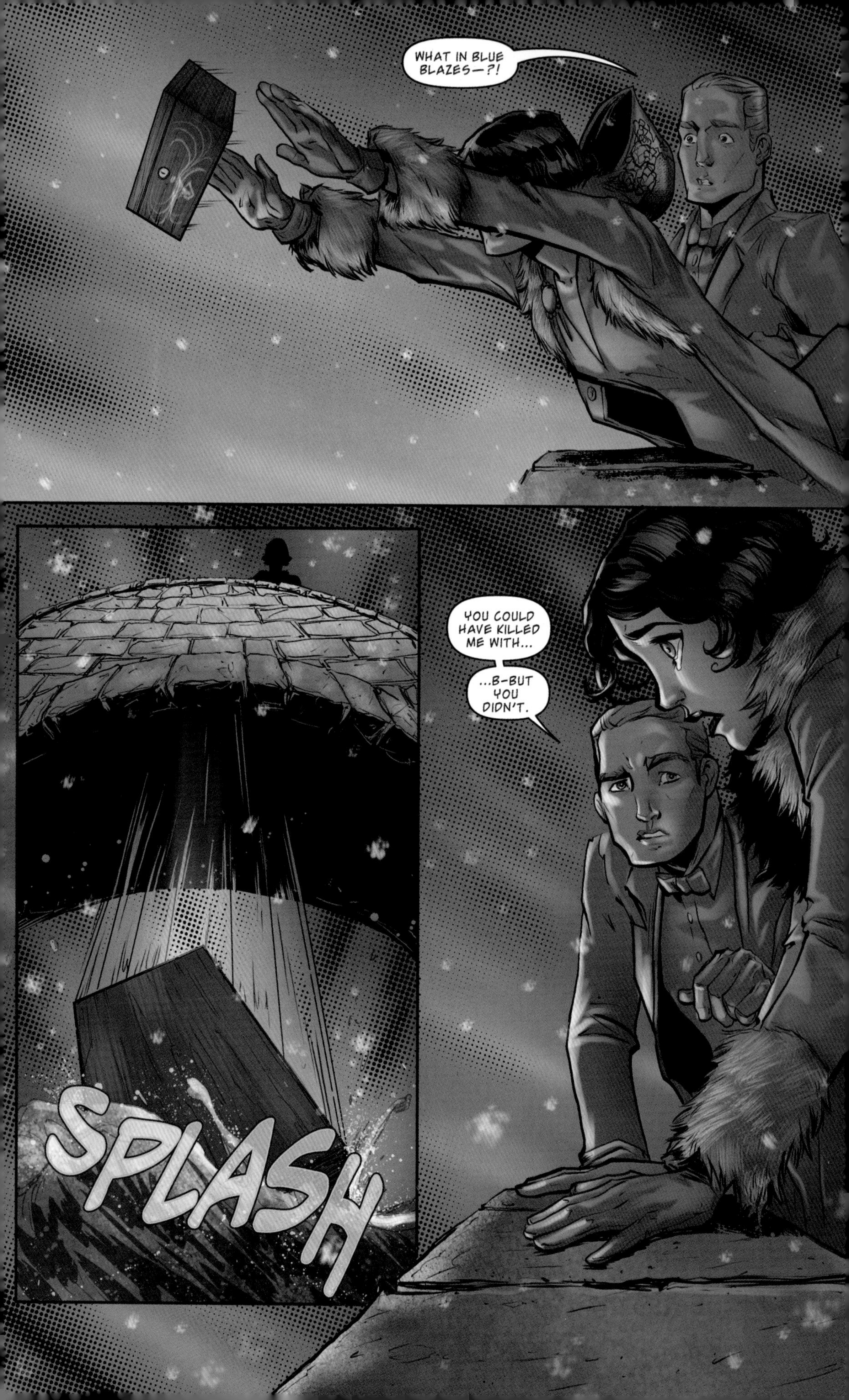
WHAT IN BLUE BLAZES—?!
SPLASH
YOU COULD HAVE KILLED ME WITH...
...B-BUT YOU DIDN'T.

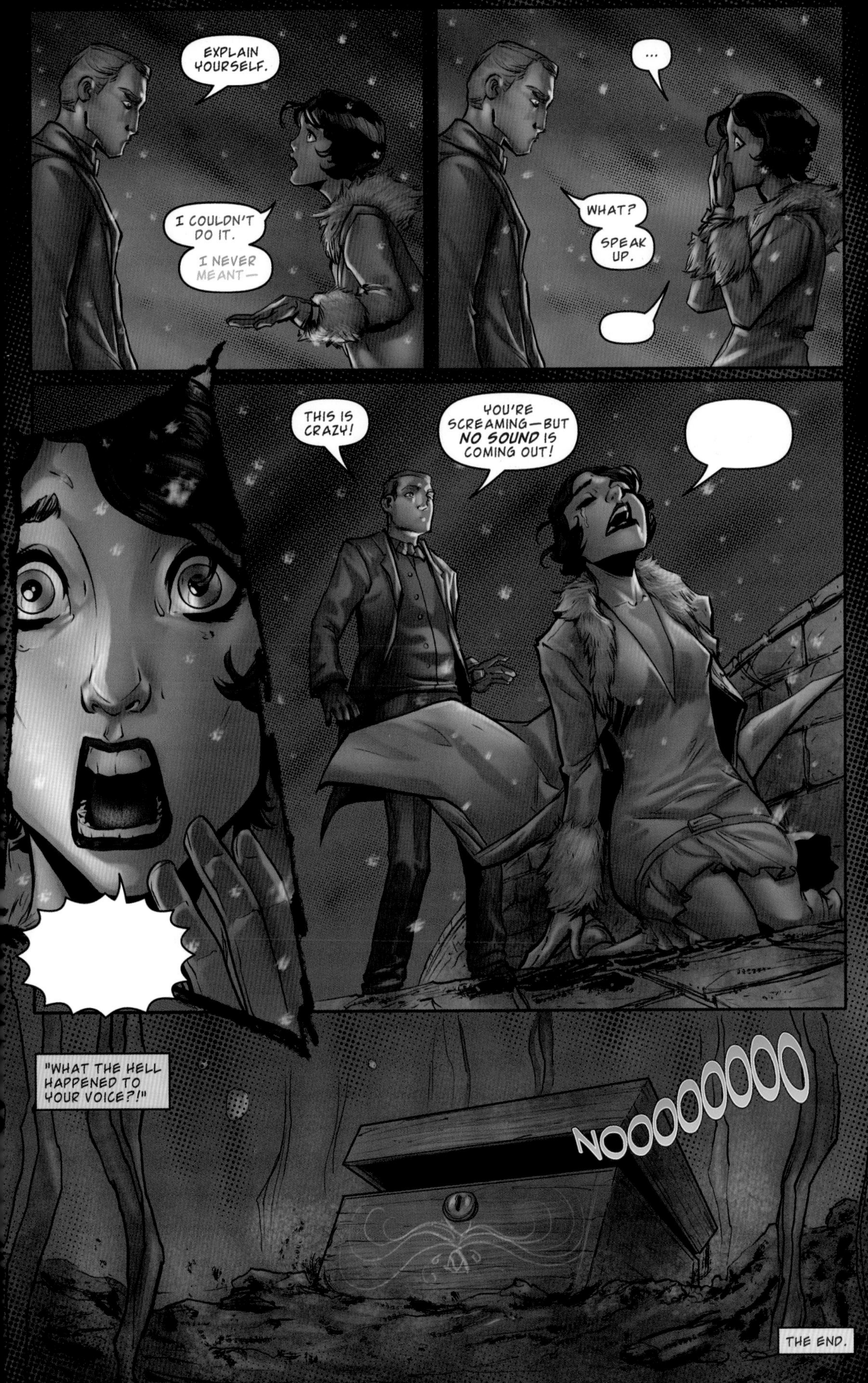
EXPLAIN YOURSELF.
I COULDN'T DO IT.
I NEVER MEANT—
...
WHAT?
SPEAK UP.
THIS IS CRAZY!
YOU'RE SCREAMING—BUT NO SOUND IS COMING OUT!
"WHAT THE HELL HAPPENED TO YOUR VOICE?!"
NOOOOOOOO
THE END.

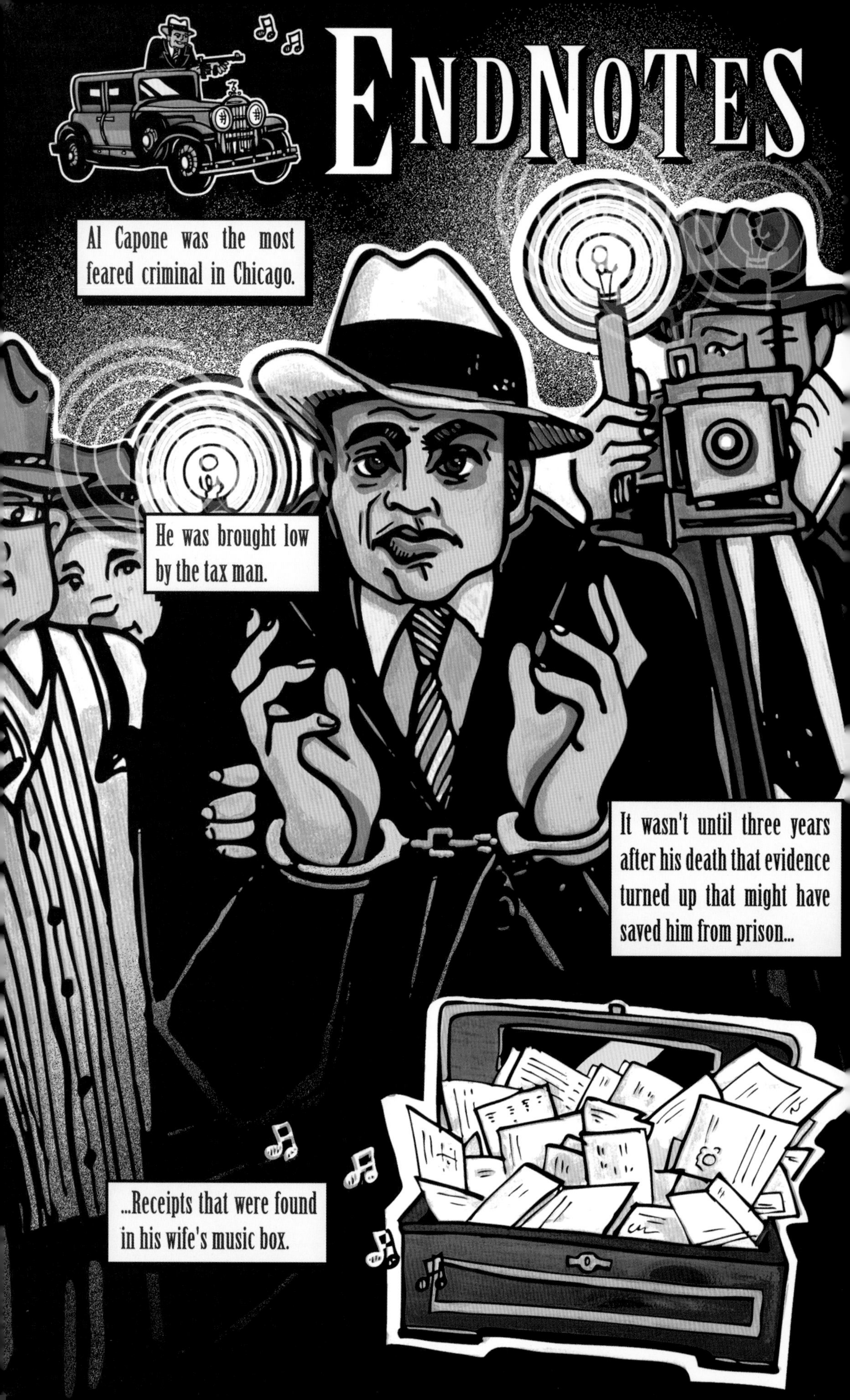
ENDNOTES
Al Capone was the most feared criminal in Chicago.
He was brought low by the tax man.
It wasn't until three years after his death that evidence turned up that might have saved him from prison...
...Receipts that were found in his wife's music box.

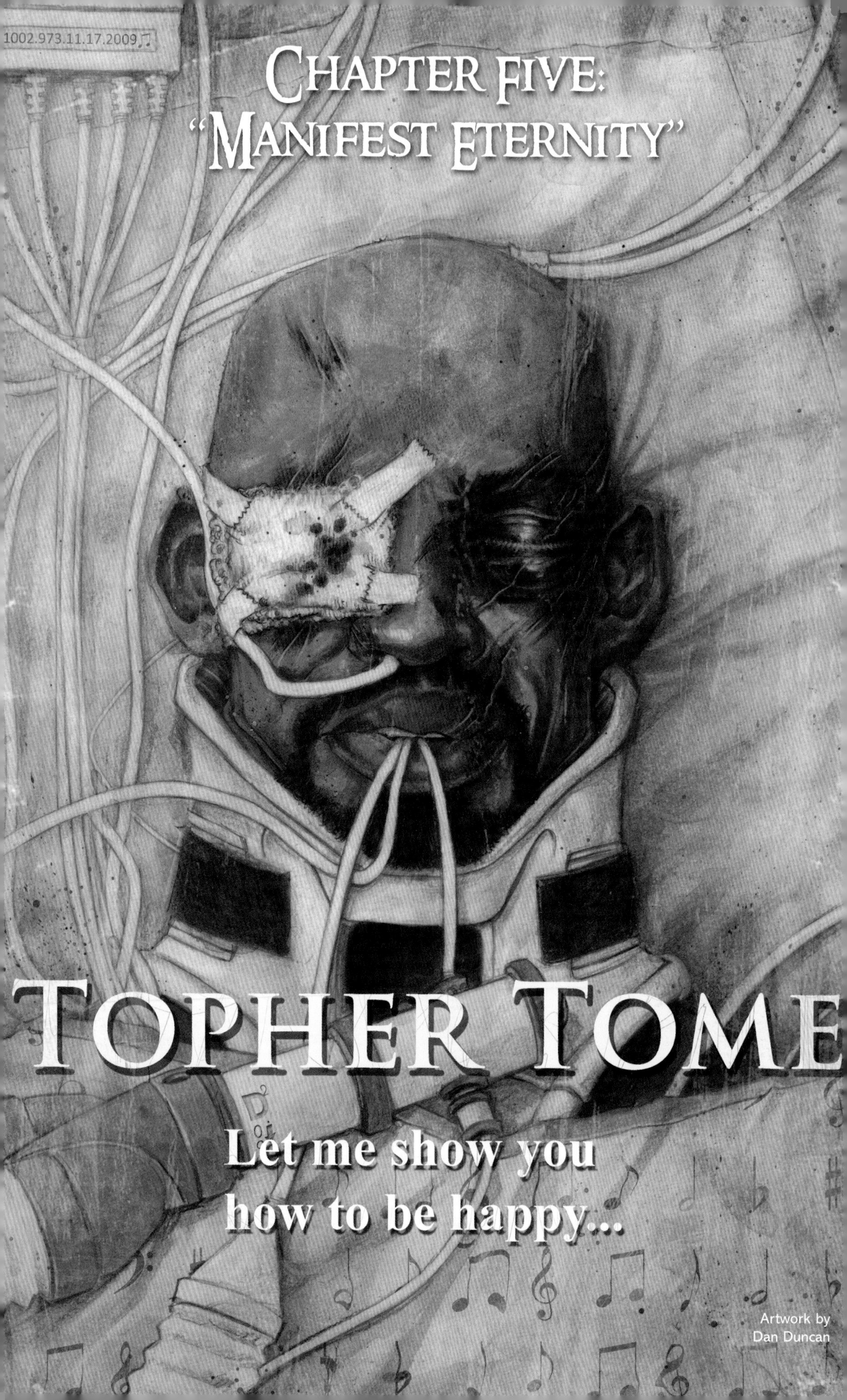
1002.973.11.17.2009
CHAPTER FIVE:
"MANIFEST ETERNITY"
TOPHER TOME
Let me show you
how to be happy...
Artwork by
Dan Duncan

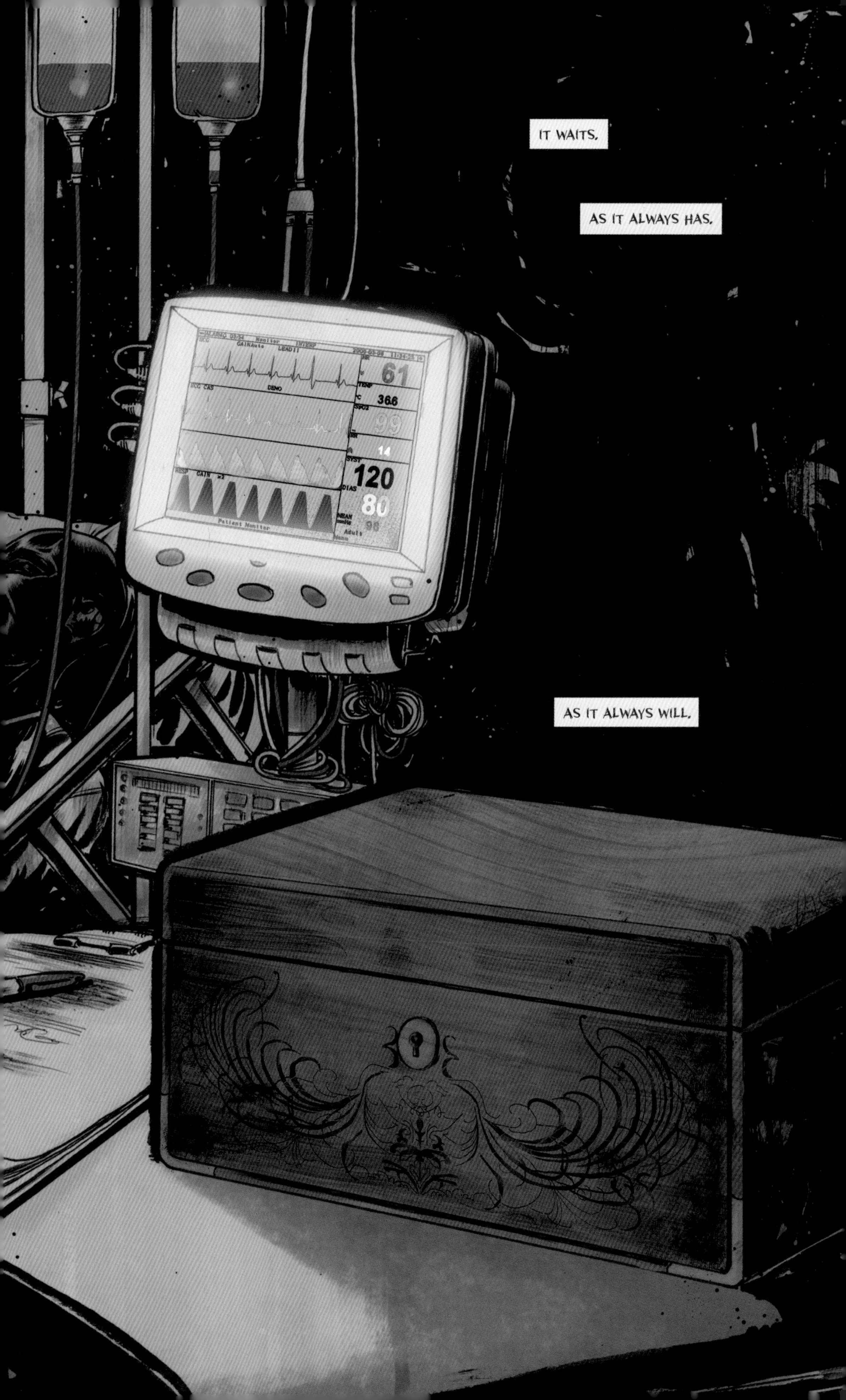
IT WAITS.
AS IT ALWAYS HAS.
AS IT ALWAYS WILL.

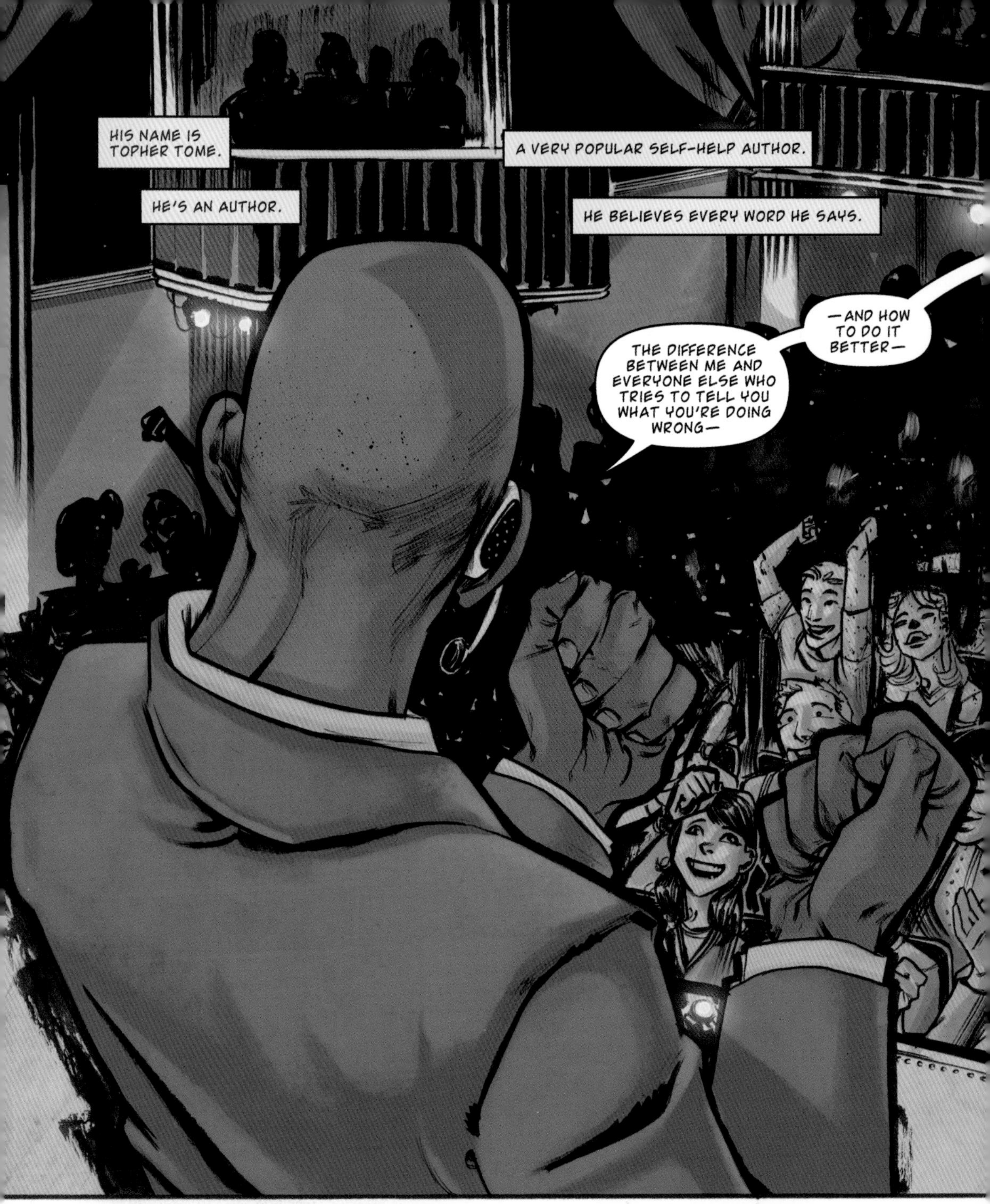
HIS NAME IS TOPHER TOME.
HE'S AN AUTHOR.
A VERY POPULAR SELF-HELP AUTHOR.
HE BELIEVES EVERY WORD HE SAYS.
THE DIFFERENCE BETWEEN ME AND EVERYONE ELSE WHO TRIES TO TELL YOU WHAT YOU'RE DOING WRONG—
—AND HOW TO DO IT BETTER—

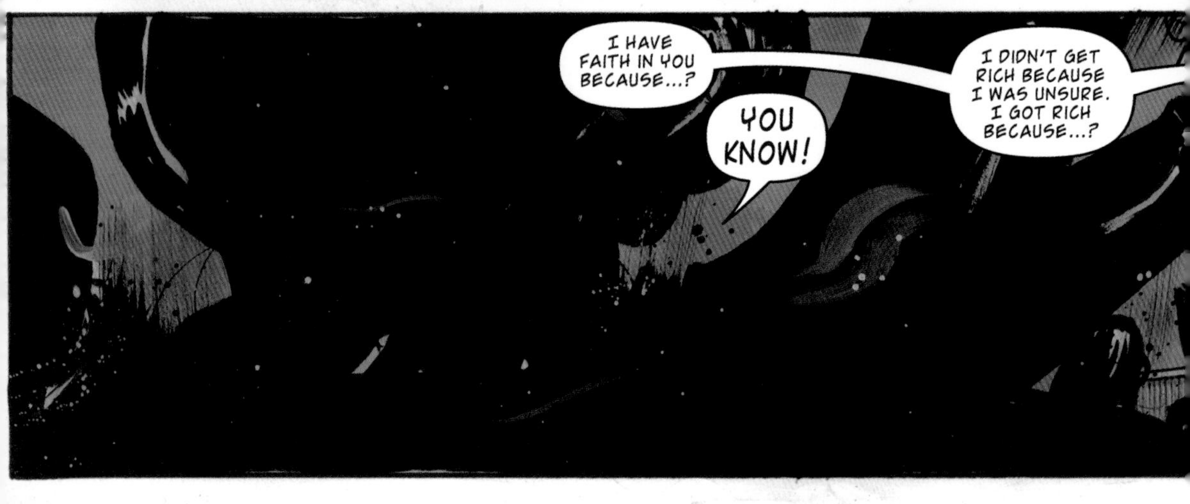
I HAVE FAITH IN YOU BECAUSE...?
YOU KNOW!
I DIDN'T GET RICH BECAUSE I WAS UNSURE. I GOT RICH BECAUSE...?

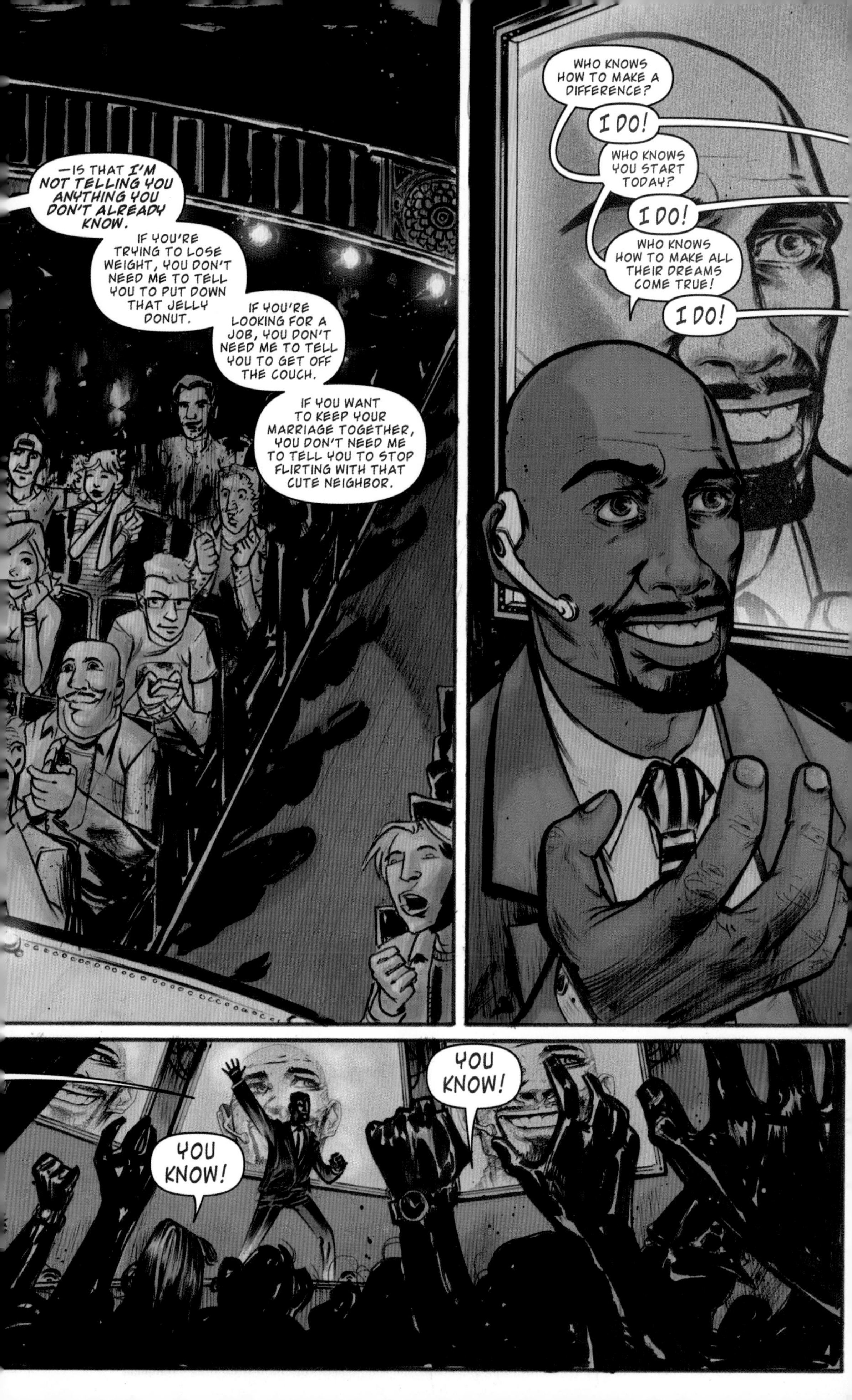
—IS THAT I'M NOT TELLING YOU ANYTHING YOU DON'T ALREADY KNOW.
IF YOU'RE TRYING TO LOSE WEIGHT, YOU DON'T NEED ME TO TELL YOU TO PUT DOWN THAT JELLY DONUT.
IF YOU'RE LOOKING FOR A JOB, YOU DON'T NEED ME TO TELL YOU TO GET OFF THE COUCH.
IF YOU WANT TO KEEP YOUR MARRIAGE TOGETHER, YOU DON'T NEED ME TO TELL YOU TO STOP FLIRTING WITH THAT CUTE NEIGHBOR.
WHO KNOWS HOW TO MAKE A DIFFERENCE?
I DO!
WHO KNOWS YOU START TODAY?
I DO!
WHO KNOWS HOW TO MAKE ALL THEIR DREAMS COME TRUE!
I DO!
YOU KNOW!
YOU KNOW!

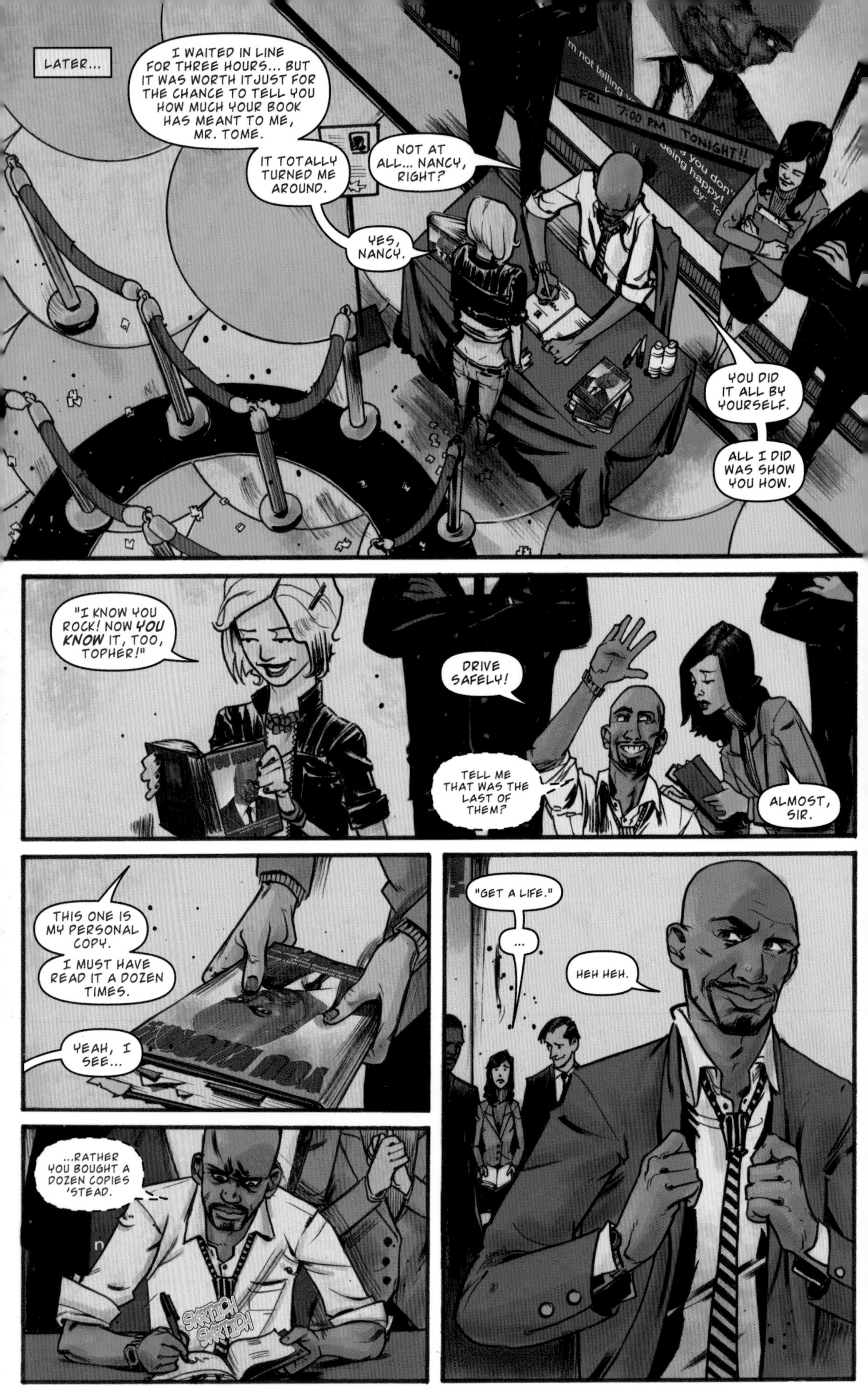
LATER...
I WAITED IN LINE FOR THREE HOURS... BUT IT WAS WORTH IT JUST FOR THE CHANCE TO TELL YOU HOW MUCH YOUR BOOK HAS MEANT TO ME, MR. TOME.
IT TOTALLY TURNED ME AROUND.
NOT AT ALL... NANCY, RIGHT?
YES, NANCY.
FRI 7:00 PM TONIGHT!!
YOU DID IT ALL BY YOURSELF.
ALL I DID WAS SHOW YOU HOW.
"I KNOW YOU ROCK! NOW YOU KNOW IT, TOO, TOPHER!"
DRIVE SAFELY!
TELL ME THAT WAS THE LAST OF THEM?
ALMOST, SIR.
THIS ONE IS MY PERSONAL COPY.
I MUST HAVE READ IT A DOZEN TIMES.
YEAH, I SEE...
...RATHER YOU BOUGHT A DOZEN COPIES 'STEAD.
SKRITCH SKRITCH
"GET A LIFE."
...
HEH HEH.

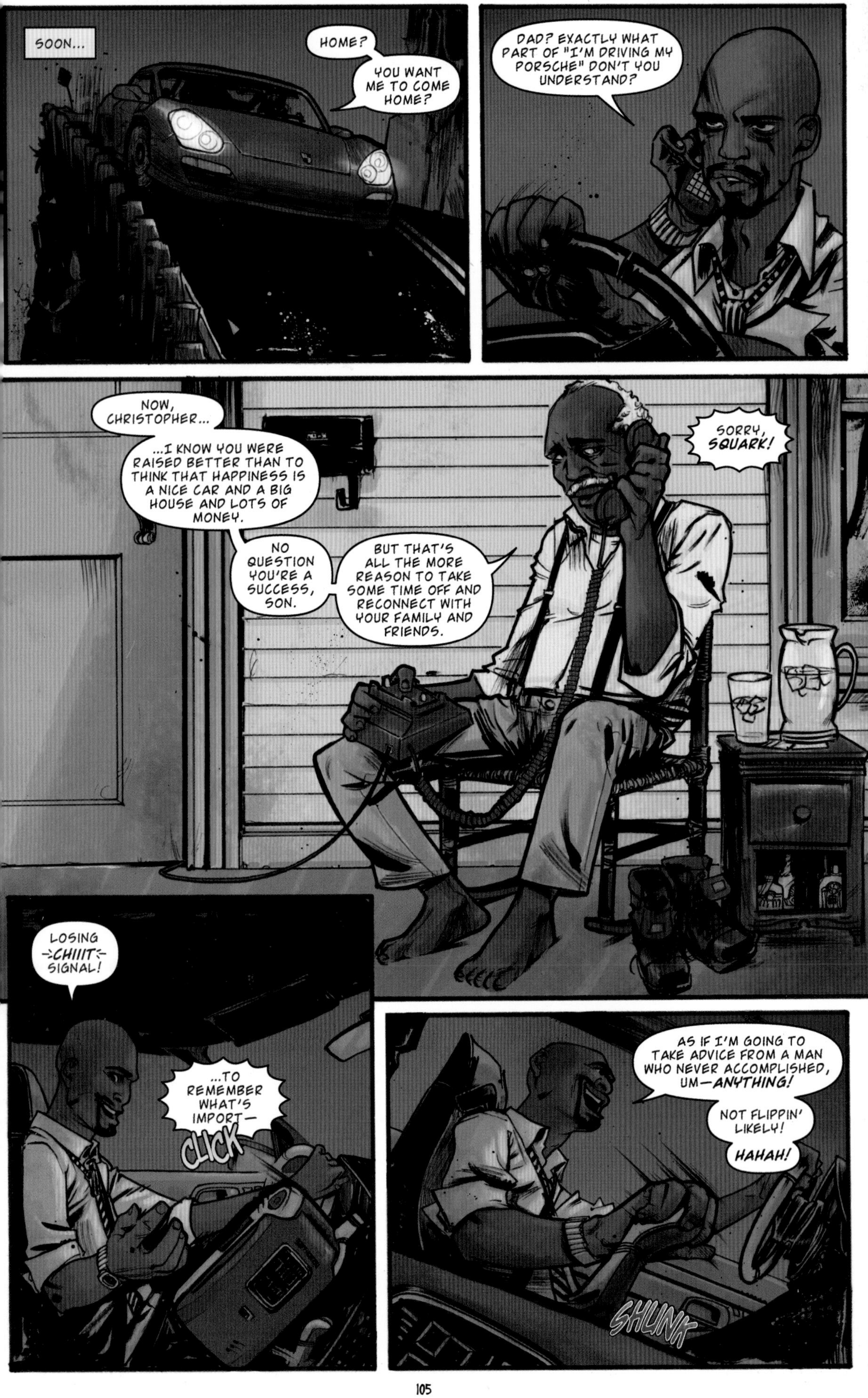
SOON...
HOME?
YOU WANT ME TO COME HOME?
DAD? EXACTLY WHAT PART OF "I'M DRIVING MY PORSCHE" DON'T YOU UNDERSTAND?
NOW, CHRISTOPHER...
...I KNOW YOU WERE RAISED BETTER THAN TO THINK THAT HAPPINESS IS A NICE CAR AND A BIG HOUSE AND LOTS OF MONEY.
NO QUESTION YOU'RE A SUCCESS, SON.
BUT THAT'S ALL THE MORE REASON TO TAKE SOME TIME OFF AND RECONNECT WITH YOUR FAMILY AND FRIENDS.
SORRY, SQUARK!
LOSING -CHIIIT- SIGNAL!
...TO REMEMBER WHAT'S IMPORT—
CLICK
AS IF I'M GOING TO TAKE ADVICE FROM A MAN WHO NEVER ACCOMPLISHED, UM—ANYTHING!
NOT FLIPPIN' LIKELY!
HAHAH!
SHUNK

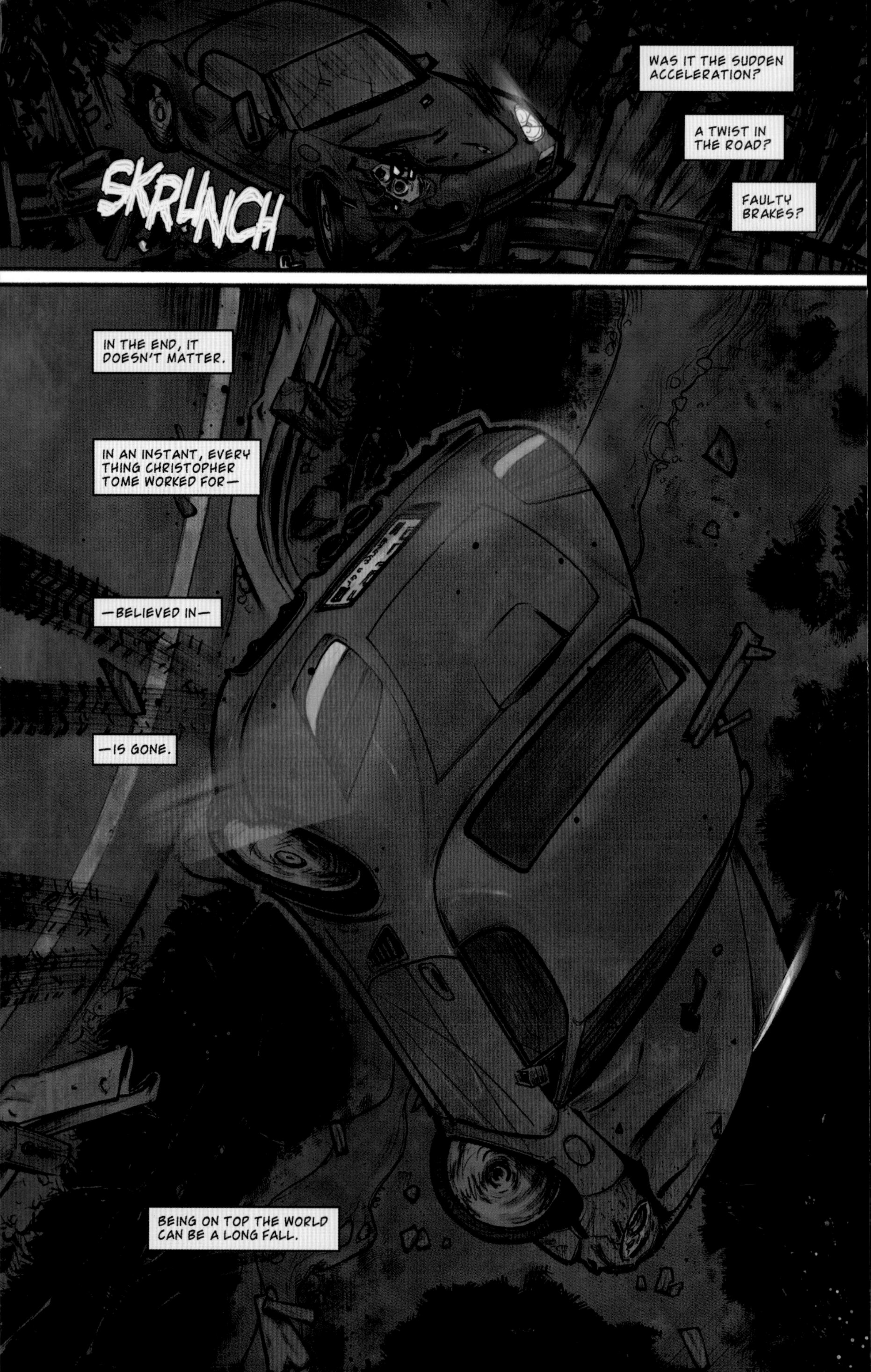
SKRUNCH
WAS IT THE SUDDEN ACCELERATION?
A TWIST IN THE ROAD?
FAULTY BRAKES?
IN THE END, IT DOESN'T MATTER.
IN AN INSTANT, EVERY THING CHRISTOPHER TOME WORKED FOR—
—BELIEVED IN—
—IS GONE.
BEING ON TOP THE WORLD CAN BE A LONG FALL.

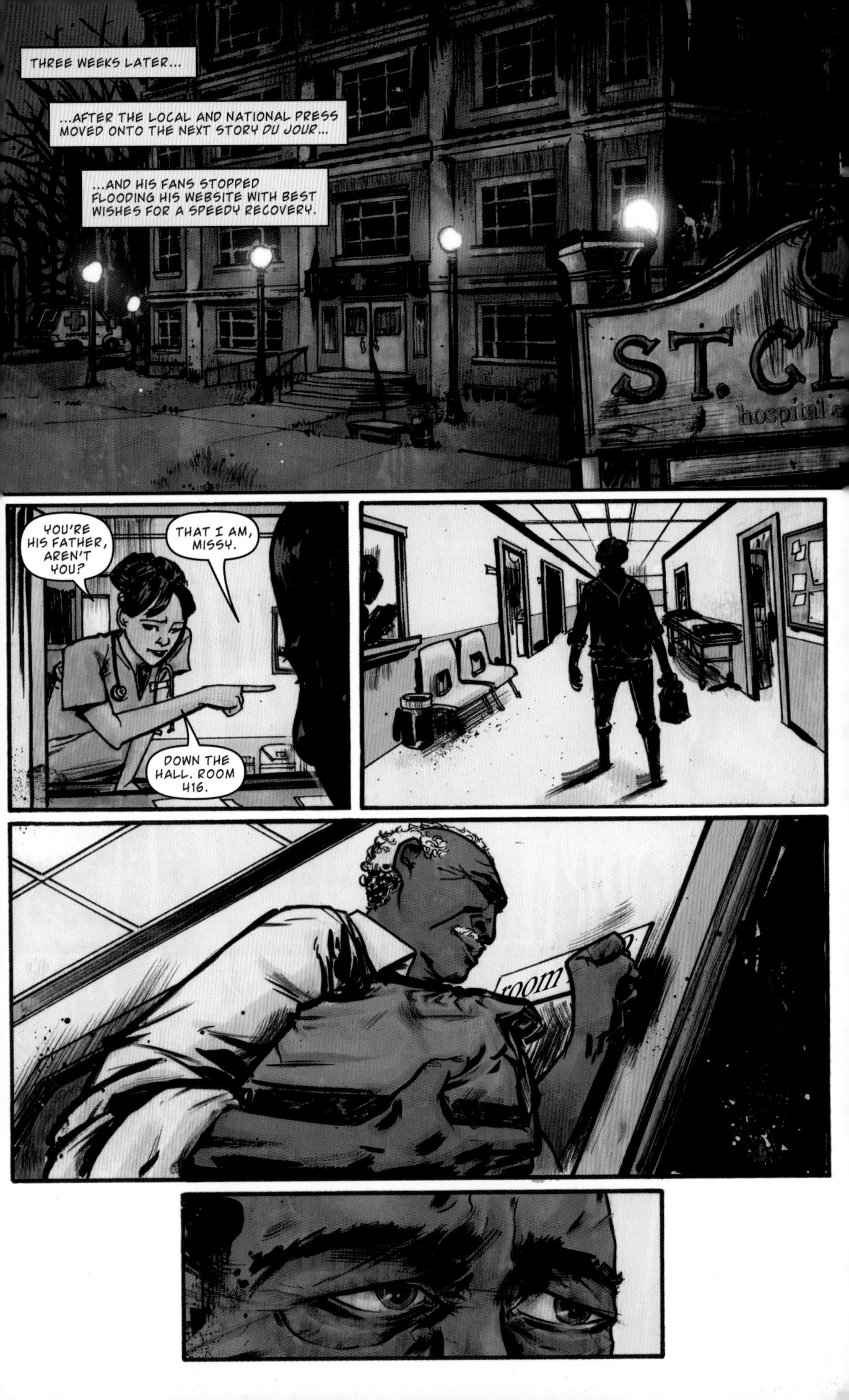
THREE WEEKS LATER...
...AFTER THE LOCAL AND NATIONAL PRESS MOVED ONTO THE NEXT STORY DU JOUR...
...AND HIS FANS STOPPED FLOODING HIS WEBSITE WITH BEST WISHES FOR A SPEEDY RECOVERY.
ST. C
hospital
YOU'RE HIS FATHER, AREN'T YOU?
THAT I AM, MISSY.
DOWN THE HALL. ROOM 416.
room

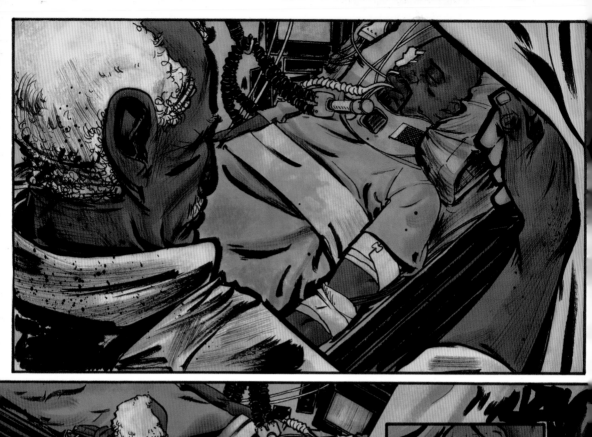

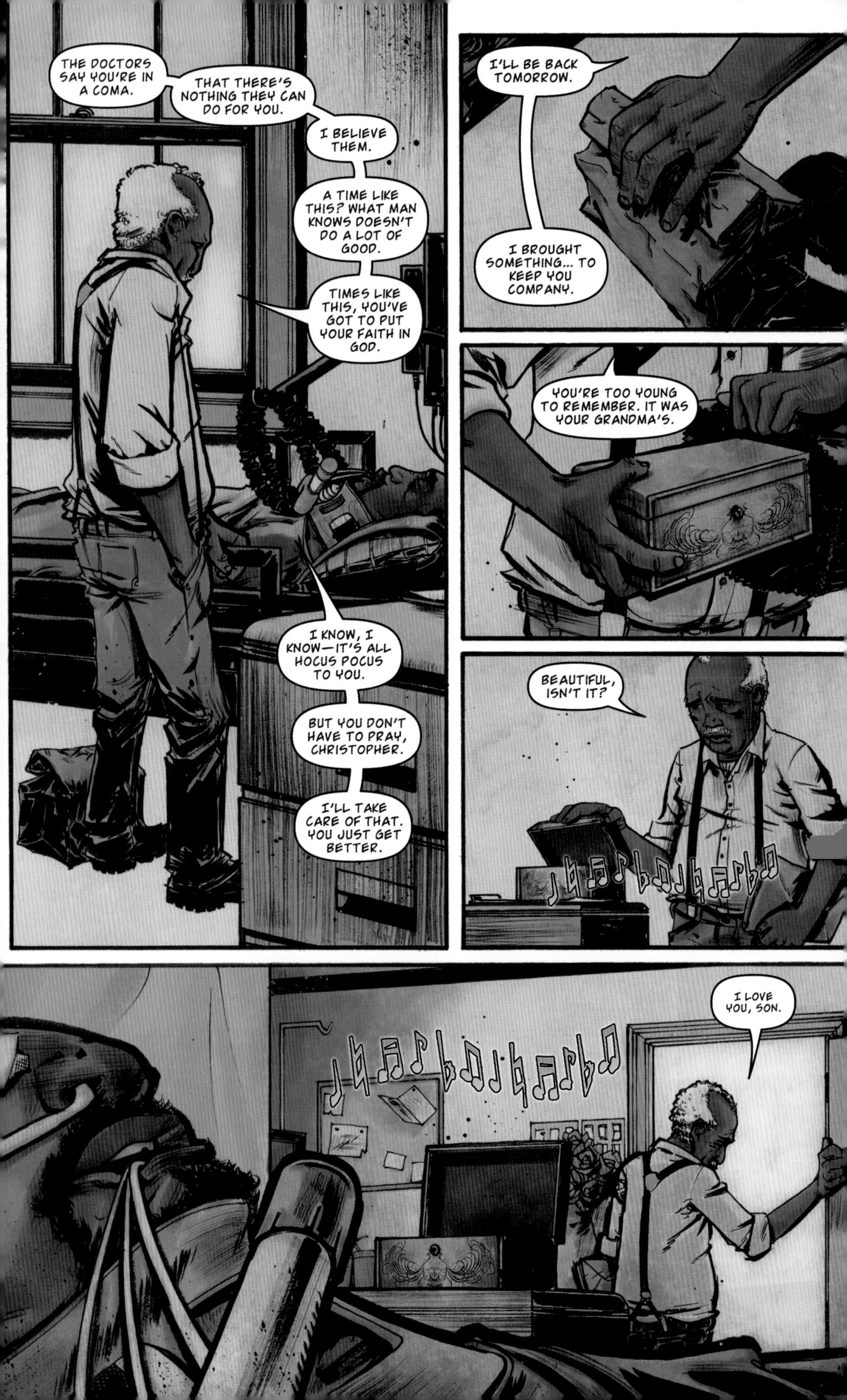
THE DOCTORS SAY YOU'RE IN A COMA.
THAT THERE'S NOTHING THEY CAN DO FOR YOU.
I BELIEVE THEM.
A TIME LIKE THIS? WHAT MAN KNOWS DOESN'T DO A LOT OF GOOD.
TIMES LIKE THIS, YOU'VE GOT TO PUT YOUR FAITH IN GOD.
I KNOW, I KNOW—IT'S ALL HOCUS POCUS TO YOU.
BUT YOU DON'T HAVE TO PRAY, CHRISTOPHER.
I'LL TAKE CARE OF THAT. YOU JUST GET BETTER.
I'LL BE BACK TOMORROW.
I BROUGHT SOMETHING... TO KEEP YOU COMPANY.
YOU'RE TOO YOUNG TO REMEMBER. IT WAS YOUR GRANDMA'S.
BEAUTIFUL, ISN'T IT?
I LOVE YOU, SON.

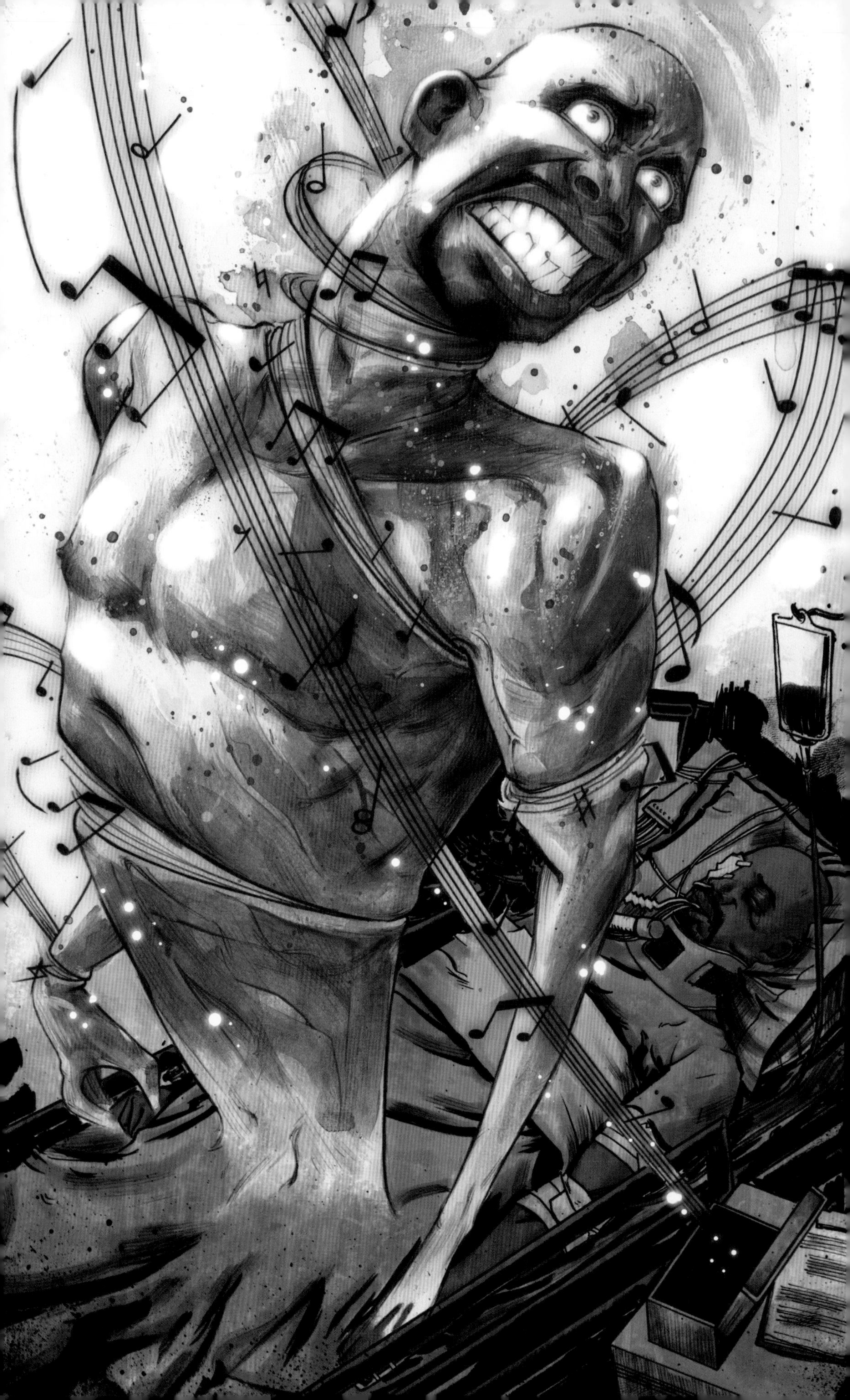

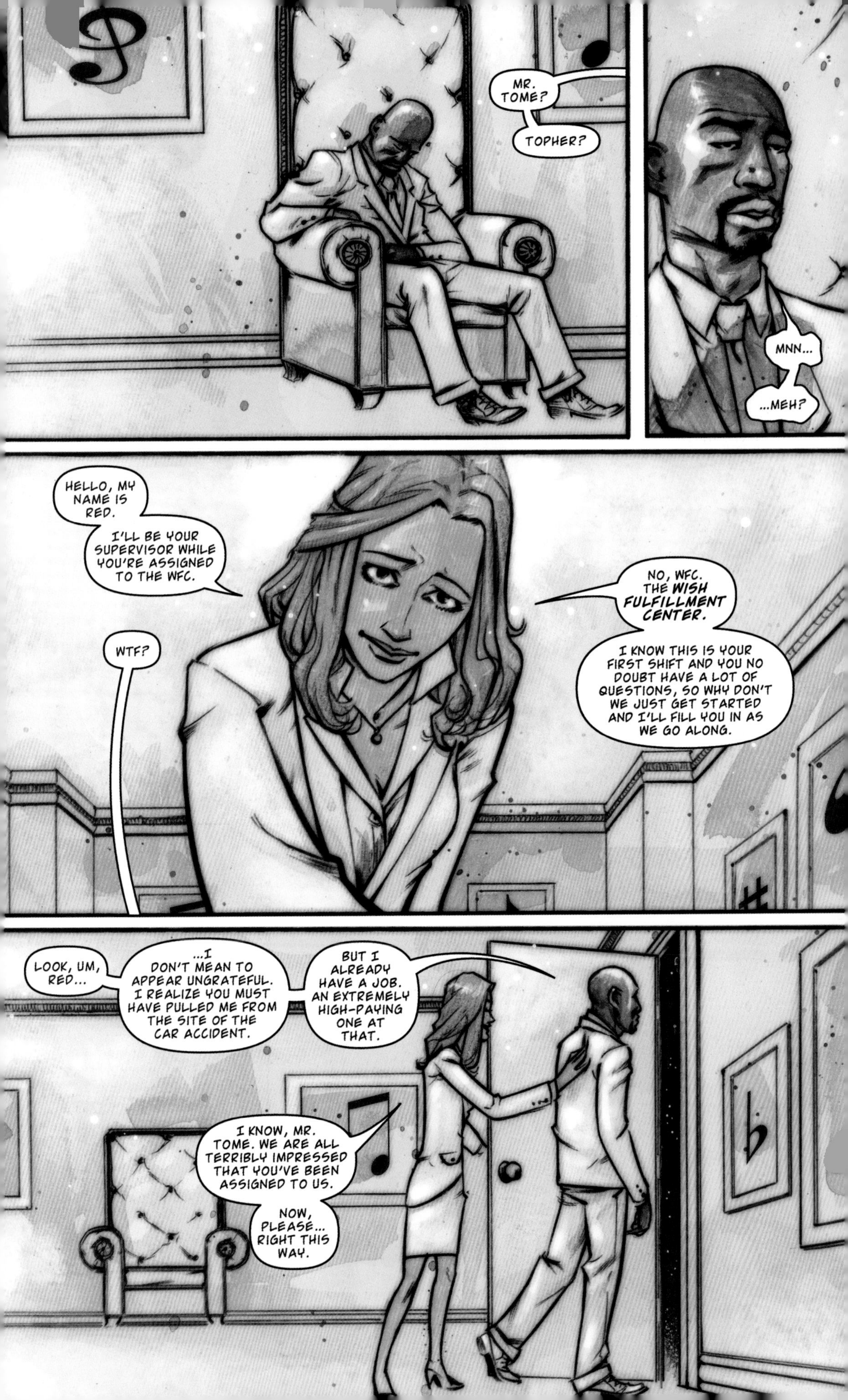
MR. TOME?
TOPHER?
MNN...
...MEH?
HELLO, MY NAME IS RED.
I'LL BE YOUR SUPERVISOR WHILE YOU'RE ASSIGNED TO THE WFC.
WTF?
NO, WFC. THE ***WISH FULFILLMENT CENTER.***
I KNOW THIS IS YOUR FIRST SHIFT AND YOU NO DOUBT HAVE A LOT OF QUESTIONS, SO WHY DON'T WE JUST GET STARTED AND I'LL FILL YOU IN AS WE GO ALONG.
LOOK, UM, RED...
...I DON'T MEAN TO APPEAR UNGRATEFUL. I REALIZE YOU MUST HAVE PULLED ME FROM THE SITE OF THE CAR ACCIDENT.
BUT I ALREADY HAVE A JOB. AN EXTREMELY HIGH-PAYING ONE AT THAT.
I KNOW, MR. TOME. WE ARE ALL TERRIBLY IMPRESSED THAT YOU'VE BEEN ASSIGNED TO US.
NOW, PLEASE... RIGHT THIS WAY.

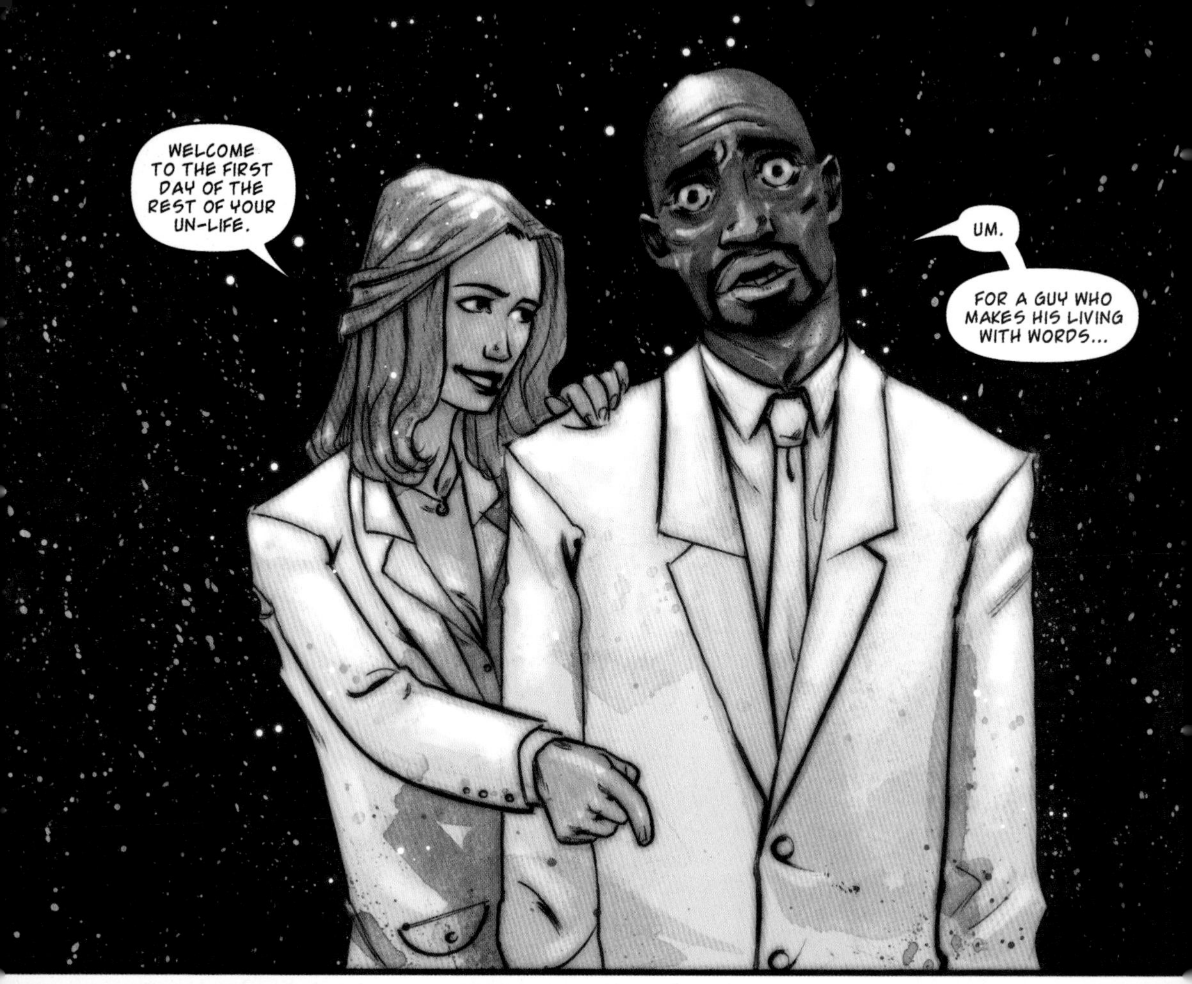
WELCOME TO THE FIRST DAY OF THE REST OF YOUR UN-LIFE.
UM.
FOR A GUY WHO MAKES HIS LIVING WITH WORDS...

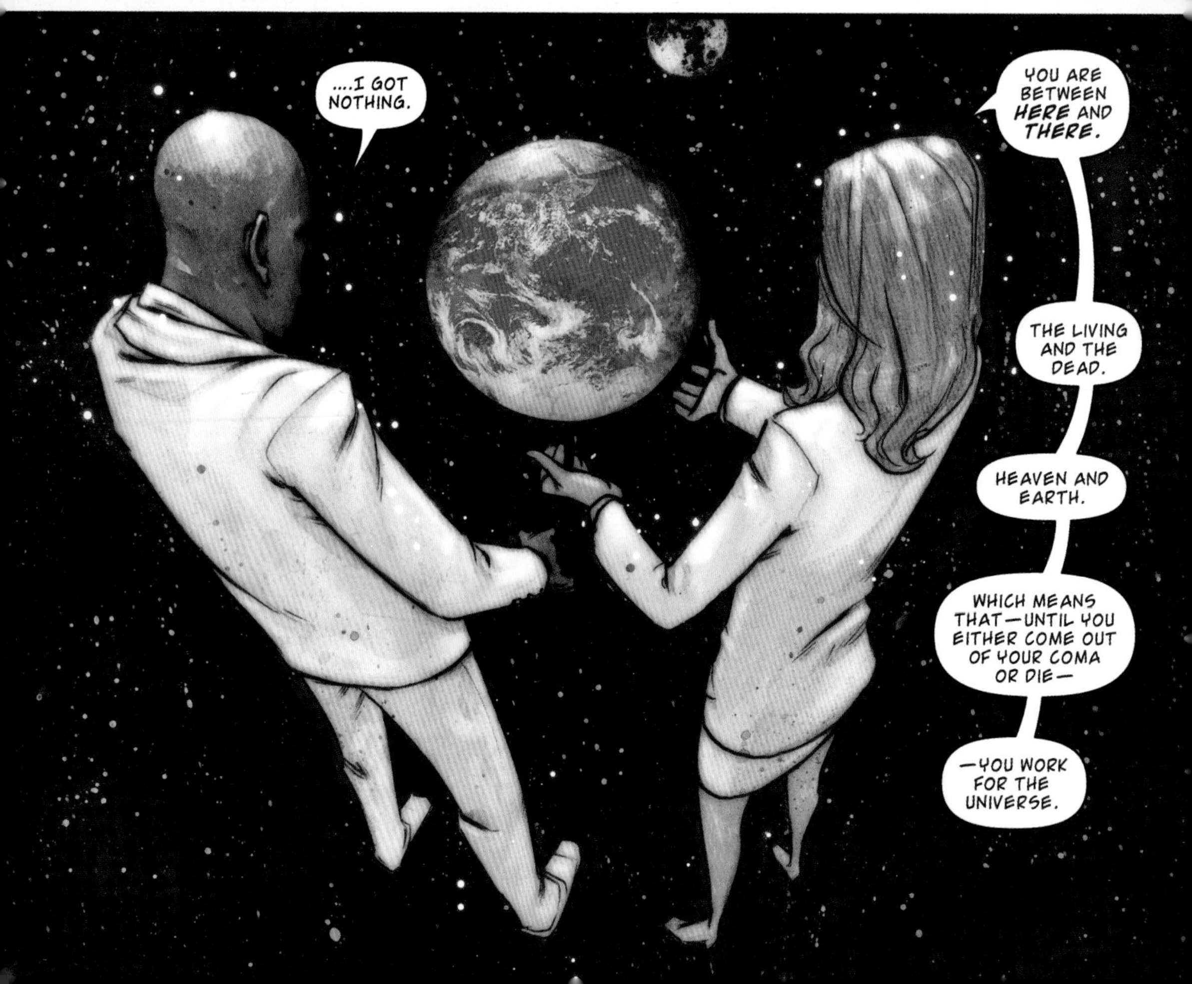
....I GOT NOTHING.
YOU ARE BETWEEN *HERE* AND *THERE.*
THE LIVING AND THE DEAD.
HEAVEN AND EARTH.
WHICH MEANS THAT—UNTIL YOU EITHER COME OUT OF YOUR COMA OR DIE—
—YOU WORK FOR THE UNIVERSE.

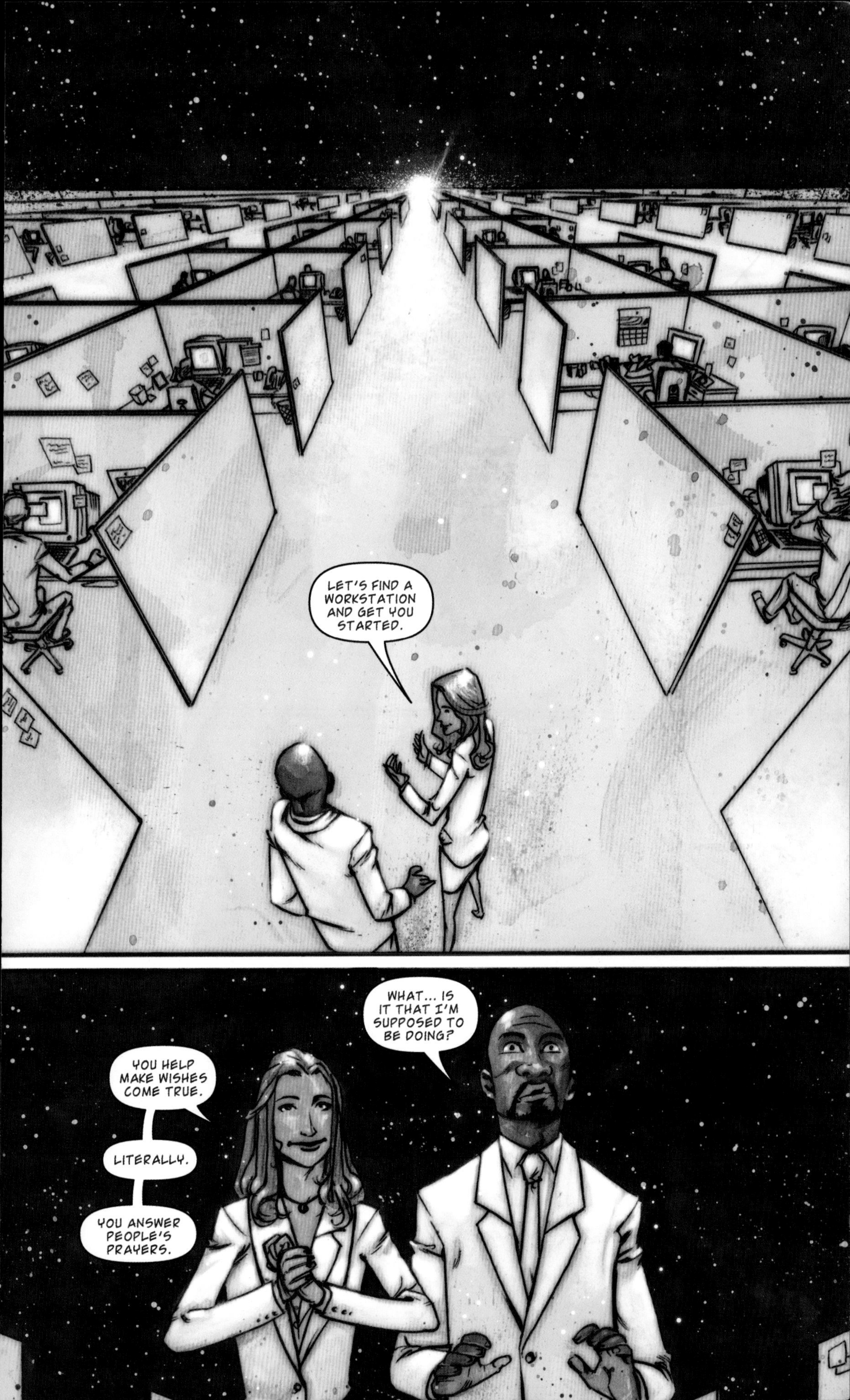
LET'S FIND A WORKSTATION AND GET YOU STARTED.
WHAT... IS IT THAT I'M SUPPOSED TO BE DOING?
YOU HELP MAKE WISHES COME TRUE.
LITERALLY.
YOU ANSWER PEOPLE'S PRAYERS.

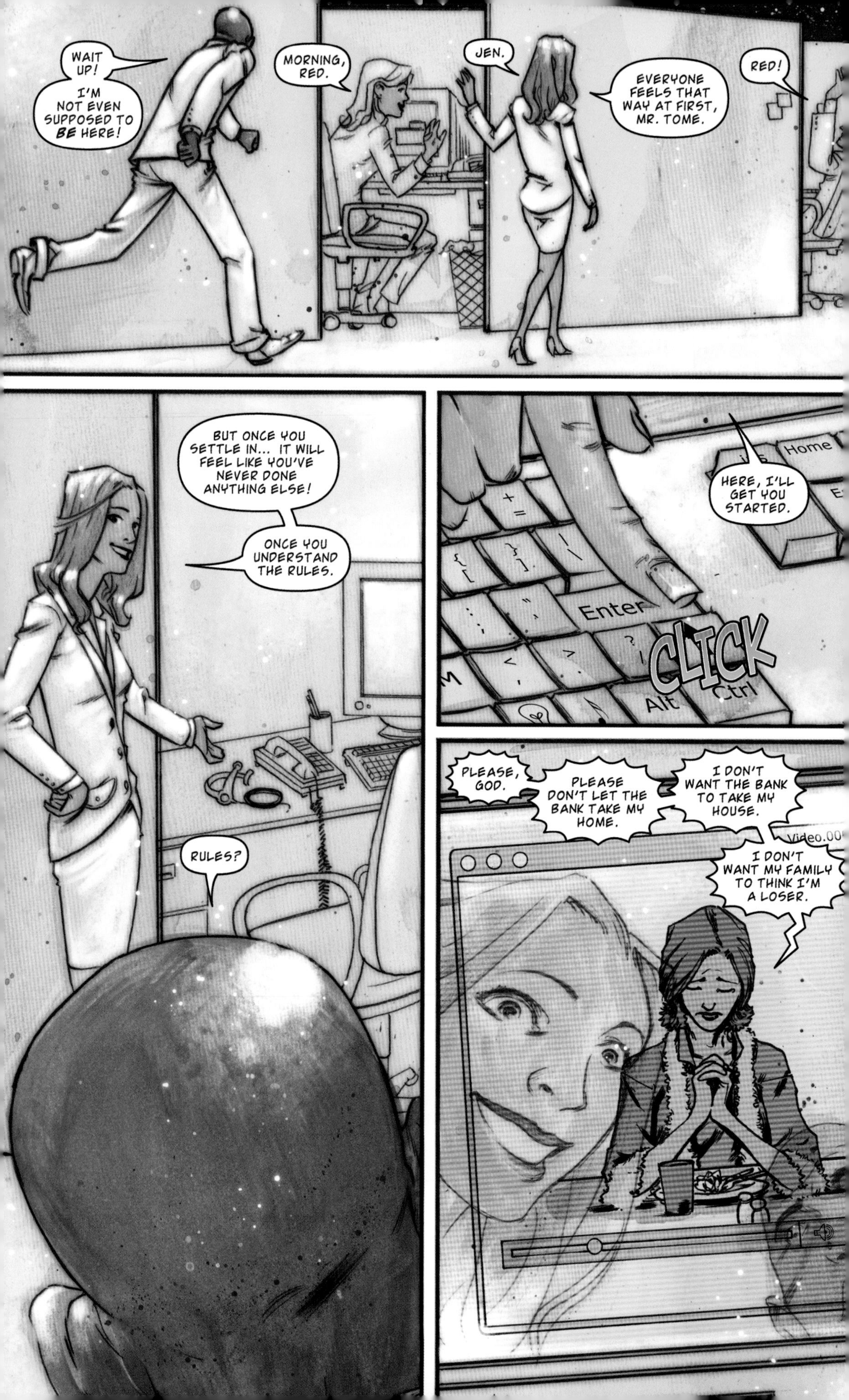
WAIT UP!
I'M NOT EVEN SUPPOSED TO BE HERE!
MORNING, RED.
JEN.
EVERYONE FEELS THAT WAY AT FIRST, MR. TOME.
RED!
BUT ONCE YOU SETTLE IN... IT WILL FEEL LIKE YOU'VE NEVER DONE ANYTHING ELSE!
ONCE YOU UNDERSTAND THE RULES.
RULES?
HERE, I'LL GET YOU STARTED.
Home
Enter
Alt
Ctrl
CLICK
PLEASE, GOD.
PLEASE DON'T LET THE BANK TAKE MY HOME.
I DON'T WANT THE BANK TO TAKE MY HOUSE.
I DON'T WANT MY FAMILY TO THINK I'M A LOSER.

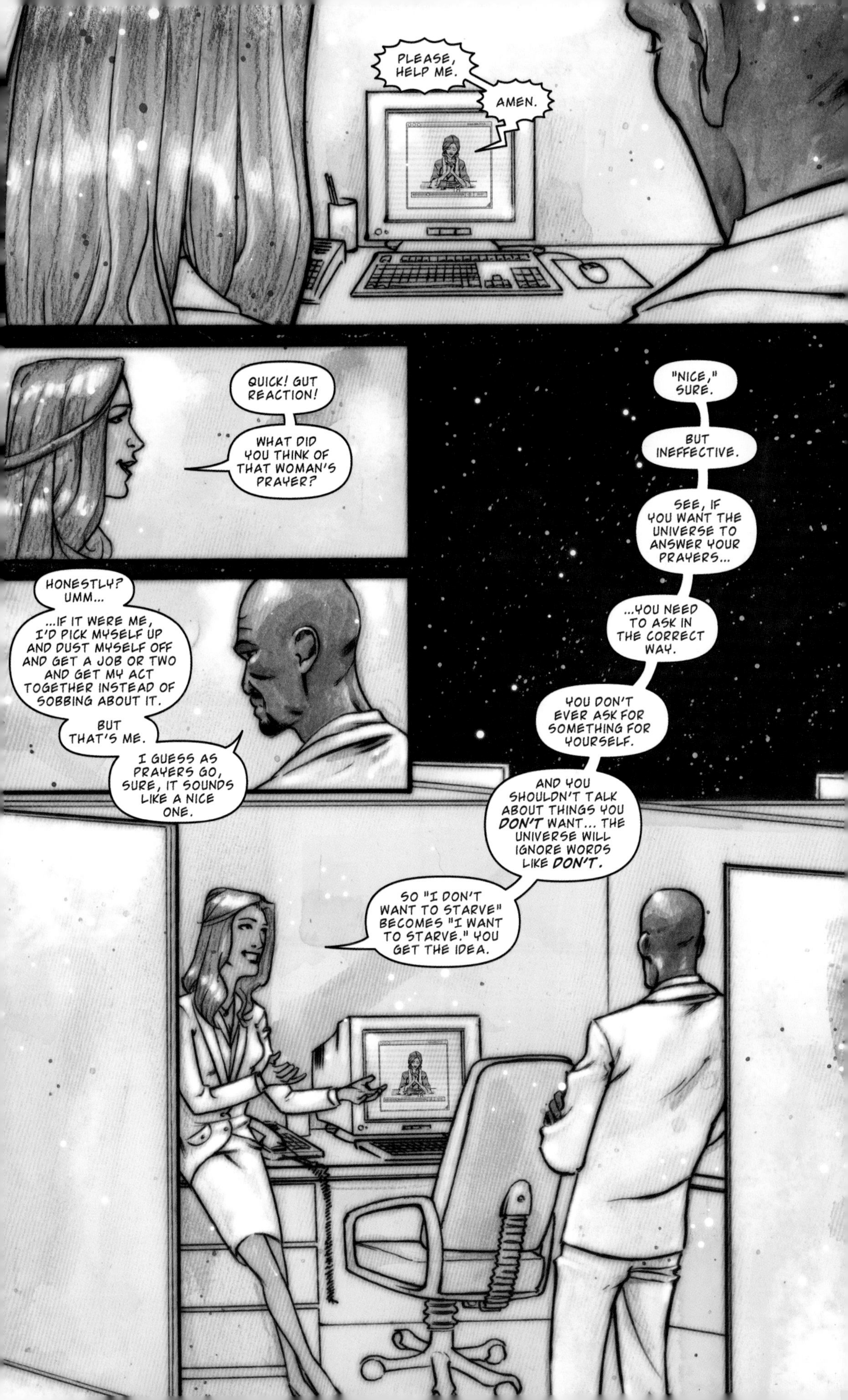
PLEASE, HELP ME.
AMEN.
QUICK! GUT REACTION!
WHAT DID YOU THINK OF THAT WOMAN'S PRAYER?
HONESTLY? UMM...
...IF IT WERE ME, I'D PICK MYSELF UP AND DUST MYSELF OFF AND GET A JOB OR TWO AND GET MY ACT TOGETHER INSTEAD OF SOBBING ABOUT IT.
BUT THAT'S ME.
I GUESS AS PRAYERS GO, SURE, IT SOUNDS LIKE A NICE ONE.
"NICE," SURE.
BUT INEFFECTIVE.
SEE, IF YOU WANT THE UNIVERSE TO ANSWER YOUR PRAYERS...
...YOU NEED TO ASK IN THE CORRECT WAY.
YOU DON'T EVER ASK FOR SOMETHING FOR YOURSELF.
AND YOU SHOULDN'T TALK ABOUT THINGS YOU DON'T WANT... THE UNIVERSE WILL IGNORE WORDS LIKE DON'T.
SO "I DON'T WANT TO STARVE" BECOMES "I WANT TO STARVE." YOU GET THE IDEA.

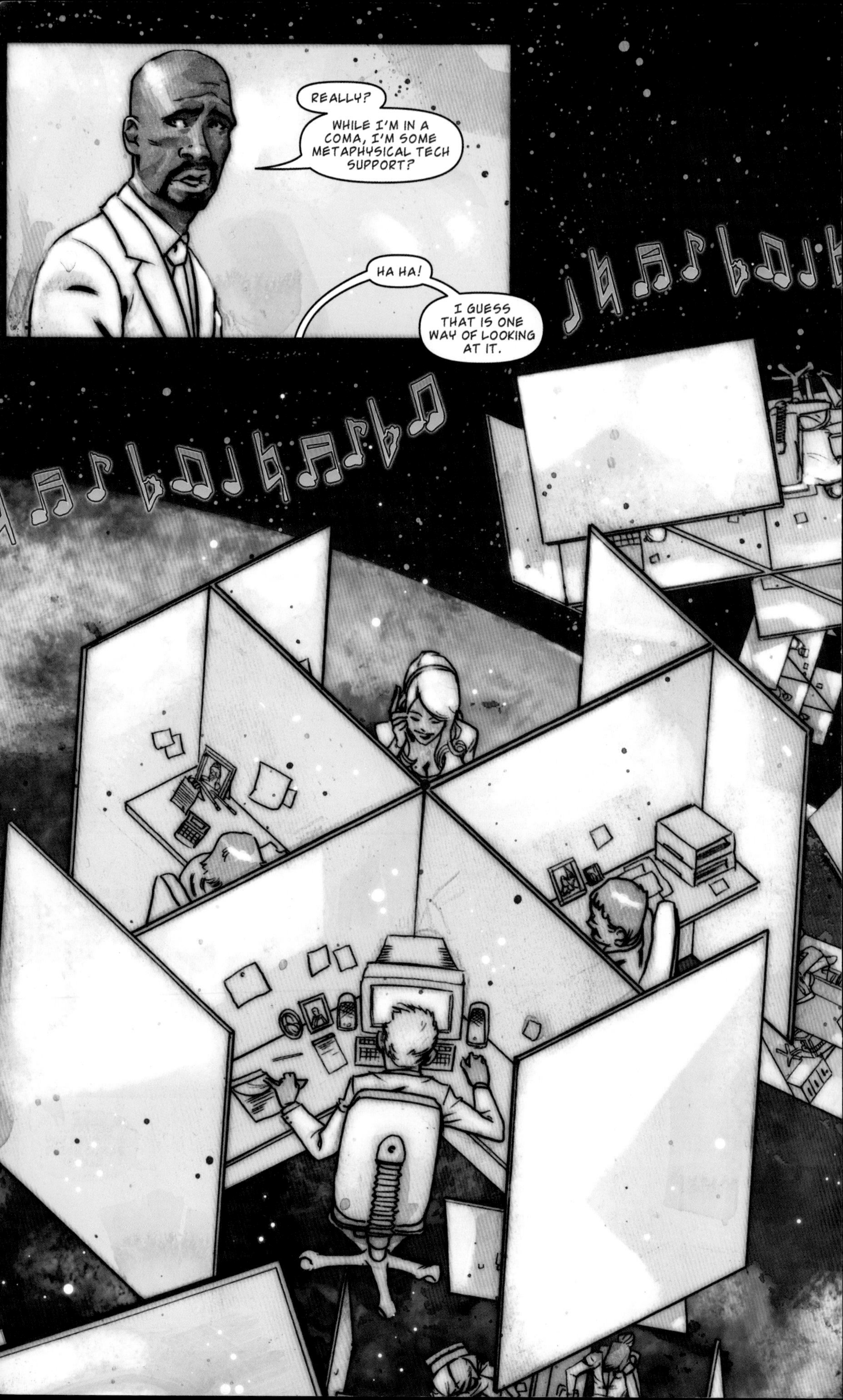
REALLY?
WHILE I'M IN A COMA, I'M SOME METAPHYSICAL TECH SUPPORT?
HA HA!
I GUESS THAT IS ONE WAY OF LOOKING AT IT.

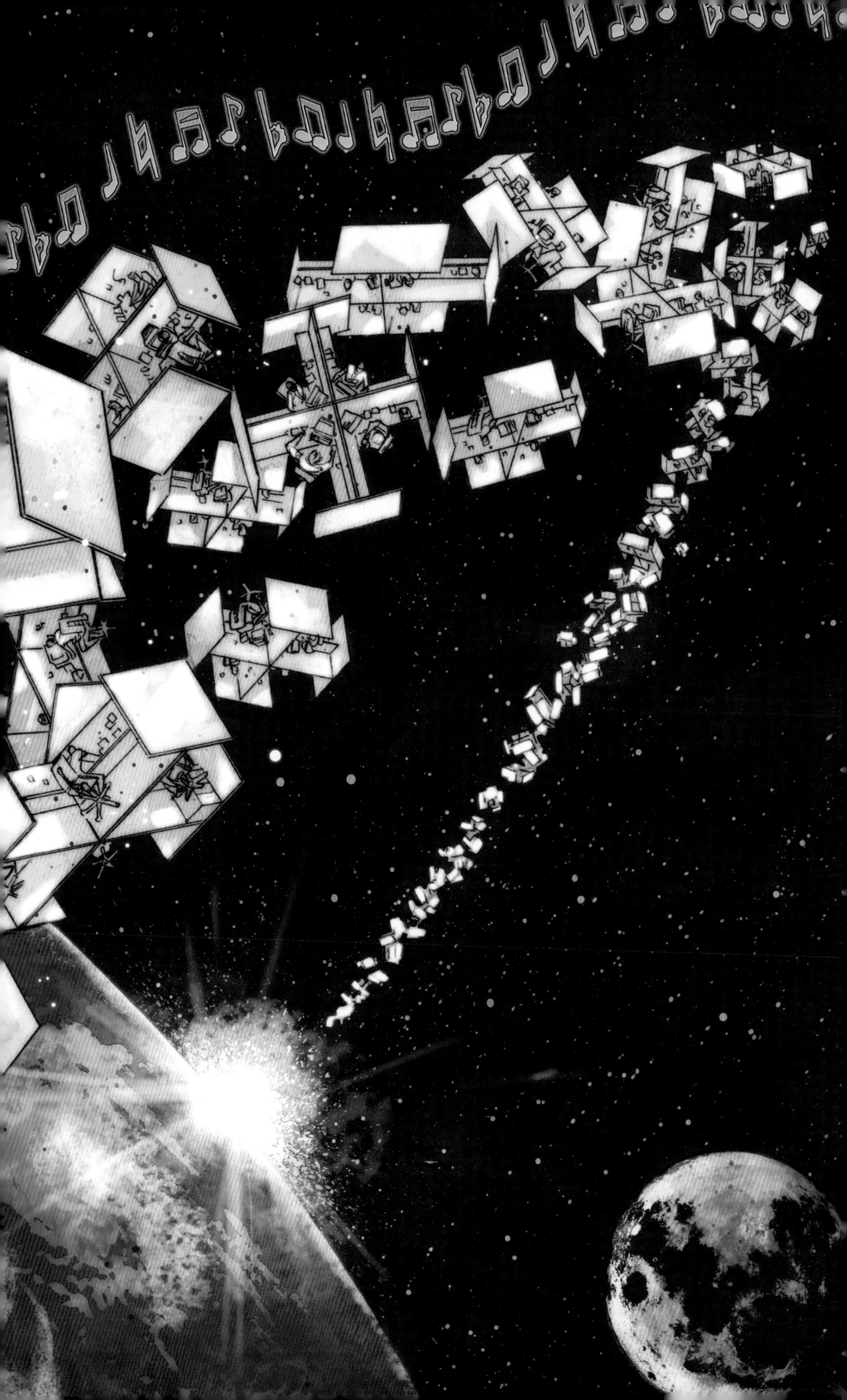

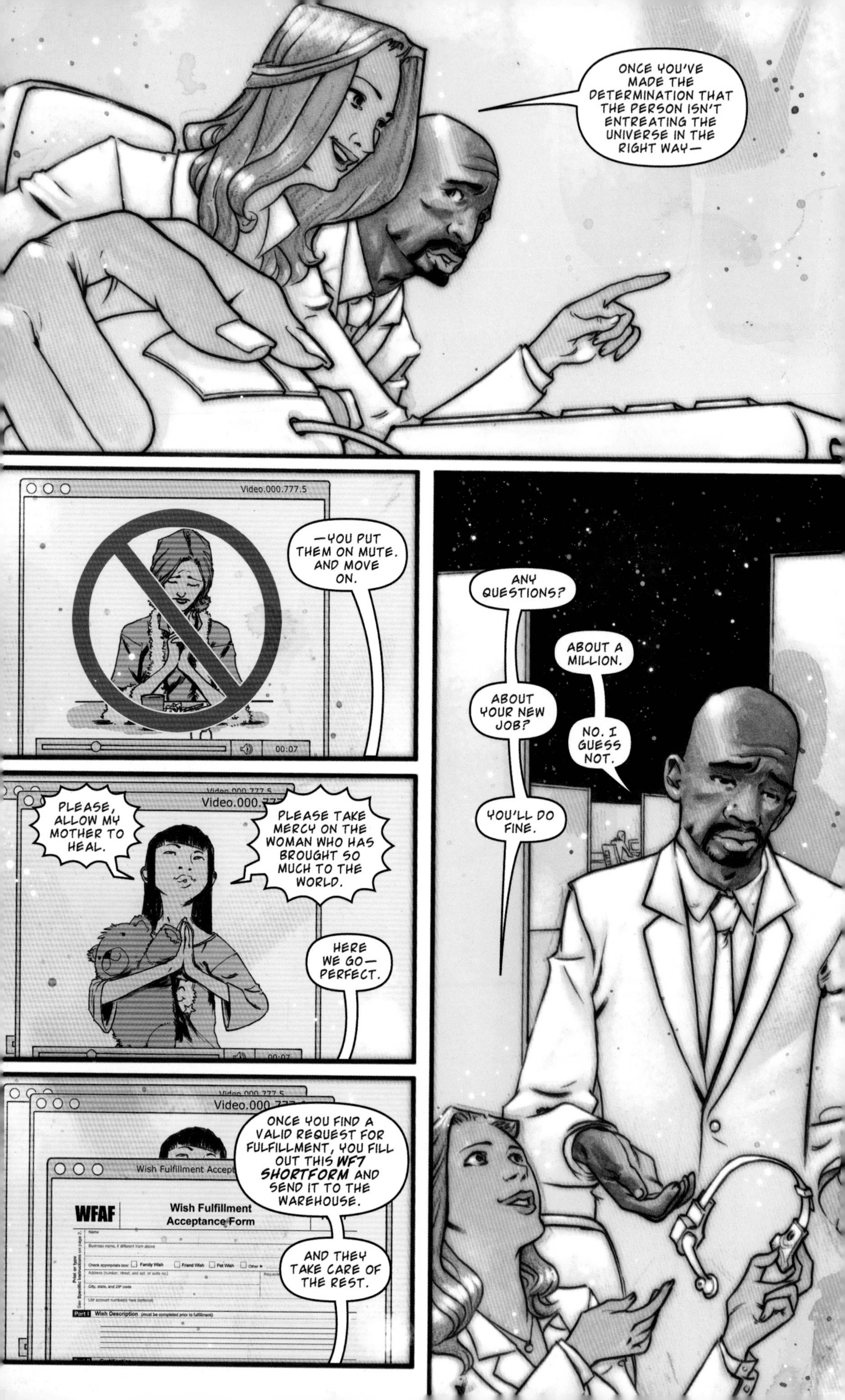
ONCE YOU'VE MADE THE DETERMINATION THAT THE PERSON ISN'T ENTREATING THE UNIVERSE IN THE RIGHT WAY—
Video.000.777.5
—YOU PUT THEM ON MUTE. AND MOVE ON.
00:07
PLEASE, ALLOW MY MOTHER TO HEAL.
PLEASE TAKE MERCY ON THE WOMAN WHO HAS BROUGHT SO MUCH TO THE WORLD.
HERE WE GO—PERFECT.
Wish Fulfillment Accept
WFAF
Wish Fulfillment Acceptance Form
ONCE YOU FIND A VALID REQUEST FOR FULFILLMENT, YOU FILL OUT THIS WF7 SHORTFORM AND SEND IT TO THE WAREHOUSE.
AND THEY TAKE CARE OF THE REST.
ANY QUESTIONS?
ABOUT A MILLION.
ABOUT YOUR NEW JOB?
NO. I GUESS NOT.
YOU'LL DO FINE.

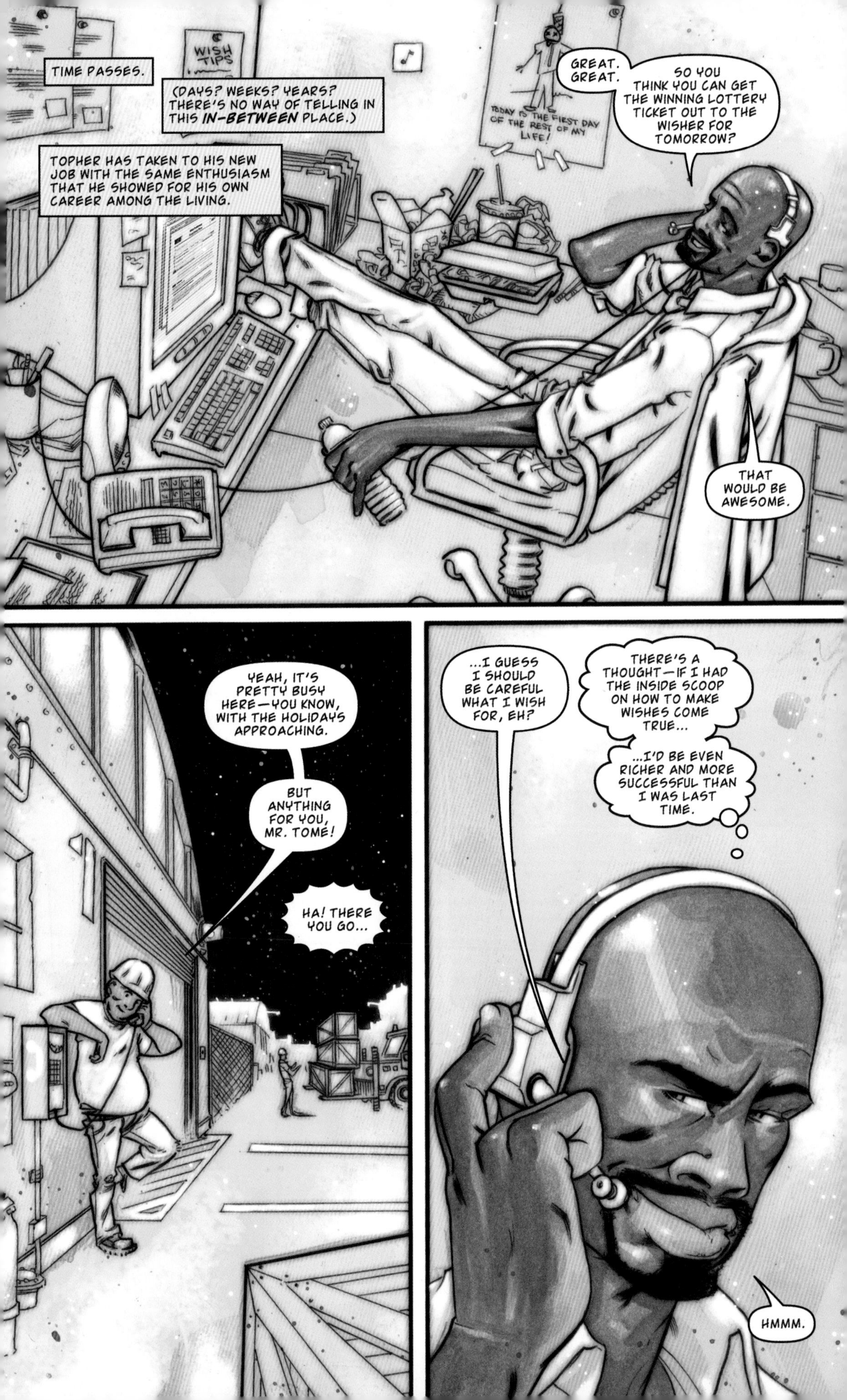

TIME PASSES.
(DAYS? WEEKS? YEARS? THERE'S NO WAY OF TELLING IN THIS IN-BETWEEN PLACE.)
TOPHER HAS TAKEN TO HIS NEW JOB WITH THE SAME ENTHUSIASM THAT HE SHOWED FOR HIS OWN CAREER AMONG THE LIVING.
WISH TIPS
TODAY IS THE FIRST DAY OF THE REST OF MY LIFE!
GREAT. GREAT.
SO YOU THINK YOU CAN GET THE WINNING LOTTERY TICKET OUT TO THE WISHER FOR TOMORROW?
THAT WOULD BE AWESOME.
YEAH, IT'S PRETTY BUSY HERE—YOU KNOW, WITH THE HOLIDAYS APPROACHING.
BUT ANYTHING FOR YOU, MR. TOME!
HA! THERE YOU GO...
...I GUESS I SHOULD BE CAREFUL WHAT I WISH FOR, EH?
THERE'S A THOUGHT—IF I HAD THE INSIDE SCOOP ON HOW TO MAKE WISHES COME TRUE...
...I'D BE EVEN RICHER AND MORE SUCCESSFUL THAN I WAS LAST TIME.
HMMM.

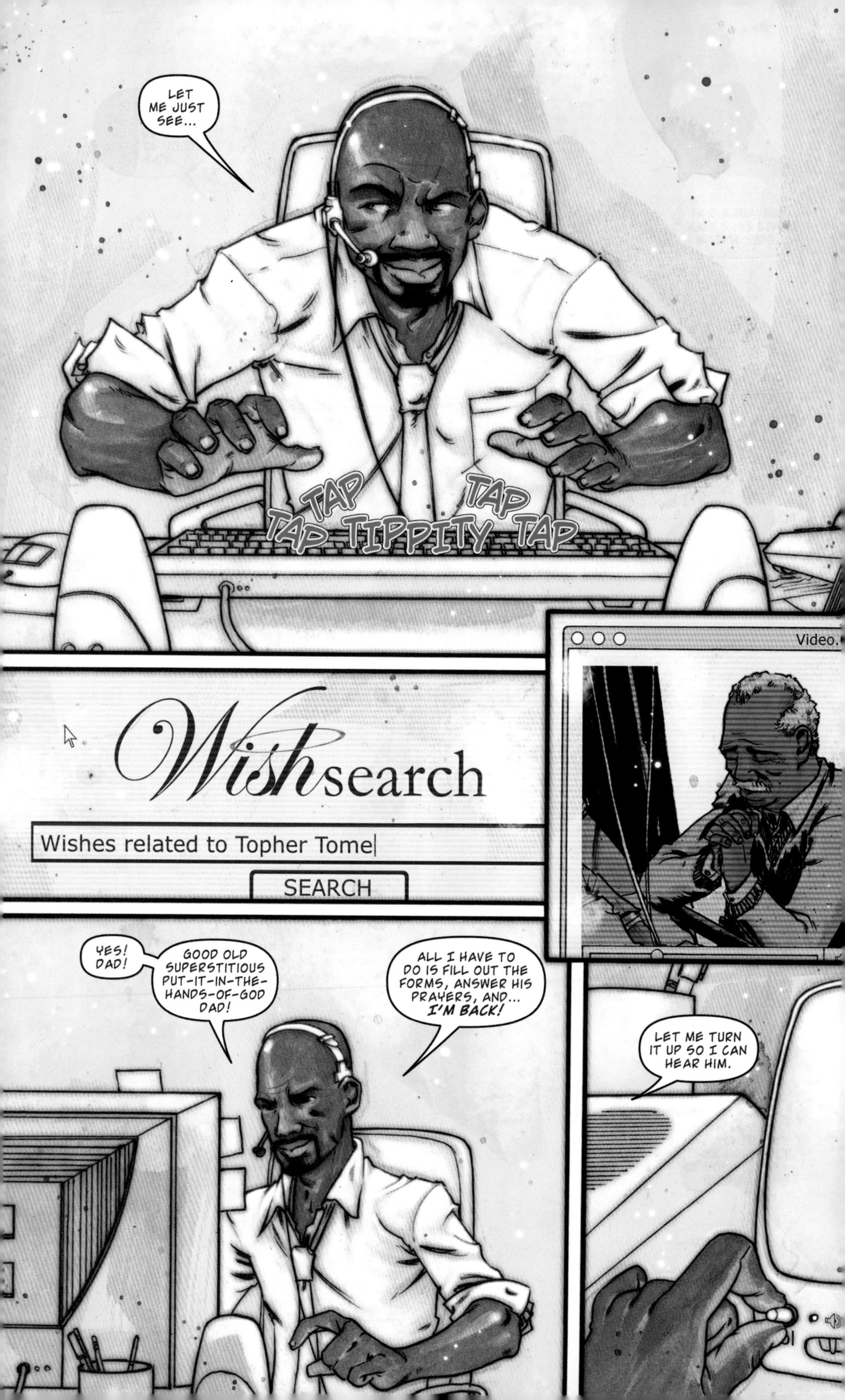
LET ME JUST SEE...
TAP TAP TIPPITY TAP TAP
Wishsearch
Wishes related to Topher Tome
SEARCH
Video.
YES! DAD!
GOOD OLD SUPERSTITIOUS PUT-IT-IN-THE-HANDS-OF-GOD DAD!
ALL I HAVE TO DO IS FILL OUT THE FORMS, ANSWER HIS PRAYERS, AND... I'M BACK!
LET ME TURN IT UP SO I CAN HEAR HIM.

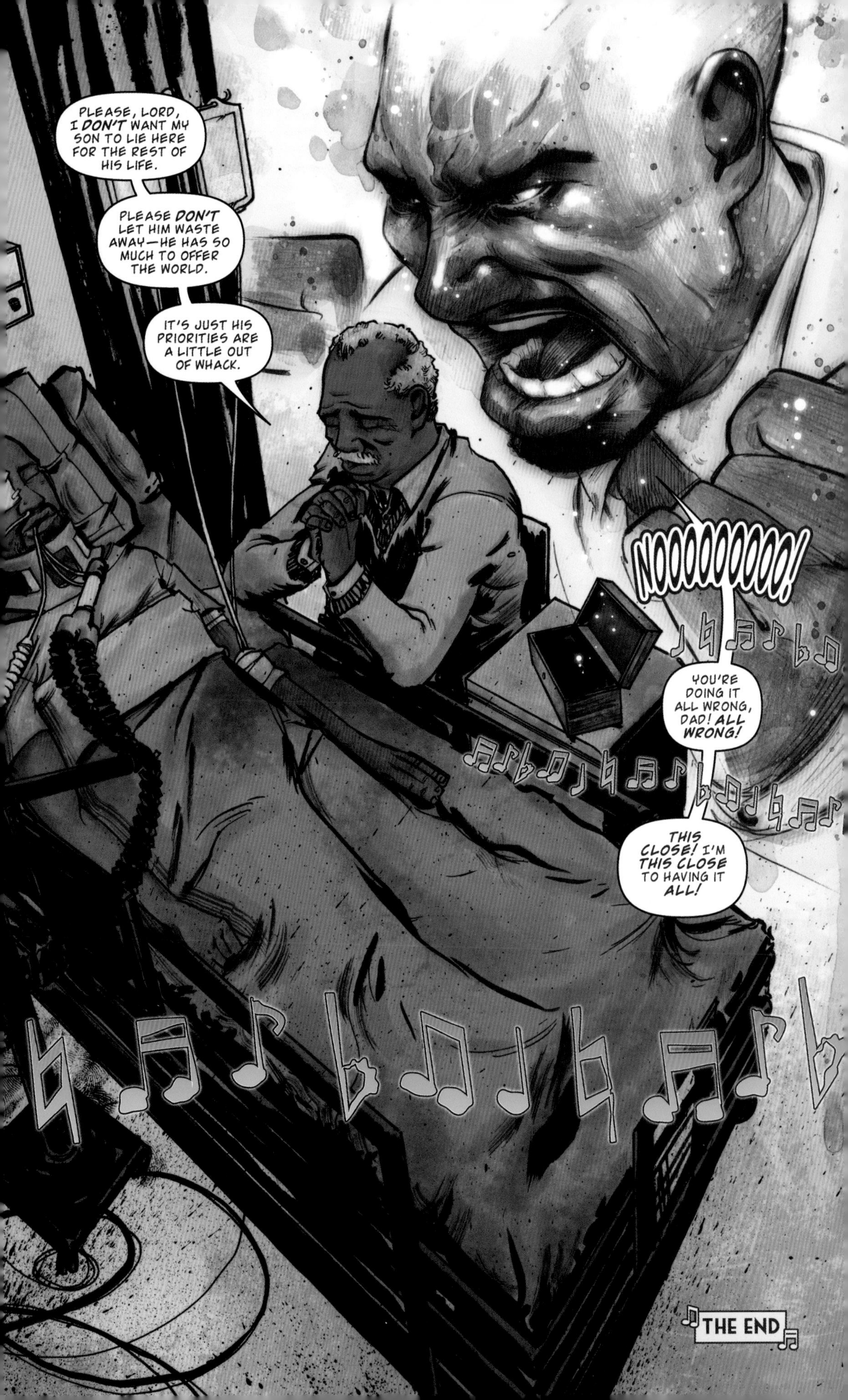
PLEASE, LORD, I DON'T WANT MY SON TO LIE HERE FOR THE REST OF HIS LIFE.
PLEASE DON'T LET HIM WASTE AWAY—HE HAS SO MUCH TO OFFER THE WORLD.
IT'S JUST HIS PRIORITIES ARE A LITTLE OUT OF WHACK.
NOOOOOOOO!
YOU'RE DOING IT ALL WRONG, DAD! ALL WRONG!
THIS CLOSE! I'M THIS CLOSE TO HAVING IT ALL!
THE END

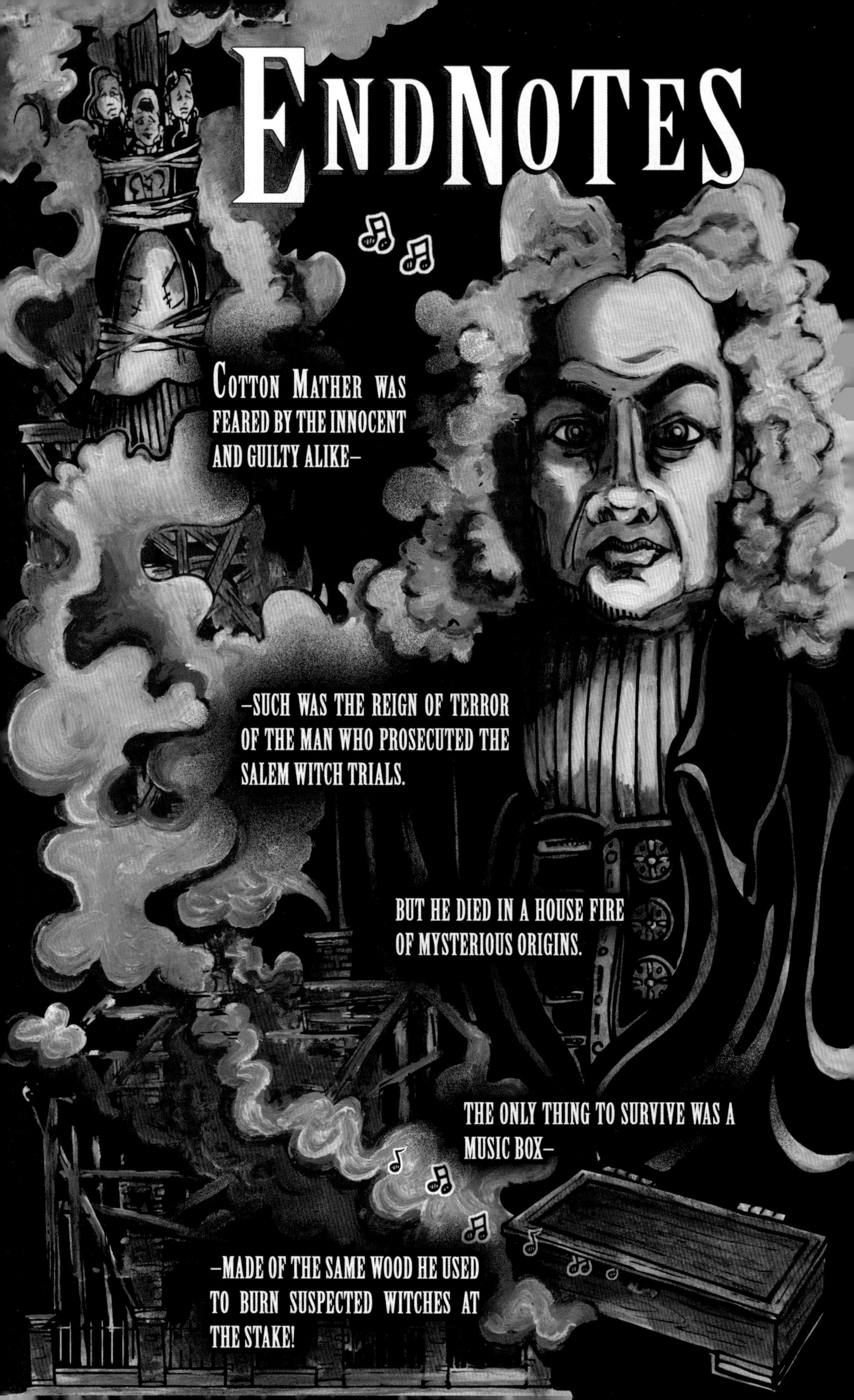
EndNotes
Cotton Mather was feared by the innocent and guilty alike–
–such was the reign of terror of the man who prosecuted the Salem witch trials.
But he died in a house fire of mysterious origins.
The only thing to survive was a music box–
–made of the same wood he used to burn suspected witches at the stake!

Jennifer Love Hewitt's

MUSIC BOX

IDW™

www.IDWPUBLISHING.com